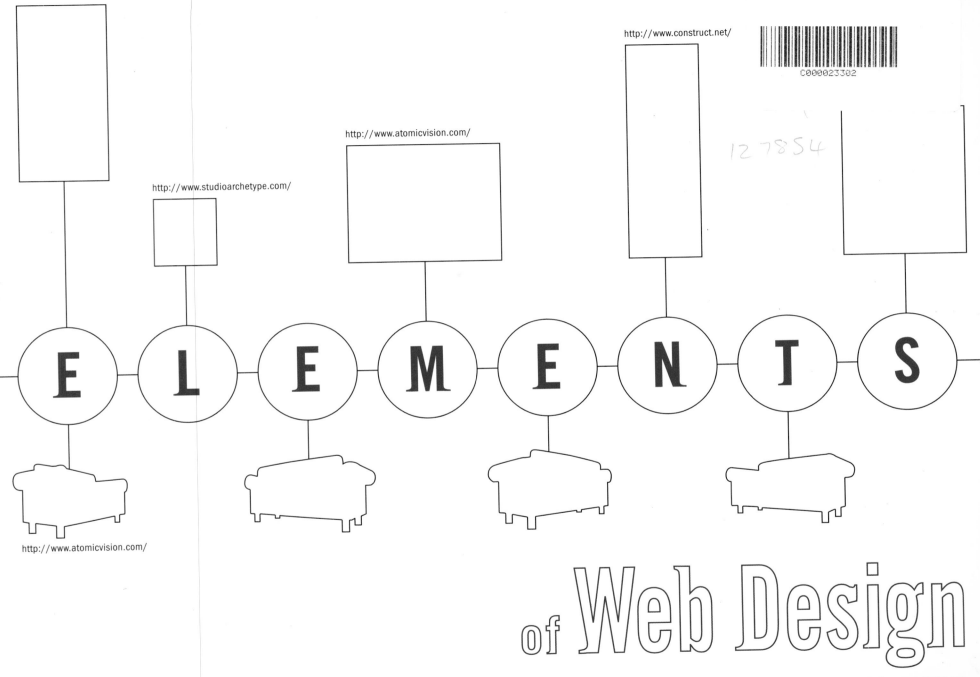

http://www.construct.net/

C000023302

127854

http://www.atomicvision.com/

http://www.studioarchetype.com/

ELEMENTS

http://www.atomicvision.com/

of Web Design

Darcy DiNUCCI with Maria **GIUDICE** & Lynne **STILES**

Elements of Web Design

Darcy DiNucci, Maria Giudice, Lynne Stiles

Peachpit Press
2414 Sixth Street
Berkeley, CA 94710
510/548-4393
800/283-9444
510/548-5991 (fax)

Find us on the World Wide Web at http://www.peachpit.com

Peachpit Press is a division of Addison Wesley Longman

Editor: Nolan Hester
Copyeditors: Tema Goodwin, John Hammett
Technical reviewer: Jonathan Feinstein
Cover and interior design: Maria Giudice, Lynne Stiles, and Ben Seibel, YO, San Francisco
Production coordinator: Kate Reber

We would like to thank all the Web designers who shared their knowledge and opinions with us as their thinking and the Web evolved. In addition to the designers profiled in the "Who's Doing Web Design?" chapter, we'd like to extend special thanks to Ryan Watkins at Dimension X (http://www.dimensionx.com/) and to Joe Lachoff of Process39 (http://www.process39.com/). Thanks also to Ted Nace, for the chance to do this book, to Nolan Hester, who shepherded it through with the patience of Job, and all the other helpsters at Peachpit Press. Special thanks to Henry Krempel for constant encouragement and occasional scripting assistance. And from Web designers everywhere, a special tip of the hat to Lynda Weinman, gracious hostess of the Web Design mailing list (http://www.lynda.com/webdesign/), a source of inspiration and advice to thousands of budding and seasoned Web design enthusiasts.

Colophon
This book was created with QuarkXPress 3.3, Adobe Illustrator 6.0, and Adobe Photoshop 3.0 on Macintosh computers. The fonts used were Franklin Gothic and Beach. Final output was on a Creo computer to plate system, and it was printed on 80# Mountie Matte at R.R. Donnelley & Sons, OH.

ISBN 0-201-88594-8

9 8 7 6 5 4 3 2 1

Printed and bound in the United States of America

Introduction

The World Wide Web has fired a fuse under the Internet, transforming it
from a mysterious buzzword to one of the hottest topics in business and
the media. It offers worldwide distribution. It's interactive. It can include
sounds, movies, and animation, in addition to text and graphics. Distribution
costs can be tiny. And starting from nowhere a couple of years ago, it's
now the fastest-growing medium on Earth.

The jump to electronic publishing—distributing magazines, marketing materials, books, and other materials in electronic form—has been predicted for ages, but now, with the advent of the World Wide Web, it has become a reality. Whether they're putting out personal e-zines or the *New York Times,* publishers see it as a way to widen their distribution at a very low cost. Businesses from one-person home offices to Sony and Disney use it as an efficient way of reaching customers and selling products. Others look to it for office "intranets," taking advantage of the cross-platform compatibility and easy navigation of Web publishing to distribute information within corporations. The Web bypasses the barriers of paper and distribution costs, allows unlimited updates, and puts information in front of its audience instantly.

For designers as for publishers, the World Wide Web is a great business opportunity. Any company that hasn't built a Web site or an intranet yet is planning one now—and that includes your current and prospective clients. As businesses throughout the world rush to establish their presence on the Web, they need the help of professional designers to help create striking and effective electronic interfaces.

Designing for the Web isn't hard. You probably already have most of the software you'll need—an image editor, an illustration program, a word processor. The popularity of the Web has driven software companies to introduce easy-to-use Web-authoring features into mainstream design and office software, and more specialized tools are often quite inexpensive and easy to learn. Thanks to these innovations, delving into multimedia, scripting, and other aspects of leading-edge Web design is becoming easier every day. And renting space on a Web server for your own Web presence can be unbelievably cheap. Many Internet service providers offer their customers Web page space on their servers for free.

There's no better time to get your feet wet than now. This book has been created to give designers a grounding in the world of the Web, guided by Web designer professionals who have set the current high-water level for innovative and exciting use of the medium. We'll help you understand how and why design for the Web differs from design for print, how to assemble the team you'll need, how to think about interface design for the new medium, how to use different types of media, and how to keep up in the ever-changing world of the Web.

Special features throughout the book help you navigate:

as a way to download images (→**106**), has attributes specially designed for this task.)

A number preceded by an arrow directs you to a page where you can find more about the topic at hand.

supports a work-alike scripting it calls **JScript**.) Visual Basic Script, popular browser support.

Terms you'll need to know are highlighted in red, defined in the margin next to their use, and gathered in a glossary at the end of the book.

START TAG

<OBJECT>

HTML quick-reference boxes show the syntax of the codes you'll use to create the effect we discuss in the adjoining text and illustrations. At the end of the book you'll find an alphabetical list of the most useful HTML tags.

stop and download things. page and hear a voice and except you will be able to
SABINE MESSNER, HOTWIRED

Quotes from our panel of expert Web designers point out tricks and pitfalls.

http://www.sandia.gov/sci_compute/elements.html
http://www.netscape.com/
Shockwave
http://www.macromedia.com

References to online sources at the end of each chapter show where you can find out more.

Table of Contents

What Is the Web?

It's Based on Hypertext

It Supports All Kinds of Media

It Can Be Interactive

Its Pages Can Be Designed

You don't need to know a lot about the technical underpinnings of the World Wide Web to design great Web pages. It will help, however, to have a little grounding in just what the Web is, how it's related to other parts of the Internet, and what a few of the terms mean that you'll run across in your work. Here's a brief introduction.

The first thing you need to know is that the World Wide Web is just one of several services available through the **Internet**, a worldwide, informal agglomeration of connected computers, linked by high-capacity lines that stretch across the country and under the oceans.

Unlike smaller networks, the Internet (often just called "the Net") isn't located in any single place, isn't based on any central computer, and isn't overseen by any network manager. It was started in the 1960s as an experiment by the U.S. Department of Defense, as a way to communicate with its contractors and re-searchers at large universities. The government laid cables between its contractors and created a **protocol**, called **TCP/IP**, that defined the way computers on the network would talk to one another. To ensure that the strategically important communications taking place

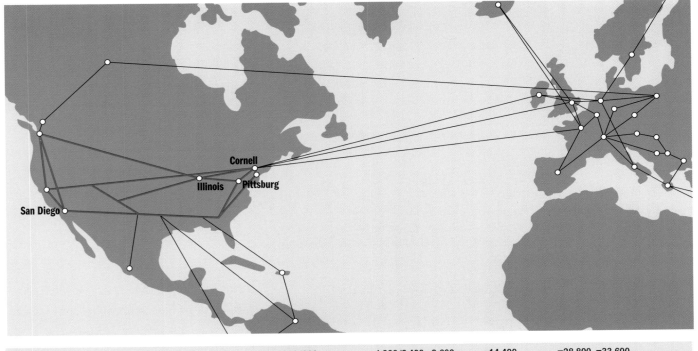

HIGH-CAPACITY BACKBONES carry Internet traffic between major hubs throughout the world. (The U.S. locations named here are the hubs of NSFNET, the National Science Foundation network that provided the skeleton of the early Internet.) Millions of individual computers are connected to these backbones by modem or cable connections.

Internet
A worldwide computer network that links thousands of smaller networks. Initially developed by the U.S. government to link its suppliers and the Pentagon, it is now used by millions of businesses and individuals.

protocol
A set of rules for exchanging information between computers over a network or via a modem connection.

TCP/IP
Stands for Transmission Control Protocol/Internet Protocol, the protocol developed for communications over the Internet and now supported by most computer systems.

Modem Speeds
▼110/300 ▼1,200/2,400 ▼9,600 ▼14,400 ▼28,800 ▼33,600

Computer Advances
▼8080 processor ▼8086 processor ▼80286 processor ▼60830 processor ▼Pentium processor
▼first microprocessor ▼68000, 8088 processors ▼HyperCard ▼QuickTime ▼PowerPC processor
▼Unix OS ▼hard disk ▼Apple founded ▼SGI founded ▼Macintosh released ▼first laptop computer
▼floppy disk ▼Microsoft founded ▼IBM PC/DOS ▼Microsoft Windows ▼Windows 3.0 ▼Windows 95
▼Pong, the first video game ▼Apple Lisa (first graphical user interface)

Number of Internet Servers
▼4 ▼23 ▼100 ▼1,000 ▼10,000 ▼100,000 ▼1,000,000 ▼10,000,000

Internet History
▼ARPAnet commissioned ▼NSFNET created (56Kbps) ▼first Internet shopping malls
▼Telnet ▼TCP/IP established ▼NSFNET upgraded to 1.5Mbps
▼first international connections to ARPAnet ▼EUNet connects European cities ▼NSFNET upgraded to 44.7Mbps
▼FTP specification ▼e-mail specification ▼ARPAnet stops ▼AOL founded ▼Microsoft Internet Explorer
▼first BBS ▼NSF allows commercial use of Internet
▼Usenet newsgroups established ▼WWW invented ▼Netscape Navigator
▼CompuServe founded ▼domain name servers introduced ▼Mosaic ▼AOL offers Internet access

9 **1970** 1 2 3 4 5 6 7 8 9 **1980** 1 2 3 4 5 6 7 8 9 **1990** 1 2 3 4 5 6 7 8 9 **2000**

Internet Services

E-mail Short for "electronic mail," e-mail is sent over computer networks, such as those inside businesses or the Internet, from one user to another. Every user has a unique address, registered with a central clearinghouse.

FTP Stands for file transport protocol, a method of sending files over the Internet.

Gopher A protocol used to create hierarchical menus, allowing users to move through information by moving through the directory structure until they find the file they need. (Named Gopher in honor of the school mascot at the University of Minnesota, where the protocol was developed.)

Newsgroups On the Internet, a collection of information on a certain topic, automatically compiled from messages sent by individual users. Newsgroups are available on just about every topic under the sun, from the Internet itself, to highway traffic laws, pets, and of course, sex.

Telnet A protocol that allows one machine on the Internet to run programs stored on another computer on the network, or a program that puts that protocol into effect.

WAIS Stands for Wide Area Information Service, a protocol used to build indexes of text pages on the Internet, allowing quick searches for information within the indexed content.

World Wide Web (WWW) The World Wide Web supports multimedia pages that are connected by a system of hyperlinks. The Web is based on HTTP, the Hypertext Transfer Protocol.

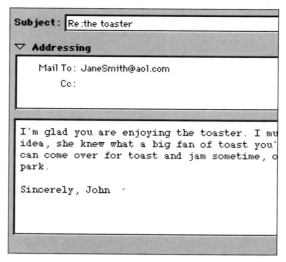

E-MAIL

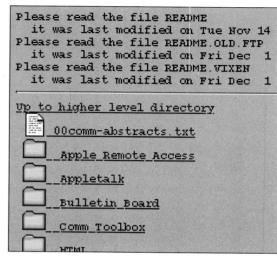

FTP

EACH INTERNET SERVICE offers a different way of publishing and viewing information on the Internet.

NEWSGROUP

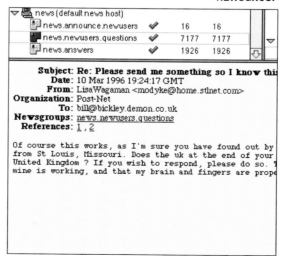

WORLD WIDE WEB

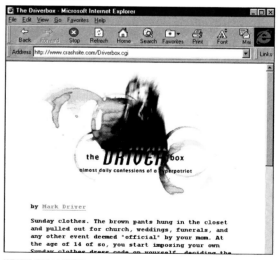

HEATH STALLINGS
http://www.crashsite.com/

over the Internet could not be interrupted by an enemy attack, TCP/IP was designed to create a decentralized system, in which any computer on the network can talk to any other, and messages on the network can be rerouted as needed, depending on what lines are free.

The Internet's facility for speeding communication through e-mail, newsgroups, and other services quickly caught on. Over the years, new methods of saving and retrieving information were created that made sharing information easier: Telnet let remote users log on to Internet computers as guests and run programs on them from their own machines; FTP let Internet users download files from remote computers; Gopher provided hierarchical menus for finding information; WAIS provided a search engine for finding what you needed anywhere in the world.

In 1991 a group of scientists at CERN, the European Physics Lab, came up with an ingenious new system for accessing information on the Internet, called the World Wide Web.

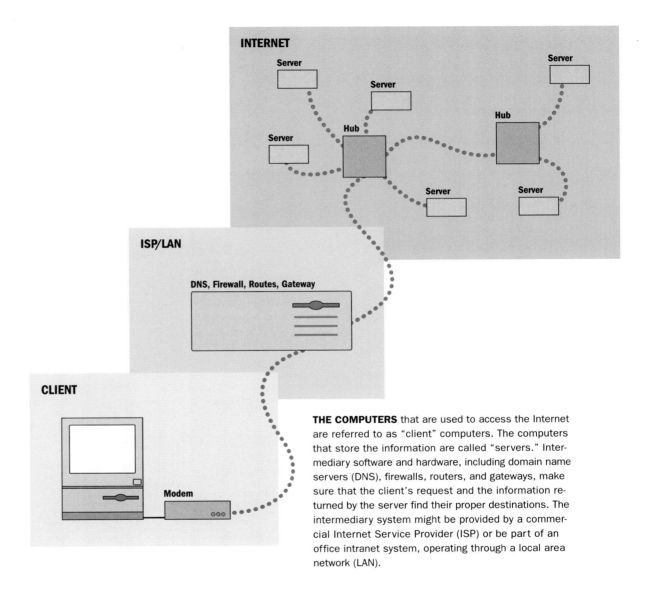

THE COMPUTERS that are used to access the Internet are referred to as "client" computers. The computers that store the information are called "servers." Intermediary software and hardware, including domain name servers (DNS), firewalls, routers, and gateways, make sure that the client's request and the information returned by the server find their proper destinations. The intermediary system might be provided by a commercial Internet Service Provider (ISP) or be part of an office intranet system, operating through a local area network (LAN).

One of our production managers says, "People talk about Web surfing, but it's really Web fishing. It's not about going somewhere, it's about casting out a line and trying to pull back what you need."

BARBARA KUHR, HOTWIRED

Like other Internet services, the World Wide Web is not based on a certain network or computer. Instead, it's a way or organizing information so that any computer around the world that operates according to the rules can access it. The rules that specify how to access and transfer files over the Web are called by the name HTTP, for Hypertext Transfer Protocol.

Hypertext Transfer Protocol

The Hypertext Transfer Protocol (HTTP) has been in use by the World-Wide Web global information initiative since 1990. HTTP is an application-level protocol with the lightness and speed necessary for distributed, collaborative, hyper media information systems. It is a generic, object-oriented protocol which can be used for many tasks, such as name servers and distributed object management systems, through extension of its request methods (commands). A feature of HTTP is the typing and negotiation of data representation, allowing systems to be built independently of the data being transferred.

News and Updates

- HTTP/1.1 and Digest Authentication become Proposed Standards New!
- HTTP 1.1 Internet draft 07 New!
- Minutes from the IETF HTTP-wg meeting

http://www.w3.org/pub/WWW/Protocols/

HTTP
Stands for Hypertext Transfer Protocol, the protocol on which the World Wide Web is based. HTTP sets rules for how information is passed between the server and the client software.

hyperlink
In a hypertext document, such as a Web page, an electronic link that calls up a specific piece of information chosen by the user.

hypertext
An electronic Information structure in which the reader controls how he or she moves through the information.

IN HYPERTEXT SYSTEMS, you can click on a hypertext anchor to call up linked information. In the example shown here, clicking on the word *HTTP* calls up a page describing the protocol.

It's Based on Hypertext

Like other Internet services, the World Wide Web is not a certain network, based on a certain computer. Instead, it's a way of organizing information so that any computer around the world that operates according to the rules can access it. The rules that specify how to access and transfer files over the Web are called **HTTP**, for Hypertext Transfer Protocol.

The Web was a breakthrough in many ways. Perhaps its most important feature, though, is its use of **hypertext**. Any text in a Web document can be made to link to any other document, anywhere in the world, that is saved on an HTTP server and connected to the Net. Let's say, for example, that you were reading the previous paragraph on line. On your screen you might see that the word HTTP was highlighted (in a different color, or underlined, for example). On a Web page, that means the word is a **hyperlink** to another page, and if you wanted to learn more about HTTP, you could just click on that word with your mouse, and another page, describing HTTP in more detail, would appear on your screen.

The text that appears may be something written by the same author and stored at the same site as the first page you were reading. Or it could be stored in Switzerland or Beijing, written by someone the first author doesn't even know. To the reader, it makes no difference: Click, and you're there.

It Supports All Kinds of Media

Anyone who has worked with personal computers in any kind of collaborative project knows that sharing files can be a headache. Too often, you may try to share a file with colleagues or friends, only to find that they are on a different kind of computer or they don't have the software they need to read it. So how do publishers on the Internet provide files that might be read by anyone, anywhere in the world?

The one sure way is to rely on **ASCII**—pure text documents, with no formatting information. Or you could specify that everyone reading your files must get special software that reads the standard formats you'll be using for your online documents. Or you could use formats such as GIF (a compressed graphics format) (→**103**) that are commonly used on many different platforms and readable by many different kinds of software. Publishers on the World Wide Web depend on a combination of all three of these tactics.

The basic format for text published on the Web is ASCII. (Really it's ASCII with a twist; the files contain certain "tags," referred to as Hypertext Markup Language, or **HTML**, that help them take on a bit of character when they're pulled up on the reader's screen.) The scheme also depends on the reader having special software, called a **browser**, that is specially made to retrieve and display HTML files and other commonly used formats and to help users navigate through the Web. Any formats that can't be read by the browser—for example, those belonging to particular applications or in a medium, say video, that the browser doesn't support—can be read by readily available, inexpensive or free programs called **helper applications**. Most popular browsers also work with a special kind of helper application, called a **plug-in**, that displays the files inside the browser window. Browsers that support ActiveX (→**173**), a software technology pioneered by Microsoft, can also use an ActiveX object called an ActiveX control (→**173**), which, like a plug-in, can be used to display a particular document format inside the browser.

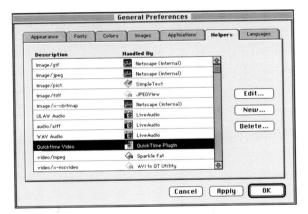

EACH FILE FORMAT and media type has an identification code called its MIME type, a two-part description you use to register it with browsers and other Internet applications. In most browsers (such as Netscape Navigator 3.0, shown here), you can specify which application you want to open each MIME type.

ASCII
Stands for American Standard Code for Information Interchange. ASCII files, sometimes called "pure text" files, can contain only text and no formatting information.

browser
Software designed to communicate with Web servers and interpret the data received from them. The two most common browsers are Netscape Navigator and Microsoft Internet Explorer.

helper application
An application launched by the browser to display files it can't read itself.

HTML
The Hypertext Markup Language, a set of codes used to mark up World Wide Web documents with tags that describe the document's structure and allow for hyperlinks to other documents on the Internet.

plug-in
A special kind of helper application that displays special formats inside the browser window.

EVERYONE WHO USES the Web must have a piece of software called a browser, which is responsible for fetching files from servers around the world and displaying the HTML file along with its associated graphics and other media.

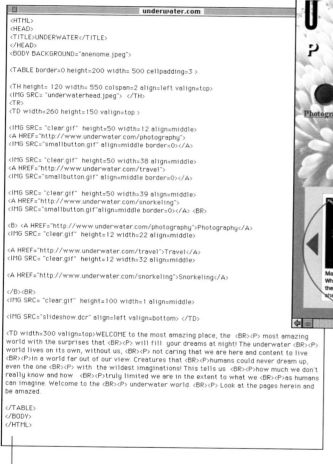

```
underwater.com

<HTML>
<HEAD>
<TITLE>UNDERWATER</TITLE>
</HEAD>
<BODY BACKGROUND="anenome.jpeg">

<TABLE border=0 height=200 width=500 cellpadding=3 >

<TH height= 120 width=550 colspan=2 align=left valign=top>
<IMG SRC= "underwaterhead.jpeg"> </TH>
<TR>
<TD width=260 height=150 valign=top >

<IMG SRC= "clear.gif"  height=50 width=12 align=middle>
<A HREF="http://www.underwater.com/photography">
<IMG SRC="smallbutton.gif" align=middle border=0>

<IMG SRC= "clear.gif"  height=50 width=38 align=middle>
<A HREF="http://www.underwater.com/travel">
<IMG SRC="smallbutton.gif" align=middle border=0></A>

<IMG SRC= "clear.gif"  height=50 width=39 align=middle>
<A HREF="http://www.underwater.com/snorkeling">
<IMG SRC="smallbutton.gif"align=middle border=0></A> <BR>

<B> <A HREF="http://www.underwater.com/photography">Photography</A>
<IMG SRC= "clear.gif"  height=12 width=22 align=middle>

<A HREF="http://www.underwater.com/travel">Travel</A>
<IMG SRC= "clear.gif"  height=12 width=32 align=middle>

<A HREF="http://www.underwater.com/snorkeling">Snorkeling</A>

</B><BR>
<IMG SRC= "clear.gif"  height=100 width=1 align=middle>

<IMG SRC="slideshow.dcr" align=left valign=bottom> </TD>

<TD width=300 valign=top>WELCOME to the most amazing place, the  <BR><P> most amazing
world with the surprises that <BR><P> will fill  your dreams at night! The underwater <BR><P>
world lives on its own, without us, <BR><P> not caring that we are here and content to live
<BR><P>in a world far out of our view. Creatures that <BR><P>humans could never dream up,
even the one <BR><P> with  the wildest imaginations! This tells us  <BR><P>how much we don't
really know and how    <BR><P>truly limited we are in the extent to what we <BR><P>as humans
can imagine. Welcome to the <BR><P> underwater world. <BR><P> Look at the pages herein and
be amazed.

</TABLE>
</BODY>
</HTML>
```

Most Web pages are saved in a format called HTML. Tags in the text file tell the browser how to structure the page on screen.

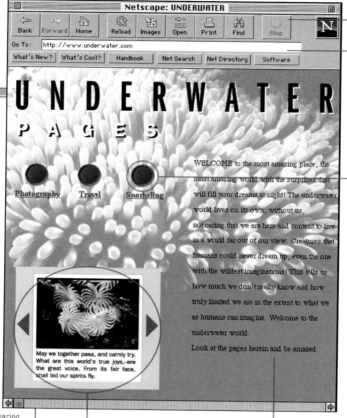

Buttons in the browser let the user navigate through the Web.

Users can view a specific file by typing its Internet address here.

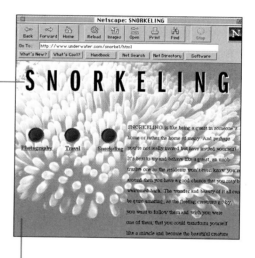

Clicking on a hyperlink calls up another page.

The most popular browsers support plug-ins, which work with the browser to display additional formats. This graphic, for example is the first frame of a Macromedia Director movie, played with the help of a plug-in called Shockwave.

HTML files and some standard formats can be displayed directly in the browser window.

It Can Be Interactive

Because the Web is based on computers, it can be interactive. Unlike material printed in a book or brochure, Web publications can respond to input by the user. The response can be as simple as returning an answer to a request for information or as complex as monitoring users' choices and controlling what they see based on their past preferences and actions.

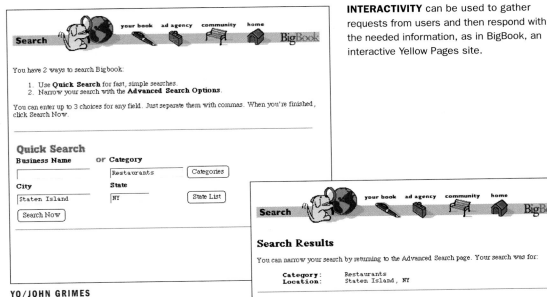

INTERACTIVITY can be used to gather requests from users and then respond with the needed information, as in BigBook, an interactive Yellow Pages site.

YO/JOHN GRIMES
http://www.bigbook.com/

What online can give you that nothing else can is live information, throbbing information that is pouring from some source. On one end of it, users are pushing the buttons, and on the other end databases are spewing out all sorts of information.

MATTHEW BUTTERICK, ATOMIC VISION

WEB PAGES can include full-color text and graphics, plus sound, animation, video, or almost anything else you can dream up, all in a hyperlinked environment that gives designers the opportunity to experiment with navigation as well as visual effects.

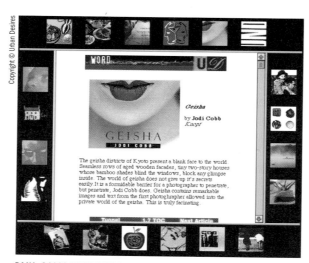

PAUL GALLI PRODUCTION/GEOFFREY BADNER
http://desires.com/1.7/Word/Holiday/roundup.html

P³⁹ **process thirty-nine**

Partner in Design, Development, and Production
Process 39 is an experienced multimedia development group helping **authors**, **publishers**, and **corporate clients** take newmedia projects from concept to finished product. Melding traditional design with technical expertise, Process 39 functions as a **digital workshop** – a place where bold ideas really get built.

Process 39 has collaborated on projects for **education**, **home entertainment**, **interactive television**, **corporate multimedia**, and the **Internet**. As a strong development partner, we have learned how to effectively contribute to **all phases** of development – from the first storyboards through the final audio tweaks.

The following sidebars explain each of our services in more detail, including real world examples from our portfolio.

Helping You Refine Your Creative Treatment

Our Role in Functional Design

Understanding Interface Development

Controlling Editorial and Content Development

The Art of Visual Design

Creating an Informative Prototype

Audio/Video Design and Production

PROCESS 39
http://www.process39.com/

Its Pages Can Be Designed

Thanks to HTML and its ability to support graphics and other media, the World Wide Web is the first service on the Internet that lends itself to any kind of graphic design. By the standards of print design, layout possibilities on the Web are still fairly meager, but they're growing at a rapid pace. Thanks to its ability to be designed, the World Wide Web is the first service on the Internet to grab the attention of the public, publishers, and businesses. And thanks to the use of hyperlinks for navigation, it presents an exciting design problem that challenges designers to create fluid and friendly interfaces, as well as attractive graphic design, to help visitors find, scan, and enjoy the material published there.

In the next chapter we'll talk about the factors that influence what can and can't be done, design-wise, on the Web. After that we'll introduce you to some of the people and companies pioneering the field. Then, with the help of those pioneers, we'll guide you through the processes of Web design, one by one.

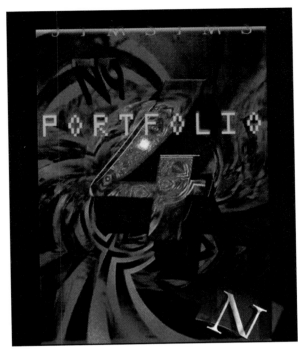

JIM SIMS/AMY BOYNTON
http://www.teleport.com/~sb/

Online: What Is the Web?

ActiveX Controls
http://www.microsoft.com/ie/ie3/activex.htm

General Information About the World Wide Web
http://www.w3.org/pub/WWW/

Helper Applications
http://vip.hotwired.com/surf/special/toolkit/basic.html

HTTP
http://www.w3.org/pub/WWW/Protocols/

Plug-ins
http://www.browserwatch.com/plug-in.html
http://www.netscape.com/comprod/mirror/
    navcomponents_download.html

If you look at the Web as an entertainment medium, it's not very exciting yet. If you look at it as an information medium, it's amazing. And when people start accessing the Web from places where they go to be entertained—like from the living room television—you're going to see the Web become more entertaining.

BRIAN BEHLENDORF, ORGANIC ONLINE

Possibilities and Limitations

The Web Is Nonlinear

You Define a Document's Structure, Not Its Presentation

HTML's Layout Controls Are Limited—But Growing

Bandwidth Sets the Standard

The Tools Are Improving—Quickly

The reputation of the Web among designers is that its design possibilities are practically nonexistent, but that isn't really so. In reality, the Web is quickly becoming one of the most exciting and flexible design media in history.

Many options, such as the choice of typeface, are, admittedly, still limited on the Web. On the other hand, the Web opens brand-new possibilities for inventive navigation schemes, a wide variety of media, and exciting interactivity, and its options for layout are growing fast. The key to satisfying and groundbreaking design on the Web—as in any other medium—is understanding the possibilities and limitations of the form. This chapter will help by explaining some important distinguishing features of design on the Web.

The Web Is Nonlinear

The first thing to remember about your site on the Web is that visitors access each page by hypertext links—from another page on your site or from another site entirely. You could lead the visitor through a controlled series of pages, but that's not what the Web is about; it's about letting the visitor choose his or her own path through the information. Your site will probably be just one among dozens the visitor will view in the space of several minutes. Visitors following a link from another site can land at any page of your site, may stay for just a few seconds, and then launch off to another site entirely.

In this context, you've got to make each page represent you or your client as strongly as every other; after all, it might be the only page of yours the visitor sees. Equally, every page should entice the visitor to explore your site further—and make it easy to do so.

How you accomplish this is wide open, of course; there's no single right way to do it. The challenge is finding the method that works best for the content you're presenting and the experience you want to invoke. One of the most exciting opportunities of design for the Web, especially in these early days, is to be one of the people finding new solutions and setting new standards for finding the way around cyberspace.

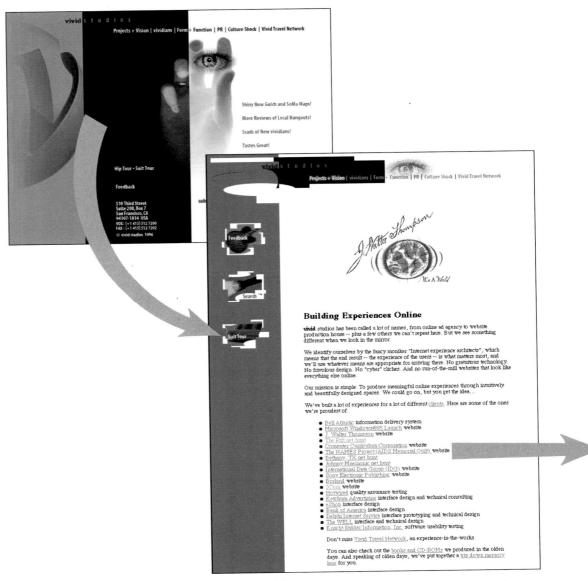

VIVID STUDIOS
http://www.vivid.com/

THE IDEA BEHIND THE WEB is to allow nonlinear access to information stored on sites all over the globe. Whatever else your design does, it must help visitors understand how to get to the information they're searching for. It must also establish an idiosyncratic identity among the dozens of sites the visitor may view in the space of a few minutes.

VIVID STUDIOS
http://www.aidsquilt.org/

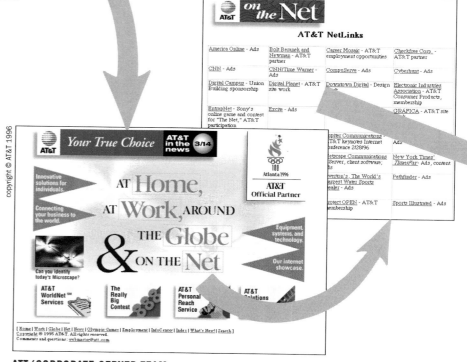

ATT/CORPORATE SERVER TEAM
http://www.att.com/

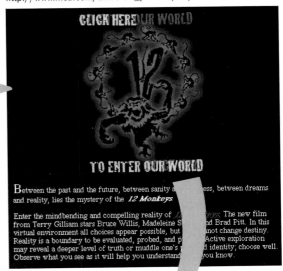

CLICK HERE OUR WORLD

TO ENTER OUR WORLD

Between the past and the future, between sanity and madness, between dreams and reality, lies the mystery of the *12 Monkeys*

Enter the mindbending and compelling reality of *12 Monkeys.* The new film from Terry Gilliam stars Bruce Willis, Madeleine S... and Brad Pitt. In this virtual environment all choices appear possible, but ... not change destiny. Reality is a boundary to be evaluated, probed, and pr... Active exploration may reveal a deeper level of truth or muddle one's ... d identity; choose well. Observe what you see as it will help you understand ... you know.

DIGITAL PLANET
http://www.digiplanet.com/

- identity
- creativity
- process
- technology
- community

digital planet

portfolio

shockwave

You are here ... have made a choice. More than anything, the interactive rev... ut choice -- your ability to chart your own ...

Portfolio

...dia's Burn:Cycle

Universal Pictures' 12 Monkeys

Universal Pictures' Casper

Universal Pictures' Apollo 13

MGM/UA Home Video

PERSONAL RESIDENCE ZONE #87645
PRISON BLOCK #87/B
CITY OF BROTHERLY LOVE

INMATE: JAMES COLE
DATE OF BIRTH: 7/13/1990
PSYCH PROFILE: VIOLENT/ANTI-SOCIAL
TERM OF SENTENCE: 25 YEARS TO LIFE

HANDY TIPS:
- YOUR CELL BLOCK COUNSELOR IS HERE TO MAKE YOU A BETTER PERSON
- CRIME IS NOT A SICKNESS-SICKNESS IS A CRIME
- POSSESSION OF PLANT OR ANIMAL MATTER STRICTLY FORBIDDEN
- NO HORSEPLAY
- VOLUNTEER-OR IT WILL BE DONE FOR YOU
- REMEMBER: COURTESY IS CONTAGIOUS!

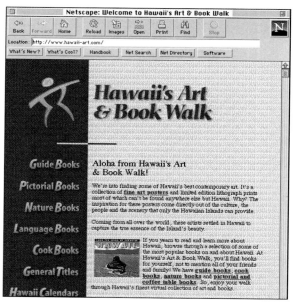

IN NETSCAPE 2.0

HTML TAGS label each element of a document—title, heading, new paragraph, and so on—but it's up to the browser software to determine just what those codes mean in terms of typography and layout. Most browsers lay out the same tags using similar specifications. To make things more complicated, though, not all browsers support all HTML codes, and individual visitors can set their own layout preferences. These illustrations show how the same HTML page may look in different browsers or with different user settings.

**IN NETSCAPE, WITH
TYPE PREFERENCES
CHANGED BY USER**

GRAPHIC COMMUNICATION
http://www.hawaii-art.com/

IN LYNX

```
Petroglyph [INLINE]
[INLINE]
Hawaii's Art & Book Walk [INLINE] Guide Books
Pictorial Books
Nature Books
Language Books
Cook Books
General Titles
Hawaii Calendars
Hawaii Videos
Fine Art Prints [INLINE]

Aloha from Hawaii's Art
& Book Walk!

We're into finding some of Hawaii's best contemporary art. It's a
collection of fine art posters and limited edition lithograph prints
most of which can't be found anywhere else but Hawaii. Why? The
inspiration for these posters come directly out of the culture, the
people and the scenery that only the Hawaiian Islands can provide.

Coming from all over the world, these artists settled in Hawaii to
capture the true essence of the Island's beauty.

[IMAGE] If you yearn to read and learn more about Hawaii, browse
through a selection of some of the most popular books on and about
Hawaii. At Hawaii's Art & Book Walk, you'll find books for yourself,
not to mention all of your friends and family! We have guide books,
cook books, nature books and pictorial and coffee table books. So,
enjoy your walk through Hawaii's finest virtual collection of art and
books. [INLINE]
```

IN NCSA MOSAIC 2.0

You Define a Document's Structure, Not Its Presentation

As we explained in the last chapter, most Web content is in the form of ASCII files, tagged with HTML, the Hypertext Markup Language. The HTML tags, which are simple codes placed between brackets within the file, label each element of the document—<P> for paragraph text, or <H1> for a first-level heading, for example. The browser software interprets the codes and lays out the document on screen accordingly.

Designers who go back to the pre–desktop publishing era will recognize the idea at work here: It's very similar to the method used for the old electronic typesetting systems. On the Web, as with such typesetting systems, the tags merely name the type of element; they don't specify its layout. The indentation, the type size and style, and other aspects of its appearance are determined by the specifications for each element programmed into the output system.

The difference on the Web is that the designer has no control over what those specifications are. Default specifications are programmed into the browser and can be changed only by the user.

Before you just quit right here, let us explain that there are a few mitigating factors. First, you should know that although there's no guarantee of it, most browsers actually use similar settings for things like typeface:

12-point Times for the basic text font and 12-point Courier for the alternate font (→**81**). And though users can change these defaults using their browser's Preferences settings, most seem to leave the settings alone. Those may not be the typefaces you would have picked, but they're the ones common to most operating systems, and at least you know what you'll be dealing with. The layout of other elements is likewise similar across different browsers.

Pages also appear different depending on the platform they're viewed on. For example, the resolution of the user's monitor can make graphics and type appear larger or smaller. Some visitors to your site will be using computers or browsers that can't display graphics—and others will have graphics turned off to make pages download faster.

This means that, although a significant portion of your audience will see your pages just as you intended, another segment will not. Successful Web design includes the art of creating pages that can be viewed successfully under a number of different conditions.

We design assuming that the basic typefaces will be Times and Courier, but you never know. Interestingly, we've noticed that PC users like to mess around with things like their typeface preferences; Mac users rarely do.

STEFAN FIELDING-ISAACS, ART & SCIENCE

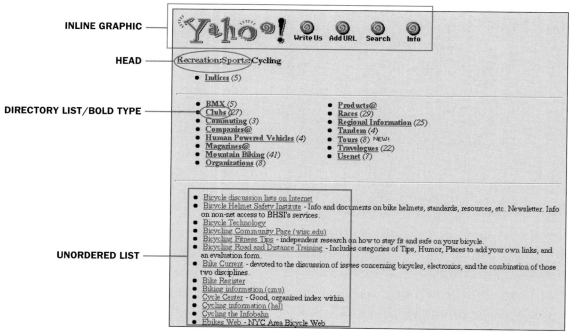

INLINE GRAPHIC —

HEAD —

DIRECTORY LIST/BOLD TYPE —

UNORDERED LIST —

CKS PARTNERS
http://www.yahoo.com/

HTML 2.0
The specification, finalized in September of 1995 by the HTML working group of the Internet Engineering Task Force (IETF), that codifies the basic set of HTML tags.

HTML 3.2
A working draft, under development by the IETF, that proposes an extended set of HTML codes.

HTML's Layout Controls Are Limited—But Growing

HTML's creators weren't thinking of blazing ground for a commercial Babel of online art magazines and corporate brochures when they defined the basic tags. What they were focusing on—and achieved supremely well—was a way of navigating the web of Internet servers through a system of easy-to-use hyperlinks. At the same time, they graciously made room for graphics and other media as well as text in their online world. The text styles included in the first revision of the language—six head levels, one standard and one monospaced font, numbered and bulleted lists, footnotes, indented quotes—solved most of the basic layout problems for the scientific papers and documentation that, just a couple of years ago, were the only kinds of documents usually found on the Internet.

The sudden popularity of the World Wide Web as a commercial publishing medium took the developers of HTML, like the rest of the world, by surprise. When the demands on HTML were noted, an industrywide standards committee was quickly formed to preside over and document the further development of the language. Its first task was to document the codes currently in use, a task that took until the summer of 1995 and resulted in a specification called **HTML 2.0**. Meanwhile, academic committees and software developers began to suggest extensions to the

language. This larger set of tags, including new proposals, is referred to as HTML 3. The current version,
as we write this, is **HTML 3.2**.

HTML 3.2 includes many features designed to take
into account the needs of graphic designers, but it
still leaves a lot to be desired. HTML 3.2 supports
centering, text-wrap around graphics, and table (grid)
layouts, for example, but not, so far, any typeface controls. We should acknowledge that it will probably be
at least a couple of years before designers moving
to the Web will have anything close to the range of
formatting features they're used to in other media.

To move HTML's capabilities forward, though, browser
manufacturers such as Netscape and Microsoft also
support some tags that they invent themselves, independently of their recognition by the standards committee. Recent developments have added quite a few
new styles to the Web designer's toolbox (→**89**), and
competition should keep the pace of innovation hot
for quite awhile.

The advantages of this rapid growth are clear. Designers
should also be aware of the other implication: the
learning curve is constant, and to stay current and
take advantage of new possibilities, designs need to
be updated often.

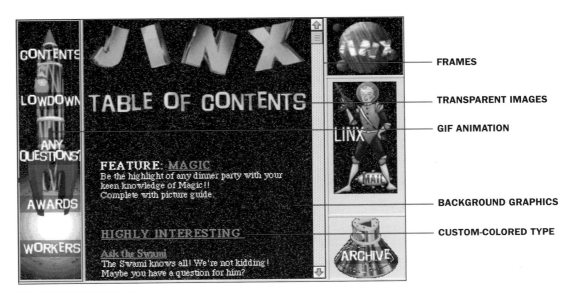

FRAMES

TRANSPARENT IMAGES

GIF ANIMATION

BACKGROUND GRAPHICS

CUSTOM-COLORED TYPE

THE BUOYANT COMPANY
http://www.jinx.com/

HTML'S BASIC TAGS, known as HTML
2.0, provide only limited layout and design
options (opposite page), but new versions
of browsers are adding support for new
features (above) at a rapid clip.

THE TIME IT TAKES to download a Web page varies with the type of connection in use. Over the next few years, telephone and cable companies are expected to make high-speed connections widely available at affordable prices, but for now, designers need to understand that most home and small business users will be using 14,400 or 28,800bps modems. This chart shows the average times it might take to download this relatively complex graphic at different connection speeds.

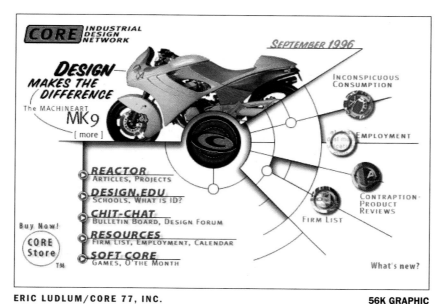

ERIC LUDLUM/CORE 77, INC.
http://www.core77.com/

56K GRAPHIC

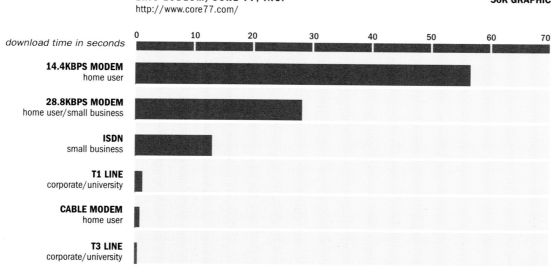

Bandwidth Sets the Standard

Designers who want more control over text styles and layout than HTML can offer are often tempted to turn to layouts based on full-page graphics, in which they can use any typefaces they want and place elements anywhere on the screen. HTTP and HTML let you embed hyperlinks in graphics (→**108**), so that the image can offer the same interactivity as HTML text. Unfortunately, there are two possible problems with that idea.

First, you've got to remember the user who has a text-only browser. Graphics interfaces won't work for that person. We'll discuss ways around that problem down the line (→**107**).

Second, graphics files—especially large and complex graphics—can take a long time to download by modem.

Designers working for print are used to seeing graphics files that weigh in at 20 megabytes (MB) or more. Successful Web designers, on the other hand, know to keep graphics to 30 kilobytes (K) or less. This takes into account the fact that lots of people who will view your work will be downloading it to their computer over a 14,400bps modem. In real terms that translates to about 1K per second—over a good connection—or 30 seconds just to get that file. This doesn't necessarily mean using thumbnail-size images throughout your site. The standard World Wide Web graphics formats—

GIF and JPEG (→**103**)—are highly compressed, and there are lots of tricks you can use to shorten download times (→**118**).

The problem is even greater when you begin to consider using time-based media such as animation, video, or sound, for which file sizes are substantially larger. New technologies for compressing multimedia files and delivering them to the user more efficiently are under development (→**135**), but for now, the Web designer's greatest challenge is to execute ideas using minuscule file sizes.

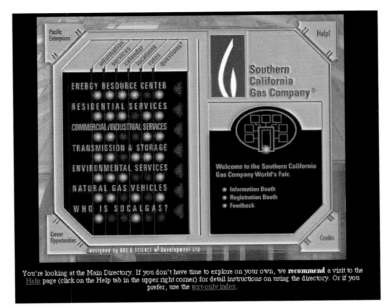

You're looking at the Main Directory. If you don't have time to explore on your own, we **recommend** a visit to the Help page (click on the Help tab in the upper right corner) for detail instructions on using the directory. Or if you prefer, use the text-only index.

ART & SCIENCE
http://www.socalgas.com/macro.html

THE GRAPHIC INTERFACE at left is created from four different graphics files (below), which many browsers can load simultaneously, significantly reducing download time. The center graphic is an animated GIF.

Design for the Web is a real art in itself. It's a lot like designing with the original Macintosh; it's defined by the limits. In the case of the Web, it's defined by bandwidth.

JONATHAN NELSON, ORGANIC ONLINE

Years from now, people will look back at what we're doing now and think it's really funny and primitive. But I remember the old days of television, when periodically the show would be interrupted and a sign would come up that said, "Please stand by. We are experiencing technical difficulties." People didn't care; they stood by. That's the stage we're in now.

BARBARA KUHR, HOTWIRED

The Tools Are Improving— Quickly

Many designers are taking a "wait and see" attitude toward the Web, holding out until the tools and design possibilities become more sophisticated. If you're tempted to wait, though, think of what happened to those who waited until the Mac had proved itself for desktop publishing—and then think of what happened to those who jumped in early and started exploring its possibilities.

The Web is in a state similar to the state of desktop publishing in 1986. It was clear that this new thing was going to be very, very big. It was also clear that it wasn't nearly up to the kind of design and production values available in other media. Same with the Web.

The difference is that the publishing industry has learned from its experiences of the last decade, and the tools for Web publishing are developing at an astonishing pace. By the end of 1995 most major desktop publishing and word processing programs could save files as HTML. Today, Adobe, Microsoft, Netscape, and other leading companies are creating WYSIWYG HTML layout tools that let designers design HTML pages using the kind of graphic tools they're used to in standard word processors, without seeing HTML at all. The leading hardware and software companies are working day and night to meet designers' demands.

It's going to take two or three years—not ten—for Web publishing tools to match—and surpass—those available for print and CD-ROM production.

Meanwhile, learning what you need to know to begin designing for the Web is a lot easier than you might think.

So our advice is, don't wait. Sure, the tools will change, and things will get easier, but there's lots to learn about this new medium. Here's your chance to blaze some new ground.

Online: Possibilities and Limitations

HTML 2.0 Specification
http://www.w3.org/hypertext/WWW/MarkUp/html-spec/
 html-spec_toc.html

HTML 3.2 Specification
http://www.w3.org/pub/WWW/MarkUp/Wilbur/

Microsoft Internet Explorer HTML Support
http://www.microsoft.com/workshop/author/newfeat/
 ie30html-f.htm

Netscape Extensions to HTML
http://www.netscape.com/assist/net_sites/
 html_extensions.html
http://www.netscape.com/assist/net_sites/
 html_extensions_3.html
http://www.netscape.com/comprod/products/navigator/
 version_3.0/layout/index.html

A year ago, everything was flat and static. Now we have pages that are dynamically generated, based on the user's software and input. The next stage will be dynamically generated information that does something, using animation and interactivity.

JEFF VEEN, HOTWIRED

Who's Doing Web Design?

Art & Science

Atomic Vision

Avalanche

CNET

Construct

HotWired

Organic Online

Studio Archetype

Vivid Studios

Web designers seem to be a whole new breed of design professional. Although some traditional design firms have taken on Web site design as part of the range of services they offer their clients, many of the leading Web design companies grew up with the medium itself—and like the Web, have gone from start-up to top of the field in little over a year. The Web came from nowhere, and only those who already had skills in both networking and design were ready to catch the first wave.

The Web designers we profile in this chapter, and whose wisdom we'll quote in the rest of this book, were among the first to ride that wave. They're an interesting mix, remarkable for their versatility and their wide variety of backgrounds as well as for their prescience in recognizing the Web's potential.

As Web publishing becomes more mainstream, as easier-to-use tools appear for Web page design and Web servers, and as the demand for Web services blossoms, Web design skills will be more widespread. But the stories of the pioneers profiled here have a lot to say about the kinds of talents required in this new medium, the kinds of jobs available in the field, and the kind of gumption that can pull great success out of modest beginnings.

Art & Science

http://www.chiba.com/

Founded in the fall of 1994, Art & Science has had in some ways a prototypical Web design history: a computer-literate nondesigner with an interest in hypertext and storytelling finds the Web, exploits its possibilities creatively, and makes it big.

Stefan Fielding-Isaacs, the company's president, graduated from a liberal arts education into work as a technical writer for Microsoft and other high-tech companies. As a freelance technical writer he worked for Taligent, Silicon Graphics, Sun, and other companies whose products would later be tightly tied to the Web, and where he first experimented with hypertext as a format for documentation. A personal project—a journal of a trip to Europe in 1993—became his first work on the Web. His experience with that won him a job doing a Web site for RSA Data Security, a company for which he'd worked as a writer. Around that time, he also met the marketing director for Joe Boxer at one of his monthly cocktail parties, and the rest is history. The playful graphics and creative navigation system Art & Science built for Joe Boxer's site won the design company notice just as Web fever was peaking in the business world. Fielding-Isaacs and an assortment of friends took office space in San Francisco's Multimedia Gulch in the summer of 1995, as jobs began pouring in.

Art & Science offers a full range of Web services: design, programming, and even site hosting and maintenance. "From our perspective offering to host sites is a necessity. Our objective is to meet our customers' needs, and if that's to build them a fast Web site, we have to also make sure it's fast once it's out there." Fielding-Isaacs acts as CEO and information architect. Out of a staff of 14, half are programmers and engineers (the team also includes a chief operating officer, an art director, a marketing director, a staff artist, plus project managers and operations staff).

ART & SCIENCE
W3 development ltd
615 third street
san francisco

千葉市

All work created by Art & Science is a result of an interactive team effort.

I'm spending 20 percent of our net revenues on R&D: learning Shockwave, Java, and so on. We have a position in the top ranks of design firms right now, and we don't want to lose that.

STEFAN FIELDING-ISAACS, PRESIDENT, ART & SCIENCE

Atomic Vision

http://www.atomicvision.com/

In the two years between graduating from Harvard and founding Atomic Vision, Matthew Butterick was a type designer, working at Boston's Font Bureau on new and revival typefaces and contributing his own experimental typeface to Neville Brody's *Fuse* magazine. Butterick started Atomic Vision in Cambridge in late 1994, and in 1995 he moved the company to San Francisco.

"I could do type design, but people have been doing that for 300 years, and I'll never be one of the best," says Butterick. "With Web design, there's the oppor-

tunity to get in on the ground floor and make something happen. In the Web I get the design and the technology, and also the components of marketing and message and editorial. And it's all completely new."

Butterick practically boils over with energy and ideas as he describes Web design, his work with new navigation structures, and his plans for his company. "I don't want to do marketing brochures," he says. "I want to find ways to extend the new medium." To that end, he has targeted a niche that he describes as "companies whose business plans have an important Web component." Atomic Vision clients such as the popular Web search service Excite and *Wired* magazine (for whom he did an online subscription program), are examples of hits in his target market.

Now with a staff of eight, including art directors, producers, and a marketing director, Butterick plans to keep his company small. "The ratio in terms of what a few people can turn out is much greater than with print," he points out. He also clearly enjoys wearing a variety of hats as head of his own small company. "I can do all this dabbling," he laughs. "I get to be this designer guy and marketing guy and programmer guy all at once."

I never refer to Atomic Vision as a Web design company. Getting wed to a particular technology is a mistake. It's information design for digital data: digital design.

MATTHEW BUTTERICK, PRESIDENT, ATOMIC VISION

Avalanche

http://www.avsi.com/

Avalanche, an interactive agency in New York's Soho, had its start as Seidler Design, an eight-year venture also headed by Avalanche's president, Peter Seidler. After relaunching at the beginning of 1995 with just Seidler and CEO Michael Block, the company now has 38 people and a client list that includes NBC, FAO Schwarz, and Elektra Records. "When we started, it was pretty clear that there was a lot of work to be done for the Web. Getting clients to understand that early on was more difficult. A year and a half ago, most people didn't know what the Web was."

Seidler describes the company's jobs as covering the breadth of interactive design, including the development of projects such as intranets, CD-ROM, and interactive press kits, but he admits that the Web is a large part of the business these days—and the culmination, as he sees it, of the short history of multimedia publishing that he has been involved in from the start. "I always felt like there were so many things we wanted to do. Now the tools are starting to catch up to the vision." When the tools are wanting, Seidler sees it as part of his company's task to create them, whether it's new compression functions for media on CD-ROM or Java interaction for a Web site.

With both his company and the field exploding, much of Seidler's energy these days goes into trying to grow fast gracefully. "I interview constantly," he says. Since the pool of talent with Web and multimedia skills is small, he says he looks for people with a good conceptual design approach. "The crew here is amazing," says Seidler. "Our systems admin, Alan Hardwick, takes care of half a dozen Sun boxes and dozens of Macs. He's a filmmaker." One of the biggest challenges for a Web company like his, says Seidler, is riding the wave without wiping out the team, a goal he describes as "trying to create our business in a way that's as beautiful as the sites we create."

Our specialty is conceptual design, design derived from the nature of the content. We put a high value on the emotional content of a site, and we're never satisfied until we can say it's totally beautiful. But a large part of that is how it works conceptually.

PETER SEIDLER, PRESIDENT, AVALANCHE

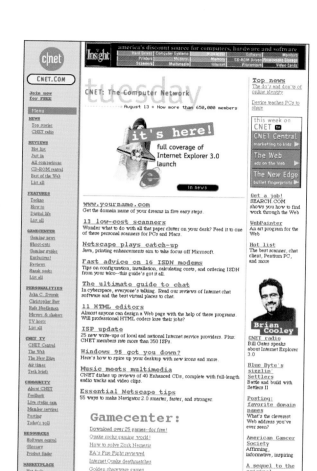

CNET

http://www.cnet.com/

CNET: The Computer Network offers computer information on the Web (with a series of sites, including *CNET* magazine, NEWS.COM, SEARCH.COM, and SHAREWARE.COM) and on television (CNET's three TV shows, *CNET Central, The Web,* and *The New Edge,* appear twice weekly on cable). Started in 1994, CNET has quickly become one of the premier purveyors of computer news in any medium and hosts some of the most-trafficked sites on the Web.

Andrea Jenkins, CNET's art director, has headed up the design and production teams involved in producing CNET's Web magazine since its launch. Working with CNET's vice president of creative affairs, Fred Sotherland, one of her first tasks was to design the magazine's distinctive look and structure. She describes her job now as "the main touch person between editorial, production, and the designers."

At editorial meetings, she helps brainstorm the structure and graphic treatments that define each story or section, then leads her staff of 12 designers and graphics production people through the execution of the ideas.

As a content provider covering the latest trends in computers and the Internet, CNET is under a lot of pressure to create leading-edge Web design. At the same time, the need for a flashy presentation must be constantly weighed against two balancing factors: first, that reader surveys have shown CNET's audience to be weighted heavily toward lower-bandwidth home computer users, and second, that the Web site is on a tight turnaround schedule. Jenkins's team is responsible for turning out two stories a week; providing content in 10 sections daily, and creating 40 promotional "front doors" every seven days—plus what Jenkins calls frequent "emergency" projects, the unplanned content that is a part of every news-based publication. In August 1996, the site was clocked at 35,000 pages and growing. The job is done with a set of design templates and basic grids that serve a variety of stories and impart a cohesive look to all parts of the site, while offering enough flexibility so that each story can get an individual, custom-made treatment.

One of our goals when we launched the site was to bring people onto the Web. We didn't want to intimidate anyone, so we made everything as simple as possible.

ANDREA JENKINS, ART DIRECTOR, CNET

Construct

http://www.construct.net/

The core group at Construct met at the Interactive Media Festival (IMF), an annual event (sponsored by Motorola) that brings together artists and businesses engaged in developing interactive electronic environments. Lisa Goldman, now Construct's president, was the festival's creative director. Mark Meadows, Construct's creative director, was the festival's webmaster. And Annette Loudon, now Construct's webmistress, was in charge of online design.

"We built a Web interface for the festival, including a private jury chamber that held one of the first HTML conferencing interfaces," recalls Meadows. "When it was time to put the gallery online, I wanted to use something that was more interactive and more spatially accurate, so I started to look into to how to make it 3-D." Thus began the group's fascination with, and expertise in, VRML (Virtual Reality Modeling Language), a format for creating 3-D interfaces on the Web. To get help with the job, Meadows turned to the Net. Messages on the WELL (a Sausalito, California–based Internet conferencing service) rounded up a group that included Michael Gough, previously a partner at the architectural firm Holt Hinshaw, now constructing virtual buildings as Construct's staff architect; Todd Goldenbaum and Adam Gould, the

company's project managers; and James Waldrop, now its technical director.

When the festival ended, Construct began. "We said, now that we know VRML, where else can we use it? We wanted to explore it further," explains Meadows. Goldman says that calls for VRML work began coming in almost immediately after the festival. The company incorporated in August of 1995, and its staff now numbers 16 full-timers. "Almost everyone has a design background," notes Meadows. "Even our tech director studied stage design—something we only realized after we formed the company."

Though much of its work centers on its VRML expertise, the Construct team stresses that VRML is just one tool among many in its toolbox. "Building virtual environments is a process that requires a lot of different skills: architecture, network programming, illustration," says Meadow. "The more we do it, the more we learn about how it all fits together."

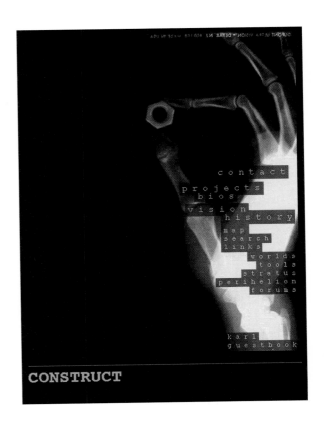

Construct is exploring shared data spaces, concentrating on the characteristics that define the online medium. We think that good Internet design welds together the aesthetic and the technical.

MARK MEADOWS, CREATIVE DIRECTOR, CONSTRUCT

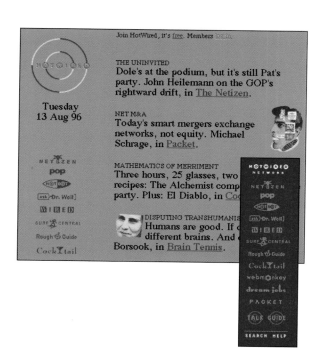

HotWired

http://www.hotwired.com/

As the first child of the marriage of ultra-hip *Wired* magazine and the World Wide Web, *HotWired* was under a lot of scrutiny when it launched in 1994. *Wired* had long been testifying about this revolution in communications, and *HotWired* was its Exhibit A.

Barbara Kuhr, who with her partner John Plunkett were the founding art directors of *Wired,* became creative director for the new venture and set about defining what a magazine might look like on the Web—a task that has continued through every day of its two-year history. It was a success. *HotWired* not only convinced the world that an online magazine can work, but along the way it pioneered ideas about what advertising might look like on the Web (*HotWired* was the first to use those ubiquitous, hot-linked ad banners), how content can be customized for each reader

(providing a "Your View" for registered users), and (with the Club Wired forums) how a site's readers can be knit together using related Internet technology.

One of *HotWired's* useful innovations was the structuring concept of "channels" online, with each channel providing an amalgam of features and departments on a given theme. The magazine's teams are also structured primarily according to those channels, with editors, designers, and production staff grouped according to the section they work on. In addition to Kuhr, we spoke to Sabine Messner, senior designer, and Jeff Veen, *HotWired's* interface director, who keeps an eye on upcoming technologies and sees to the development of systems and interfaces for sections, such as *HotWired's* forums, that span the entire site.

Ideas come from whoever's at the table, and that's very different from other media. It starts to approach the process of filmmaking. That way of telling stories is what Web design is going to be all about.

BARBARA KUHR, CREATIVE DIRECTOR, HOTWIRED

Organic Online

http://www.organic.com/

Jonathan Nelson, CEO of Organic Online, remembers making cold calls on corporations in 1993 trying to convince their marketing departments that they needed Web sites, with no luck. Nelson, along with his brother Matthew (Organic's chief production officer) and Brian Behlendorf (chief technology officer) had been offering Web design and networking services as a part-time business, keeping their day jobs until about the summer of 1994, when, says Nelson, those companies starting calling him back. "It was about the time that *Time* magazine put the Internet on the cover," he remembers. Nelson gave up the sound engineering he'd been doing to devote full time to the Web.

As one of the earliest companies to pitch the idea of communicating on the Web, Organic was perfectly poised to ride the first wave of commercial interest in the new medium. Behlendorf was an early web-master for *HotWired*, and its first clients were some of *HotWired's*—and thus the Web's—first advertisers, including AT&T, Volvo, and Saturn.

Organic offers clients what it calls "turnkey Web solutions." Clients can take advantage of any or all of the company's services, from consulting up front; to the design, writing, programming, and production leading up to the launch of a site; to online publicity and statistical and demographic analysis after the site is live. Most of Organic's clients keep their sites on its servers, says Nelson.

"If you would have told me a few years ago that we would be working with Nike and McDonald's, I would have thought you were crazy," says Nelson. "Now we say, OK, we've got Nike and McDonald's. Who don't we have?"

If you think of us as an **HTML** shop, you're missing the point. That's a handful of people in a company of 50. We do interactive communications. We develop content, special technologies, and marketing plans for strategic issues.

JONATHAN NELSON, CEO, ORGANIC ONLINE

Studio Archetype

http://www.studioarchetype.com/

Formerly known as Clement Mok designs, Studio Archetype was founded in 1988. The band of designers, information architects, and multimedia professionals headed by Clement Mok quickly grew to be recognized as leaders in high-tech design, both because many of the firm's clients were based in the Silicon Valley and because the company was one of a handful doing new media projects such as CD-ROMs and show-floor kiosks in the '80s. As Studio Archetype, the name the business adopted in early 1996, the studio has continued to help clients build brand identities that span different media types. In mid-1996, the firm, based in San Francisco, had a staff of more than 60.

John Grotting and Peter Merholz, who spoke for Studio Archetype in this book, are two of those recent additions. Grotting is one of the company's six design

directors. Merholz, previously in charge of producing the Web site at Voyager, the New York new media publisher, is an online producer. "On our Web projects, I'm the one who keeps abreast of the technology to see what we can do. I tell the producers and designers the limitations as well as the possibilities of the technology," says Merholz. Grotting, like the company's other designers, moves back and forth between print and new media projects, a mix he sees as a definite advantage for the company. "It forces you to approach each project fresh," he says.

Studio Archetype's long history in new media (Mok helped launch HyperCard as creative director for Apple in 1986), its eclectic mix of talent, and a reputation for clean and colorful design draws high-profile clients who demand innovative and ambitious solutions befitting their reputations as industry leaders. QVC came to them when it needed an interface for its online version, iQVC, for example. The work Studio Archetype may be proudest of, ironically, most people never see; a large component of the studio's work is helping clients develop strategies for how technology can be used to evolve their businesses—imagining applications that can't even be achieved with current technology.

It's the range of disciplines you get involved in that allows you to make connections and bring different experiences to the work. What we're really good at doing is being in many different spaces, and where we add value is making those connections between different industries and different media.

CLEMENT MOK, FOUNDER AND CHIEF INFORMATION ARCHITECT, STUDIO ARCHETYPE

Vivid Studios

http://www.vivid.com/

Vivid Studios has gone through myriad incarnations since its founding in 1990. Known then as Vivid Publishing, it specialized in software for the NeXT machine and books dedicated to helping people understand technologies of all kinds. (*Understanding Computers* was its first title, followed by *Multimedia Demystified* and *Careers in Multimedia*.) Its three-person staff consisted of Nathan Shedroff as creative director (he's still in that role), a programmer, and a marketing director—a constellation of skills that could be seen as a recipe for a successful Web design firm, which is what the company had morphed into by 1994. Now headed by Henri Poole, a multimedia producer whose company merged with Vivid in 1992, Vivid defines itself as a firm that creates "online experiences." Based in San Francisco, the company was 45 strong in mid-1996, split into five groups: management, "experience," engineering, producers, and operations.

"You've got to remember that your competition isn't other Web sites; it's everything else people might be doing: roller blading, scuba diving, or watching TV," says Shedroff. That attitude shapes Vivid's approach to the Web sites it creates, which are planned in terms of "adaptive" technologies and interaction.

In keeping with that concept, the lead designers on Vivid's project teams are called "interaction designers." "They own the experience," explains Shedroff. "They're in charge of being inspired." Vivid's workday operations are designed to encourage both interaction and inspiration. Weekly design meetings keep all the firm's staff apprised of how others in the company are approaching design problems, and field trips to theater, sports events, and museums help prod new ideas.

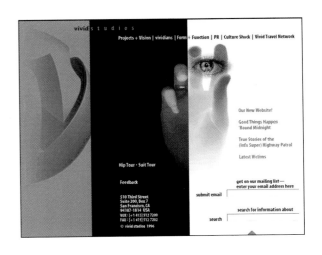

As a company, we are trying to concentrate on online experiences that are truly interactive.

NATHAN SHEDROFF, CREATIVE DIRECTOR, VIVID STUDIOS

The Process of Web Design

When approaching the Web or any other new medium, just remember: Underneath the mix of unfamiliar job titles, file formats, and terminology, the job still comes down to design, production, and distribution—the same tasks you'll find in any publishing venture. In this chapter, we'll describe what those steps entail in a Web publishing project and talk about ways some teams split up those jobs.

The World Wide Web is such a new medium that no models have really been established for who does what and how the team members interrelate. The situation is made harder to describe by quick changes in technology. Just as desktop publishing tools like PageMaker changed the role of print designers, new tools for HTML page layout and interactive scripting may quickly put some of the tasks usually handled by production engineers into the hands of Web designers. And as bandwidth improves and sites become more media-rich, producing a Web site could demand all the skills of producing a film, requiring professional video and sound production—even actors.

The Web Site Development Process

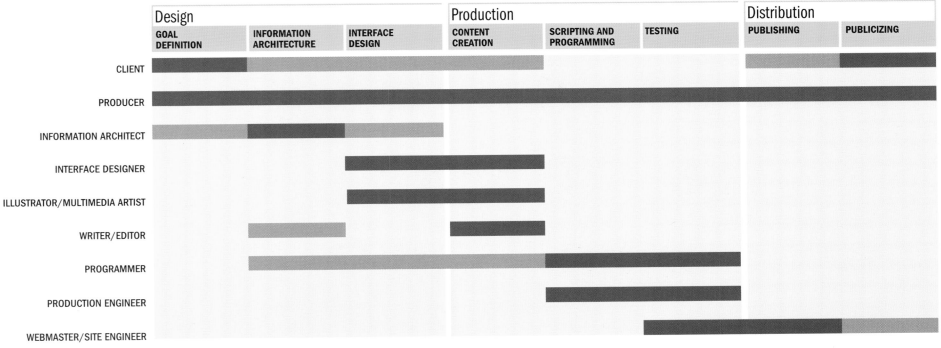

	Design			Production			Distribution	
	GOAL DEFINITION	INFORMATION ARCHITECTURE	INTERFACE DESIGN	CONTENT CREATION	SCRIPTING AND PROGRAMMING	TESTING	PUBLISHING	PUBLICIZING
CLIENT								
PRODUCER								
INFORMATION ARCHITECT								
INTERFACE DESIGNER								
ILLUSTRATOR/MULTIMEDIA ARTIST								
WRITER/EDITOR								
PROGRAMMER								
PRODUCTION ENGINEER								
WEBMASTER/SITE ENGINEER								

WEB PUBLISHING IS COLLABORATIVE by nature, calling on the skills of a variety of team members. The dark bars here show the areas of each team member's main responsibility. The light bars show where those people play a consulting role.

At HotWired, each channel has a team, consisting of an editor, a designer, a production manager, and an engineer. Without collaborating we would never get things to work.

SABINE MESSNER, HOTWIRED

Managing the Project

As in any publishing project, the job of pulling together the ideas and expertise of individual team members into a coherent plan is generally given to a single manager, who might be called the project manager, project editor, or—most often these days—the producer. Whatever the title, the job is the same: to define the project, pull together an appropriate team, and, as the job progresses, oversee the project from a bird's-eye view, communicate the project plan to team members, and make sure the project is implemented according to that plan.

If the job is being done for an outside client, an account manager may also be involved in order to represent the client's wishes to the team and communicate the team's ideas and progress back to the client.

On the Web, project managers often have a special challenge, created by the newness of the medium. Most clients have no experience with the Web, and even more than with other media, the manager will need to take special pains to help the client understand just what to expect from the process. Careful delineation of what you need from the client and what the client can expect from you will help smooth the road.

As soon as we win a project, we take a deposit and do a detailed needs analysis. What the client really needs will quickly rise to the surface. We'll come back at them with a contract that includes a timeline and a statement of work that includes the deliverables, a staff list, and a creative brief. Everybody signs it, and we go.

JONATHAN NELSON, ORGANIC ONLINE

The Webmaster

One of the most common yet loosely defined roles in the world of the Web is "webmaster" or "web-mistress." Depending on the site, it can mean the chief programmer, the head editor, the lead producer, the site engineer (the person who oversees the setup and maintenance of the server)—or just about anything else. Often, it just means the person who was the first to take an interest in the Web at that particular company and who headed up the initial effort to launch a site. Given the history of the Web, that often means someone who has a background in Unix computers and network management.

Defining the Site's Goals

The first step of any publishing project, of course, is to define the publication's goals. If an outside client is involved, the job of establishing the publisher's goals usually involves discussions between the client and the account manager. For an in-house project, it might be the job of the project manager, in conversation with any of the managers whose departments will be served by the Web site. There is no single way of getting the needed information, and each design group will look for different types of information. Most of the information you need to obtain is the same as for any publishing project: an understanding of the audience you're trying to reach and the message you want them to understand. With Web design, though, there are some special needs to ascertain. Since Web design often requires a trade-off between download speed and flashy effects, it's important to reach an understanding of which end of that spectrum the client is aiming for. And since certain effects can be viewed only by visitors using certain browsers (→**21**), the target software must also be defined.

This step should end with a document describing the goals of the project—a **creative brief**—which should be signed off on by any managers who will need to approve the design. Such a document will ensure that everyone involved shares the same expectations and will help inform decisions as the site develops.

Phase 1: Conceptual Development

GOALS AND MESSAGES

Determine the Following
1 Primary and secondary goals of the product
2 Primary and secondary goals of the client/publisher
3 Primary and secondary audience description (interests, needs, skills, capabilities, assumptions)
4 Audience capabilities (platform, browser/app, connection speed, degree of Net savvy and Net experience)
5 Platform descriptions (make, models, RAM, hard drives, CD-ROM, data load for each)
6 Top three messages the product needs to convey
7 After you've thought through these issues, rethink the goals.
8 Are they the true goals or merely the obvious ones?

Content
1 Does this product use primarily existing content?
2 If yes, how is it to be repurposed? In what ways will it be made appropriate to the interactive medium?
3 If new, how will it be captured and created? How much will there need to be?
4 Does this product use data entered by users? If so, how much and in what forms?
5 What can be done with it once entered?

Structure and Interpretations
1 What is the primary organization of the content?
2 What are other organizations that can be made available for other modes of searching, viewing, browsing, learning, exploring, and understanding?
3 What are the main presentation ideas of the structure of the title/project?
4 What are the most important and compelling features?
5 Are there any novel interactions? If so, what are they?
6 Will any new or emerging technologies be employed?
7 Will the audience be able to use them (or will the audience be given the necessary means and support to use them)?
8 What is the level of interactivity?
9 Are there any adaptive technologies employed?
10 Which ones and how?
11 Are there any cocreative features?

Sensorial Design
1 Describe the overall visual elements and styles of this product (use adjectives if necessary).
2 Describe the overall auditory elements and styles of this title.
3 Describe the text elements and written portions of this title.
4 Describe any ideas about animation style and use.
5 Describe any ideas about video style and use.
6 Describe the sophistication of programming needed.
7 Describe any current authoring systems that are intended for use or modification.

Market Testing
1 What are the environmental issues that concern the user of this product?
2 Which of these are most important to them?
3 Who are the competitors for this product?
4 How do these competitors rate on the environmental issues?
5 What are their strengths and weaknesses?
6 How can these strengths and weaknesses be addressed?
7 What are the best opportunities, and how can these be used to an advantage?
8 What are the most critical weaknesses, and how can these be eliminated?
9 Where are the best positions within the field of competitors?

Team
1 Who are the primary members of the production team? What are their roles and responsibilities?
2 What is their experience?
3 Are there technical, programming, marketing, and media professionals represented on the team?

WEB DESIGN USUALLY STARTS with a formal fact-finding procedure, during which the design team determines the client's requirements for content, look and feel, and function. This illustration shows the document Vivid Studios uses to gather this information.

creative brief
A statement of the goals of a design process.

Site architecture requires very tight right-brain/left-brain integration. You have to be able to organize the information and then also realize how that's going to work on the screen.

STEFAN FIELDING-ISAACS, ART & SCIENCE

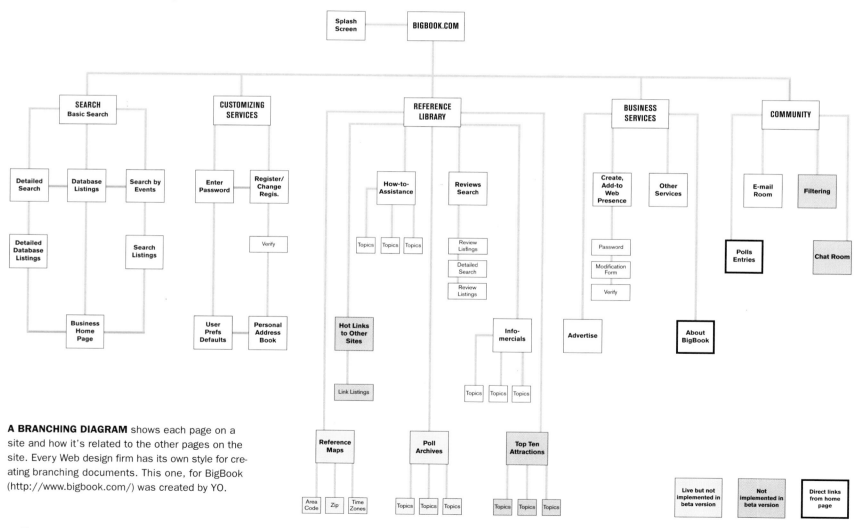

A BRANCHING DIAGRAM shows each page on a site and how it's related to the other pages on the site. Every Web design firm has its own style for creating branching documents. This one, for BigBook (http://www.bigbook.com/) was created by YO.

Information Architecture

Once the site's goals are understood, the planning of content can begin. Here again, exact job titles are hard to define, but more and more, the industry seems to be adopting the title **information architect**, a term very descriptive of the task at hand, which is building a structure for the site that will hold the information and offer the functionality described in the creative brief.

Defining what the site contains is a fairly straightforward and familiar process. For sites for which the main goal is the distribution of information, the design team may get most of the content from the client or publisher. For sites in which the purpose is more playful or less well-defined, the team may pull in the services of a copywriter to plan a creative approach to the message.

With the content defined, the next decision is how the content will be organized in the hyperlinked structure of the Web—probably the most challenging and specialized form of Web design. Complex enough when the fairly straightforward interfaces of text, graphics, and hyperlinks defined the Web, it's even more complicated now that the options are enhanced by a variety of technologies for animation and interactivity. For this reason, the planning of a Web site usually depends on the collaboration of a whole team of talents, including programmers as well as information architects. The programmers can keep an eye on the technical implications of any design directions being discussed: Will a particular type of interaction require too much traffic on the server, and thus cause slowdowns? Can a particular effect be realized using Java or another programming language, or not? How much time would it take to implement? Is an even more elegant solution possible using the newest tools?

The process of arriving at an "information architecture" for a site usually involves a series of meetings for discussing possibilities. It results in a document that defines the structure: at least an outline, but more helpfully, a **storyboard** or a **branching diagram**, showing what pages the site will include and what information each page will contain.

The architecture determines what's going to go on the page. Then, once you know what's there, you start to think, "What are we trying to say, what kind of technology are we going to use, and what mood are we trying to set?"

JOHN GROTTING, STUDIO ARCHETYPE

branching diagram
In Web design, a diagram that shows what pages a Web site contains and how they are related to one another.

information architect
For any publishing project, the person responsible for determining how information will be organized for the publication. In Web design, the information architect is responsible for deciding how the information will be arrayed on the pages of a Web site and how it will be accessed by the user.

storyboard
A document that shows the planned sequence of frames for video or any other time-based storytelling form.

Everyone on our team knows what's possible on the Web, but you still need an engineering person to help you plan. A particular idea may be possible, but the engineer knows whether or not it's practical to implement.

BARBARA KUHR, HOTWIRED

Planning for a site that assumes any kind of interactivity should also result in a **technical specification**, which describes the expected user experience and the way the site should respond to users' actions.

The branching diagram and the technical specification together form the backbone on which the interface designers, writers, and programmers can begin building. They also provide the information the project manager will need to predict talent and scheduling needs—whether special skills such as programming or animation will be required, for example.

These documents also provide the information the project manager or site engineer needs to define directories and filenames for the final files—an important detail for building a working site, with functioning hyperlinks, later in the process.

technical specification
A document that describes the expected user experience and the way the site should respond to users' actions. A technical specification codifies the expectations for any programmed interaction on a site.

Interface Design

Once the information architecture is complete, documented, and approved by the client, the team knows what information and functions need to be on each page of the site, and a more detailed, page-by-page design phase can begin.

This stage can also be broken into a couple of parts. The first stage might be called **page architecture**, in which the designers decide what standard elements will be on each page, how they will relate to one another on screen, and how they will interact with the site as a whole. This will probably include creating a navigation system for the site: a standard set of icons or other links that users can quickly learn for navigating through the pages. This step might be thought of as determining how the pages *work*.

Only after that do we finally get to how the pages *look*—the stage that might be called graphic design. The page designer defines a "look and feel" for the information, directing the work of illustrators and HTML coders to create a logical, attractive, and appropriate interface. Many designers think in pictures and develop ideas visually, so sketches for possible looks and graphic elements may begin much earlier in the process, but it's only at this stage, with the structure and function of the pages solved, that the design can be finalized.

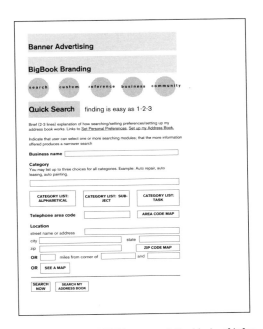

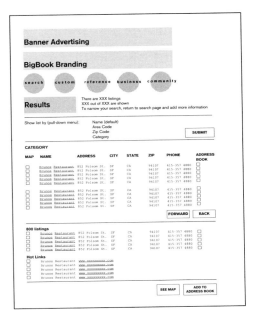

PAGE ARCHITECTURE maps out the kinds of information on each page, or each type of page, in the Web site. It's at this stage—after the site architecture is complete and the content of each page is determined—that the designer can determine such interface issues as which elements of each page will be text and which will be graphics.

page architecture
A plan for the placement of information on a page.

GRAPHICS, TEXT, and the other elements of a Web site may go through several iterations as the site's requirements are refined. The idea of using a dog as an agent in the BigBook Web site navigation graphics (right) evolved early in the design process. Later stages refined the department names, icons, and the size of the navigation bar.

INTERFACE DESIGN VERSION 1

INTERFACE DESIGN VERSION 2

YO/JOHN GRIMES
http://www.bigbook.com/

FINAL INTERFACE DESIGN

Creating the Content

With the structural plan in hand and the look and feel understood, the content creators can begin the job of fleshing out the site.

An extensive team can be required to create the content for a site. Writers will be responsible for creating concise, effective copy for each page; editors and copy-editors will be required to fine-tune it.

Graphic artists, animators, and sound and video specialists may be called in to create the site's visual identity and multimedia sequences, working with the production engineers as necessary to prepare the media in the small file sizes and specialized formats required on the Web.

As the team members whip up their copy and artwork, the project manager puts out fires, obtains (or gives) any necessary approvals, and ensures that everyone is working toward the common goal and deadline.

Once we've negotiated the format and we have some idea of the content—or the direction the content needs to go in—we come up with some sort of artistic direction. We do pen and inks and let the client see them. It might take a week or two to finalize the direction. Then we go back into Photoshop or we render it in 3-D.

STEFAN FIELDING-ISAACS, ART & SCIENCE

Programming and Scripting

Simple tools for interactivity—the ability to jump from page to page using hyperlinks, the ability to send e-mail to a specified address—are built into HTML. Anything that goes beyond that—collecting data from forms, or returning any response to user input—requires programming.

Programs for some of the simplest, most common actions—counting visitors to the site, responding to a click on a portion of an image—are available free on line. Most others will require a programmer to construct **scripts**: lists of instructions for the computer to follow in response to a user's input.

The writing of simple scripts is often one of the jobs assigned to production engineers, whose tasks include HTML production as well as scripting (→**48**). As programming possibilities grow, though, so will the need for more specialized programmers, who can create interactive interfaces, hook in back-end databases, and create other custom behavior for Web sites, using programming languages such as Java (→**168**).

As Web pages become more complex, the link between programming and design will become even tighter, and success will rely on the ability of designers and programmers to collaborate to make ideas come to life using all available technology.

Production

In many ways, the world of Web production has a lot in common with the world of print production in the early days of desktop publishing. Before desktop design software automated many production tasks, those tasks were performed by typesetters and paste-up artists.

By late 1996, the first "desktop publishing" programs for the Web had begun to appear, but they were not sophisticated enough to replace specialized HTML experts. While WYSIWYG HTML editors (→**77**) such as Adobe's PageMill, Microsoft's FrontPage, and Macromedia's Backstage can help designers develop rough layouts, they aren't yet able to produce clean, final pages. Someone still has to hack the HTML. In the next year or so, software for laying out Web pages may become as sophisticated as software for producing pages for print is now. Until that happens, though, the jobs of design and production will be split on most Web teams, with designers creating prototypes and production teams taking care of the mechanical aspects: preparing the graphics, coding the HTML files, and the rest.

Since basic HTML is relatively simple to learn and use, many designers opt to do at least basic coding themselves. It's important to remember, though, that HTML is not simply a layout tool. It works hand-in-hand with HTTP, scripting languages, various browsers, and

script
A simple program that lists a sequence of actions to be followed by the computer.

```
┌─────────────────────────────────────────────────────────────┐
│ ▤▤           www.peachpit.com                          ▤ │
│ 26 items          88 MB in disk          117.7 MB available  │
│   Name                      Size  Kind              Label  L │
│ ▽ 📁 peachpit                 —   folder             —       │
│ ▷   📁 asktell               —   folder             —       │
│ ▷   📁 features              —   folder             —       │
│ ▷   📁 forums                —   folder             —       │
│ ▷   📁 maps                  —   folder             —       │
│ ▷   📁 meetus                —   folder             —       │
│ ▽   📁 order                 —   folder             —       │
│         📄 cancel.order.gif      7K   GIFConverter 2.3.... — │
│         📄 change.order.gif      7K   GIFConverter 2.3.... — │
│         📄 checkout.gif          7K   GIFConverter 2.3.... — │
│         📄 continue.browsing.gif 7K   GIFConverter 2.3.... — │
│     ▽   📁 faq               —   folder             —       │
│             📄 order.faq.html    11K  SimpleText docum... — │
│         📄 internat.order.faq.html 7K Microsoft Word do... Hot │
│         📄 order.buttons.bookstore.... 4K GIFConverter 2.3.... — │
│         📄 order.buttons.gif     4K   GIFConverter 2.3.... — │
│         📄 order.buttons.orderlist.gif 4K GIFConverter 2.3.... — │
│         📄 order.checkout.html   7K   Microsoft Word do... — │
│         📄 order.html            7K   SimpleText docum... — │
│         📄 order.list.html       21K  Microsoft Word do... — │
│         📄 review.your.order.html 4K  Microsoft Word do... — │
│         📄 send.order.now.gif    7K   GIFConverter 2.3.... — │
│ ▷   📁 titles                —   folder             —       │
│     📄 welcome.html          7K   SimpleText docum... —     │
│     📄 whatsnew.html         7K   SimpleText docum... —     │
└─────────────────────────────────────────────────────────────┘
```

THE COMPLETED FILES—HTML files, maps, images, and other media—are all sorted into logical directories (folders) on the server. The location and name of each file should be planned early in the production process, because that information is required to create working hyperlinks to the pages. (This directory is from the Peachpit Web site at http://www.peachpit.com/.)

all the other technologies that are part of a working Web system. Using HTML wisely requires familiarity with the ins and outs of all those parts. There's no reason, of course, that a designer can't master all that, and every Web designer should at least be knowledgeable about what HTML can and can't do with page layout (→**80**), but because HTML coding is time-consuming and requires skills that don't necessarily overlap with those of a designer, HTML production is usually handed off to specialized production engineers.

In a nutshell, a production engineer's job is to pull together the disparate files—graphics, text, sound, animation, video, scripts—into pages that work over the Web and with the target browsers. Production engineers' responsibilities include some or all of these tasks:

- Setting up the directory structure for the files on the server and making sure the files are named and distributed correctly within that structure

- HTML coding, or verifying and fine-tuning HTML files supplied by the designers

- Preparing graphics and other media for low-bandwidth transmission

- Writing any necessary scripts

- Creating and testing links to inline media and to other Web pages

Publishing

The final stage of Web site development, as in any other publication process, is the "publishing" itself: making the final product available to its audience, whether that means the employees inside a company or the world at large. On the Web, this stage is much easier than in any other medium. When the files are deemed ready to go, the production head just copies the final files into the appropriate directories on an HTTP server. Anyone on the network—the Internet or a corporate intranet—who knows the right address can then log on and retrieve the files.

Many companies use an internal **staging server** on which they can post the final files and test the links, scripts, and other functions before the site goes "live." To work correctly, this server should be an exact replica of the real server, with the same files, directories, and scripts.

Design companies working for outside clients may or may not offer to host their clients' Web sites on their own servers, but a small, select portion do, adding to the value they can offer clients. Setting up a Web server needn't be difficult, but Web site hosting is a challenging job, requiring round-the-clock trouble-shooting. Remember, the site is available only as long as your server is working correctly. If a visitor is turned away because the system is down or the bandwidth is insufficient, that visitor may never return.

Publicizing Your Site

The ease of publishing on the Web has a flip side. The publisher is saved the trouble and expense of mailing the publication to subscribers or shipping copies to bookstores, but if your work doesn't appear in readers' mailboxes or catch their eye on a book-store shelf, how will they know it exists? The role of publicity is arguably more important in Web publishing than in any other medium. Luckily, there are several good ways to pull readers to your Web site.

Perhaps the most important step is to register an easy-to-remember **domain name**. If you've registered your company name as your domain name, potential readers can go directly to your site by typing the name in their browser. It's often the first method people try for finding a site. Ask your Internet Service Provider about registering your domain name, or do it yourself through **InterNIC**, the service that handles domain names for the entire Internet. As we write this, registering a domain name costs $100 for the first two years ($50/year thereafter), plus any handling charges your service might charge for processing the request.

The standard marketing tools open to any business also can be powerful tools for publicizing your Web site. Everyone has seen television commercials, magazine advertisements, and even billboards that list Web addresses for everything from microbreweries to the latest movies. Every magazine that has an

domain name
A name by which an Internet server is known (e.g., "peachpit.com"). The first part of the domain name provides a unique, plain-language identifier for the Internet server. The part following the period is usually a three-letter code signifying the type of site: e.g, *.com* for commercial, *.edu* for educational institution.

InterNIC
The service that registers domain names for commercial Internet users.

staging server
A server that has the same directory structure as the server that will be used to publish Web files, used to test pages on line before they are made publicly available.

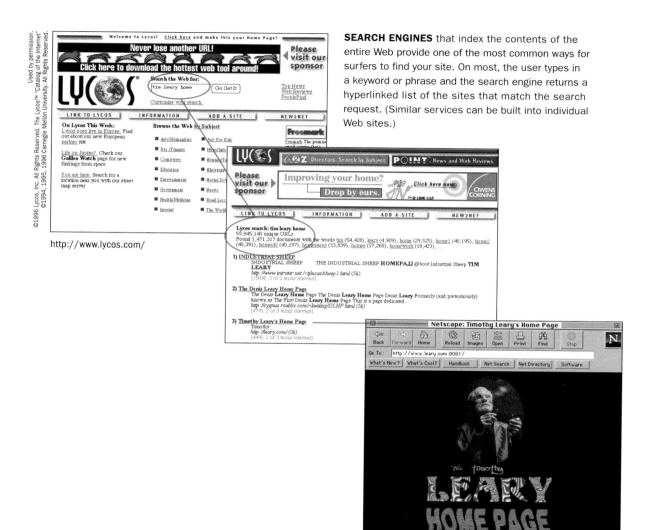

http://www.lycos.com/

SEARCH ENGINES that index the contents of the entire Web provide one of the most common ways for surfers to find your site. On most, the user types in a keyword or phrase and the search engine returns a hyperlinked list of the sites that match the search request. (Similar services can be built into individual Web sites.)

search engine
A program that searches through electronic information. Web search engines such as Lycos and InfoSeek search through indexes of the entire Internet in response to user queries.

CHRIS GRAVES/JOEY CAVELLA/RETINA LOGIC
http://www.leary.com/

online edition lists its Web address on its masthead or table of contents. Marketing materials mailed to clients can also highlight the advent of a new Web site. A company that spends significant amounts on customer support could quickly recoup the cost of advertising its Web address once customers start looking to the Web site, instead of to more costly sources such as 800 numbers and customer support departments, to answer their questions. The payback is also clear, of course, if you sell products from your Web site.

If you don't have an advertising budget, though, you'll be glad to know that effective publicity tools are also available, for free, on the Web itself.

Many people find what they need on the Web through online **search engines**. Although there are lots of these, just a handful of key ones are referred to by the vast majority of Web users. They include Yahoo, Excite, and Lycos, to name a few. Registering your site with these services makes it possible for potential visitors to find your site by simply typing a keyword on the service's search page. In addition to a search facility, Yahoo and other directories list registered sites in subject categories, so that users can click on narrower and narrower topics to get to sites that serve those interests.

Next, look for other sites on the Web that reach the same people you'd like to reach, and let their publishers know you're there. Many sites have a page of links that point their readers to sites of related interest. It's also a good idea to look for Internet newsgroups that serve your audience and post news of your site there. (You can find relevant sites and newsgroups by doing your own search in the kinds of places we name in the preceding paragraph.)

Last but not least, if you think your site is something special, propose it to one of the many "cool site" listing pages. These sites are run by self-appointed taste-makers who scan through the thousands of sites presented for their attention and anoint a select few to be called "cool." Getting on one of these lists can bring the largest audience of all, since they're followed by many thousands of readers with a wide variety of interests. Cool Site of the Day is the most famous; we name some more in the "Online" list on this page.

What's Your Role?

The term *Web design* is a loose one—it can include one or all of the processes described in this chapter. Many Web design firms limit the services they offer to the "design" parts of the process: information architecture and interface design. Others take on HTML production as well. Some offer a complete set of services, including programming and production, and even host sites on their own servers. To fill gaps in their resources, many Web design firms seek out strategic partnerships with companies that offer skills they don't have in-house, teaming up with independent writers, programmers, and Internet service providers.

Especially in the early days of Web design, the soup-to-nuts services may have an edge. Since Web publishing is such a new field, few companies that need a Web site have any in-house expertise for managing the process and so will look for consultants who can guide them through the steps and find the necessary talent for bringing a Web site to life.

As you saw from the examples in the last chapter, though, successful Web design companies come in all shapes and sizes. Here, as with almost every aspect of Web design, the rules that are made to be broken haven't even been made yet.

Online: The Process of Web Design

"Cool site" Services
http://www.projectcool.com/sightings/
http://cool.infi.net/
http://www.highfive.com/
http://www.pointcom.com/

InterNIC Registration Service
http://www.internic.com/

Site Registration Services
http://www.submit-it.com/
http://barnsides.com/links.htm

Web Search Services
http://www.excite.com/
http://www.lycos.com/
http://www.yahoo.com/

Structuring the Site

A Web site's pages are linked to one another—and to the rest of the Web—by a series of hyperlinks. Any page can link to any other anywhere in the world. Given that the movement through a site is so unpredictable, with each page linked to any number of others, what do we mean when we talk about a Web site's structure?

Although no designer can control the path a Web user chooses to travel through information on the Web, it is a Web designer's job to make the content of a site available and enticing to every visitor who finds his or her way there. That requires both a careful analysis of the content you're presenting—determining its main messages or components—and skills for helping visitors find and understand those messages. Doing this successfully combines the tasks of information architecture—the creation of a structure for the site's information—and interface design—the crafting of tools that help visitors navigate that structure and find information that will be of interest to them. Those are the tasks we'll discuss in this chapter.

Information Architecture: What Goes Where

The structure of a Web site grows from the way you want visitors to, first, understand and, second, get to the information you post there.

Your initial conversations with your client during the site definition stage we talked about in the last chapter (→**41**) should uncover the basic outlines of the content you'll be presenting. This phase should define what information the client wants to have available, what interactions the client wants to offer, and the client's broader marketing goals: the ideas and impressions visitors to the site should take away with them. For example, an online flower shop might want its customers to have access to a complete catalog of available bouquets (content), to be able to order flowers on line (interaction), and to learn that ordering on line is more convenient and inexpensive than any other method (marketing message). A bank may want to detail its checking, savings, and investment plans (content), let users make contact by e-mail with "personal bankers" and check their account balances on line (interaction), and create the impression that this bank is doing more than any other to make banking convenient for online customers (message). All three facets are key in planning any site. The site's final content and the way it presents itself to the user must achieve all these goals.

Most sites we visit are stuck in an old school of thought: if you drew a map, it would look like a pyramid. We like to encourage a navigational mechanism that allows you to navigate laterally or to anywhere else on the site.

STEFAN FIELDING-ISAACS, ART & SCIENCE

A Structure That Allows for Change

The contents of a Web site will—or should—change constantly (→**176**). Visitors must feel that the site will hold something new for them each time they visit, giving them a reason to return to the site again and again. Planning and designing a Web site is therefore a lot like creating a new magazine. Content planners must think in terms of content categories ("departments"), not specific content, when planning the site's sections.

This factor affects the interface as well as the structural design of a site. Designers should think in terms of rules, or templates, for styling the content, thinking ahead to the uses to which each element might be put. That's not to say that new features can't have their own individual design, but as with a magazine, the site's graphic identity should remain constant while the specific content changes.

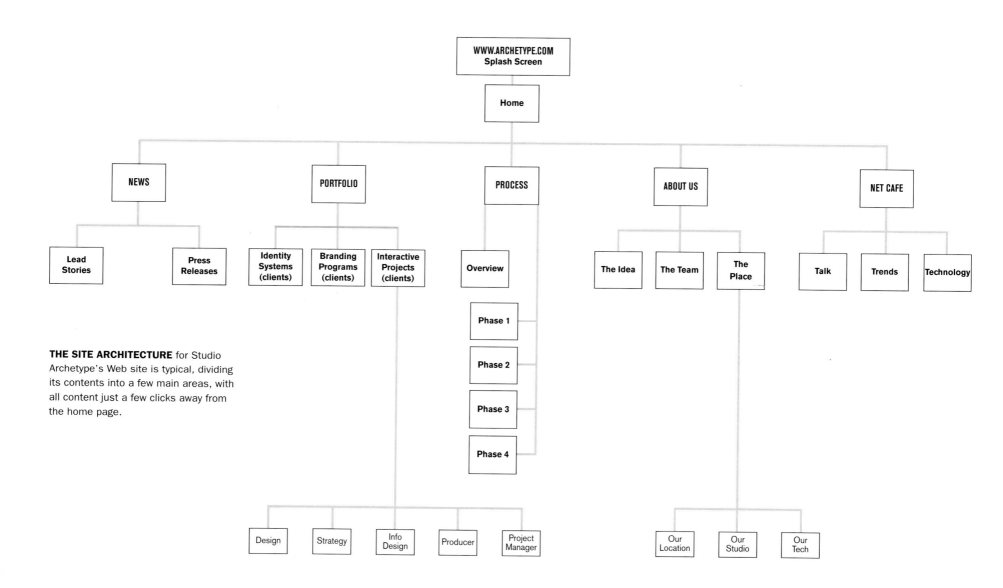

THE SITE ARCHITECTURE for Studio
Archetype's Web site is typical, dividing
its contents into a few main areas, with
all content just a few clicks away from
the home page.

With the goals understood, the challenge becomes how to achieve those goals creatively and effectively using the technology of the Web. Despite everything we've said about the Web's current limitations, it is potentially the most flexible of media. Using basic HTML tools, the Web can work like an encyclopedia (random-access reference information), a book (sequential pages), a magazine (graphically presented "departments"), or a promotional brochure (an unfolding "pitch"). Adding multimedia to the mix, it can mimic more familiar electronic media such as television (an active, animated presentation), a slide show (sequential, bite-size messages), or a computer game (mysterious clues). The latest trends in Web technology, including tools such as Shockwave (→**130**) and Java (→**168**), can turn a Web page into online software, providing real-time interaction and access to up-to-date, searchable information based on back-end databases. An interactive site might allow visitors to use online questionnaires to determine the right personal banking plan or bouquet.

There are countless ways to execute and combine such effects, so it's impossible to lay down rules for right and wrong ways to create a Web site's structure. At the same time, though, a few simple tests (described on the next page) can help you gauge the effectiveness of your site plan.

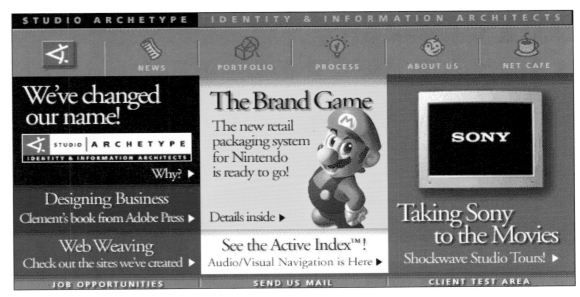

STUDIO ARCHETYPE
http://www.studioarchetype.com/

STUDIO ARCHETYPE'S HOME PAGE gives an overview of the site's content, showing the five main areas (plus a link for the home page) in an iconic navigation bar.

Ask yourself these questions:

Have you created a logical structure that represents the view of the information that you want to convey? In most cases, a visitor to your home page should be able to see at a glance what information your site has to offer, a goal best achieved by determining and offering a limited set of content categories. Common wisdom and cognitive psychology experts hold that the set should be limited to no more than about seven basic groups, the number of separate items that most people can grasp at one time.

Does the content of each page represent a logical module of information? The hyperlinked structure of the Web counts on the ability of users to get straight to the information they need, from a variety of different starting points. The best way to achieve that is to limit each page to one topic. Imagine the banking site we talked about earlier. Rather than combining information for all its checking plans, it might put a description of each plan on a separate page. The site might then link to the page on business checking plans from a page about checking plans in general and also from another page on the site that details special services for businesses. Keeping each module of information on its own page also makes updates easy; when the information needs updating, you change it in only one place.

Does the structure pass the three-click test? No important information should be more than three clicks away from the home page and, if possible, no more than three clicks away from any page on the site. On the Web, remember, each click costs the visitor valuable time, so the information you want everyone to see, or the information most likely to be looked for, should be as close as possible to the top of the structure. And as we'll describe in the next section, you can put more information within easy reach by using thoughtful navigation strategies.

It's all interrelated. Sometimes working on the architecture provides insight into how the navigation should work, and sometimes the interface provides insight into the architecture.

JOHN GROTTING, STUDIO ARCHETYPE

home page
Sometimes a generic name for a Web site, but now usually referring to the top page of a site structure, providing access to all other pages on the site.

Site Navigation: Making Content Accessible

With the basic site structure defined, the next task for the designer is making it easy for visitors to find the information they need on the site. On the Web, that means creating a system of hyperlinks that will allow visitors to move around the site efficiently.

Web designers can count on a built-in set of navigation controls that are standard in Web browsers. These include **bookmarks**, **history lists**, and Forward and Back buttons. Users will learn to depend on the browser's controls for such functions, and designers shouldn't confuse the issue by duplicating them in their site's interface.

Creating site-specific navigation tools requires, first, deciding which pages will be linked to what others. Part of this is ad hoc and logical. (The bank's business services page would clearly need a link to the business checking plan page, for example.) The other part is more systematic—coming up with a sitewide plan for putting as many pages as possible at the visitors' fingertips, no matter where they are on the site.

The simplest way to do this is to offer a link to the site's home page from every other page on the site; once users return there, they can find their way back down the hierarchy to any other piece of information on the site. A somewhat more powerful option is a

I'm a strong hierarchy person, so that's the way I approached the CNET design. I'm not sure it's necessary that people know where they came from last; the important thing is to know how to get to the rest of the story.

ANDREA JENKINS, CNET

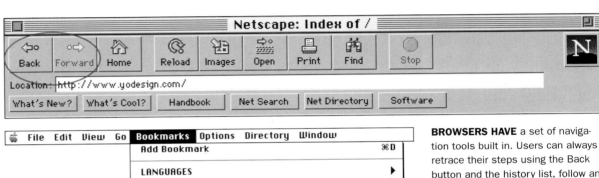

BROWSERS HAVE a set of navigation tools built in. Users can always retrace their steps using the Back button and the history list, follow an earlier path again using the Forward button, and mark often-visited pages with bookmarks.

bookmark
An electronic record of a particular page's URL, stored with a user's browser Preferences, allowing the user to return to that page by choosing the page's name from a menu.

history list
A list of pages that the user has visited during that online session, usually listed in a browser menu so that the user can choose the page's name to return to it.

GRIFFIN CHERRY
http://www.tweak.com/

WITH FRAMES, a navigation bar can be supplied in a separate window.

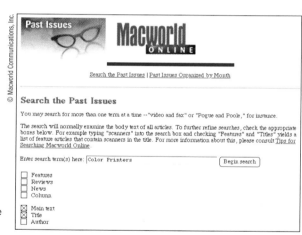

TRIAD, INC.
http://www.macworld.com/

A SEARCH FEATURE helps visitors find the page they want by entering a word or phrase describing the content they're looking for.

A SITE TABLE OF CONTENTS helps visitors find their way to any page on the site from a central location.

navigation bar
A row of hyperlinks, usually in the form of icons or text links, that offers access to a standard set of pages—usually the top pages of the site's main sections.

navigation bar, a standard element that lists the site's main sections on every page, offering a deeper level of access with a single click. For more complex sites, a site index or table of contents is a popular tool. And particularly large sites often offer a search function that allows the visitor to look for occurrences of particular words or concepts anywhere on the site.

The latest versions of HTML support frames (→**96**), a way of dividing a browser window into separate, independently scrollable regions, each holding a different HTML file. One particularly effective use for frames is to isolate a site's navigation elements into their own frame, which stays constantly on screen while pages requested by hyperlinks appear in other sections. The <A> tag for creating hyperlinks (→**75**) can also flow pages into any specified frame.

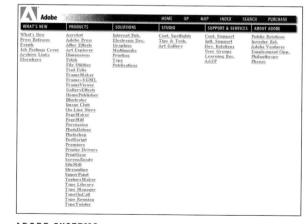

ADOBE SYSTEMS
http://www.adobe.com/misc/sitemap.html

Integrating Look and Feel

After the essential structure of the site is documented and you've decided how to provide access to its different levels, it's time to think about interface: the way your site presents itself to the user. Interface design is responsible for creating a strong subjective impression as well as an easily understood overview of how it all works. Ideally, a strong interface seamlessly melds navigational tools and the graphic identity that gives a Web site its character.

Anyone creating site-specific navigation methods must first be aware of the navigation assumptions and tools already built into Web browsers. For example, visitors will work on the assumption that at every site they visit, text hyperlinks will look the same. Preferences for whether or not they are underlined and the color they are displayed in can often be set in each browser, but all Web users know that colored text (and bold text on some nongraphics systems) signals a hyperlink. Web designers need to respect that convention and refrain from coloring any text that's not a link. The flip side of this is that they can take advantage of that convention to identify links in graphics by showing them as colored text.

Another convention of graphical browsers is to have the pointer turn into a pointing hand when it passes over a hyperlink. Designers can count on that interface to tip off users that a graphic is "live." Likewise,

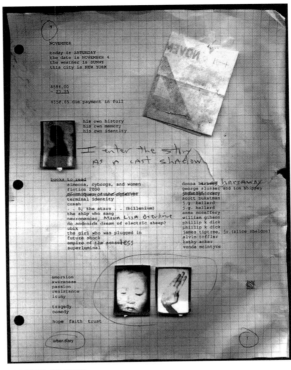

JOSEPH SQUIER
http://gertrude.art.uiuc.edu/ludgate/the/
place/urban_diary/

GRAPHICS AND LAYOUT combine to create a graphic environment that complements the content. At left, a notebook of childhood memories is presented as a typewritten scrapbook, and each image acts as a hyperlink. Below, a playful online magazine uses frames to turn the screen into a board game, with animated buttons leading to different destinations.

THE BUOYANT COMPANY
http://www.jinx.com/

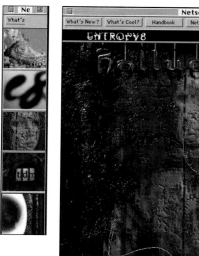

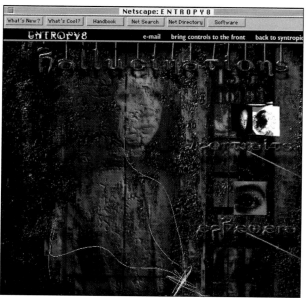

A MYSTERIOUS LAYERED LOOK identifies Entropy8, a personal site (and design business calling card) by Auriea Harvey. The navigation bar, in a separate window, lists the site's sections by graphic identity rather than by name.

AURIEA HARVEY
http://www.entropy8.com/entropyindex.html

SOUTHWEST AIRLINES uses a metaphor every visitor is familiar with. You want to get flight information? Go right to the airport counter.

SOUTHWEST AIRLINES
http://www.iflyswa.com/

they should make sure to replicate that interface when creating non-HTML interfaces for Web sites using tools like Shockwave (→**130**) or Java (→**168**).

These conventions aside, any other clues about how to move around your own Web site—and reasons the visitor might want to—are up to the site's own user interface to convey. The art of interface design is to create a graphic environment that includes the information users need in a more quickly assimilated and attractive manner.

As with site architecture, interface design has too many possibilities to be subject to simple rules, yet there are a couple of guidelines against which you can test your ideas.

Ask yourself these questions:

Does the interface convey a "look and feel" appropriate to your client's message? Illustrations, metaphors, and layout should all combine to convey the image your client has named as a goal—friendly, sophisticated, businesslike, whatever.

Will the use of your site be obvious to first-time visitors? A site's use will be more obvious to visitors if you use familiar metaphors and conventions—a map for navigating a geographic area, a labeled door for entering a new area, a question mark icon indicating a help section, or a beveled interface indicating a clickable button—but that's not to say that there's no room for originality. It's almost impossible, of course, to know whether what seems like a clear interface to you will be equally obvious to others. Providing a set of instructions isn't necessarily a bad idea, but if you're depending on visitors to read them before they use your site, you know you're in trouble. The only way to really find out whether your interface is working is with user testing: Running tests with people who have never used or seen your site can tell you how likely it is that someone who has no history with the site and its development will understand your solutions.

Are cues and feedback consistent? Any interface has to be learned to some extent. Even when an interface uses only the most time-honored conventions, a user starts by testing his or her assumptions about how it will work. If a tool works as expected—if clicking an upward-pointing arrow takes you to the top of the page, for instance—the user learns a skill (getting to the top of a page), is encouraged to explore more, and learns to trust the interface. If on another page the upward-pointing arrow behaves differently, that trust is broken, the skill is unlearned, and the user is discouraged from exploring. A hallmark of a good interface is that it uses metaphor, location on screen, shape, color, sound, and every other cue consistently, reassuring visitors that their efforts will be rewarded.

The navigation graphics are part of the site's identity. They're not purely for getting to information.

JOHN GROTTING, STUDIO ARCHETYPE

SOCIO X
http://www.papermag.com/

THE NEON-LIGHTED GRAPHICS of PaperMag appropriately evoke the nightlife of New York, which is the site's topic.

User Testing

An interface that seems perfectly clear to its designer may be extremely opaque to someone who hasn't been involved in its development, or to someone to whom the color red—or any other interface cue—simply has a different connotation. Because the success of a Web site depends on the ability of a wide variety of users to understand its clues, it is of prime importance that designers understand just how a broad range of people react to the interface choices they've made.

Anyone developing a very high profile site might find time spent testing designs with broad-based focus groups a worthwhile investment, but most projects, and most schedules, won't be able to afford such formal testing. Most designers can, however, get time with friends, colleagues, and others who won't mind looking over prototypes at different stages of development. While a second, third, or fiftieth opinion may not be more worthwhile than your own, extra feedback is bound to point out some issues you may not have thought of and, perhaps, point the way to more universal solutions.

The interface design and the architecture are inseparable. During the planning stages, I'm going to be changing the structure to accommodate the interface, or vice versa. Otherwise you end up with a pretty interface that's impossible to use.

STEFAN FIELDING-ISAACS, ART & SCIENCE

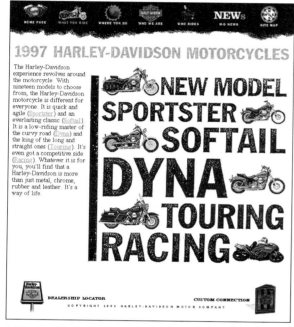

ORGANIC ONLINE/VSA PARTNERS
http://www.harley-davidson.com/

AT HARLEY-DAVIDSON, the icon for the current section is animated to show visitors what section they're visiting. The Shockwave animation also makes visitors feel at home with evocative "vroom-vroom" sounds.

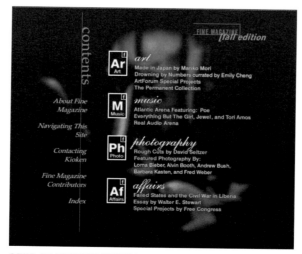

GENE NA/KIOKEN/KAHNG NA DESIGN
http://www.finemagazine.com/

Does the design accommodate lowest-common-denominator systems? Too often, designers depend on graphics to convey important navigation information and content, making the site unusable to visitors on text-only systems. This is not to say that you can't use graphical navigation systems on your site. It only means that you may sometimes need to provide alternate paths for text-only browsers, and you should be careful to take advantage of the methods for accommodating text-only systems that are built into HTML's image codes (→**107**). Likewise, if your target audience includes users on low-bandwidth systems and older browsers, you should be careful to plan interface elements with minimum file sizes and avoid using Shockwave or other specialized media to execute your ideas.

FINE MAGAZINE features fine arts in a suitably elegant interface. The "periodic table" section identifiers carry through all the site's pages as a graphic navigation bar.

The Home Page

The term *home page* is used in a couple of different ways. Often, it is used as a synonym for Web site, as in "Bob has just posted his own home page." More and more, though, it refers to the "front page" of a site: the one you land on if you type the site's domain name, and the one from which all the other pages on the site can be reached.

As, usually, the first—and sometimes the only—page any visitor to your site will see, the site's home page is arguably its most important feature, and so worth a little special attention in this chapter. Like the cover of a book or magazine, or the opening credits of a TV show, its primary role is to state your message—whatever that may be—loud and clear.

Web designers have struggled to find the right balance of content and style on their home pages. One school of thought argues that the home page should highlight, and provide direct links to, as much of the site's content as possible. Another abhors the crowded and confusing page that such an approach can cause and opts for simple home pages with nothing but links to the site's main sections. Some models mimic magazine covers or newspaper layouts. The samples shown here illustrate some possible approaches.

AGENCY.COM LTD.
http://www.agency.com/

A HOME PAGE usually has several standard elements: the company branding, a map of the site's main sections (often offered in both graphic and text views), a feedback link, and copyright information.

THE MINIMALIST APPROACH creates a sort of "cover" for the Web site, setting the tone but offering very little information.

REBECCA ODES
http://www.gurl.com/

The front page is your first chance. This is where people have to decide whether they want to use your site or not. I like to make home pages that you actually get something out of—you're not required to click on anything to get to the basic information.

MATTHEW BUTTERICK, ATOMIC VISION

THE PLACE, by poet, photographer, and teacher Joseph Squier, lures visitors in with a timed splash screen leading to a mysterious environment labeled with evocative section titles. The idea here is to encourage exploration.

JOSEPH SQUIER
http://gertrude.art.uiuc.edu/ludgate/the/place.html

THE MORE INFORMATION you offer on the home page, the more likely a visitor will see something of interest. The '80s Server shows a colorful, tabloid-style home page.

STEPHAN WILLIS
http://www.80s.com/

Accommodating Advertising

More and more, Web designers face a challenge that magazine designers have contended with for decades—advertising. The basic issues are the same in any medium: How to give advertisers prominence without overwhelming the site's own content, how to make clear what is an ad and what isn't, and how to accommodate a hodgepodge of graphics that aren't under the control of the site designer.

Unlike magazines and newspapers, the Web has yet to establish standard sizes for ads. A narrow banner extending the width of the browser window is one common shape, but the exact width and depth vary from site to site. Other formats are also beginning to appear. In print, the high costs of prepress make it hard to create custom ads for each publication, but those costs are minimal for the Web. That, and the fact that there are still relatively few outlets for Web advertising, make it more likely that advertisers will be willing to prepare ads in any size a site requires.

Web designers are also still experimenting with the challenge of differentiating ads from a site's own content. Different sites use rules, borders, space, frames, and other devices to create the requisite graphic distance.

Where to place ads on a Web page is another question with a variety of answers. Advertisers, of course, prefer that their ads appear as close to the top of the page as possible, to be visible on screen without scrolling.

As advertisers take advantage of eye-catching effects such as animation, ads create even more competition for attention on the page—a real threat on the Web, of course, since the advertiser's goal is to entice the viewer to click on the ad and be transported to the advertiser's own site, and away from yours. The best solutions to this tug-of-war for attention will only emerge over time—and through experimentation by creative designers.

MAKING ADS STAND OUT from the site's own content is the biggest challenge facing designers of ad-supported Web sites. Slate (above) creates a border by building ads into its page banner. Web users are learning to recognize standard banner ads like the one used in Urban Desires (left).

HTML Basics

We introduced HTML, the Hypertext Markup Language, back in the first two chapters of this book. You already know that it was created along with the Web to provide a hyperlinked interface to the content of the Internet; that it's the basic format for all Web pages; that it marks the structure, not the design, of documents; and that it's developing quickly, as industry coalitions and commercial interests do their best to keep up with the needs of Web designers. In order to design for the Web, you're going to have to get to know HTML a lot better than that.

HTML is the backbone on which Web pages are built, and its strengths and limitations determine what you can and can't do on the Web. It's not hard to learn, but it has lots of idiosyncrasies you'll need to understand in order to create great Web pages.

We'll cover specific HTML techniques for controlling page layout, graphics, sound, video, and interactivity in other chapters. Here in this chapter, our task is to give you some context for understanding just how HTML works and what you'll use it for.

Viewing the Source

Basic HTML is really quite easy to master. Many of the codes it uses are simple descriptive words (e.g., *align=center*) or abbreviations (*B* for bold, for example) for the effect they create. In fact, probably the hardest thing about learning HTML is reading the HTML specifications, which are written in the style of programming language documentation.

The quickest way to learn HTML is to take advantage of a command you'll find in almost any browser: View Document Source, which lets you see the HTML that makes up any page you read on the Web. Compare the tags in the HTML file to the results in the browser, and you'll quickly see what can be done, and how.

The basic information you'll learn in this chapter—the parts of an HTML file, the anatomy of a tag, the different types of tags, and the different versions of HTML—should be all you need to understand how the HTML files work. You'll find more help in the quick reference boxes in this book, which show the syntax of individual tags as we discuss them, and from the HTML reference in the back of this book (→**184**).

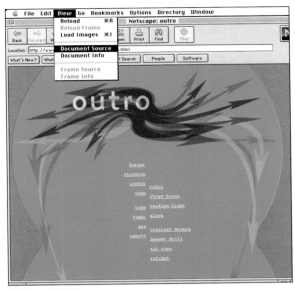

ATOMIC VISION
http://www.atomicvision.com/outro/index.html

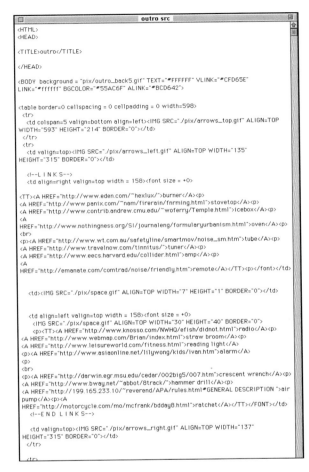

VIEWING THE SOURCE CODE of HTML documents is the quickest way to learn HTML. The Netscape Navigator interface is shown in the screen at left, but most browsers have a similar command.

HTML is becoming just a kind of container. It will be a way of getting the media to the browser. In the future, an HTML document might be just 20 <OBJECT> tags. You're going to embed applets to do what you need.

MATTHEW BUTTERICK, ATOMIC VISION

SGML: The Parent of HTML

HTML springs from an international standard for electronic document exchange known as SGML (Standard Generalized Markup Language), a system widely used in government and educational organizations. Familiarity with the ideas behind SGML may help Web designers understand why HTML is like it is and where it might be headed.

SGML was designed to allow publishers to reuse the same documents in several different media, with several different applications, or in several different layouts without recreating the file each time. Because the file is stored in ASCII format, organizations need never fear the danger that otherwise threatens electronic files: that the software or system for which the document was created will become obsolete, and the files will thus become unreadable.

There are many different flavors, or "applications," of SGML, all of which share the same method, defined by the standard, of marking up files. The difference between the styles is simply the set of tags they use. HTML is one of those flavors.

What Is HTML?

HTML is not a file format in the sense that QuarkXPress or Microsoft Word have file formats. As we explained earlier, HTML documents are pure ASCII—text only—and can be read by practically any application. HTML is actually a set of codes, or "tags," that are embedded in these text files, between angle brackets.

Most people think of HTML as a language that describes the layout of text in an HTML file, but that's really just part of the picture. Most HTML tags affect the layout of the file, but HTML can more accurately be thought of as a browser programming language. Along with information that tells the browser what part each piece of text plays in the file, HTML commands can also tell the browser to load other files on the Web (through the <A> tag) (→**75**), accept user input (the <FORM> tag and its associates) (→**150**), run scripts (the <SCRIPT> tag) (→**166**), and find and run external programs (<OBJECT>) (→**164**). In fact, it's possible that as Web pages depend more and more on programming languages (→**160**) and multimedia plug-ins (→**11**), an HTML file might not hold any of the text and images the user sees; instead it might simply hold pointers to external programs.

Types of Tags

Although it's clear that there are several different types of HTML tags, it's hard to define just what those types are. HTML has grown like a many-armed monster. It got its start as a well-structured branch of SGML (see the sidebar on the opposite page), but it quickly grew extra limbs as software makers added the tags they needed to accomplish new tasks.

In one sense, there are essentially two types of tags: those that belong in the head of an HTML document, supplying any general information about the file, and those that belong in the body, providing the content that is shown in the browser window.

For designers, though, perhaps the most useful breakdown, which takes into account the new types of tags being recommended by browser vendors as well as those in the official HTML specification, is to think of the tags as falling into three main groups:

Structural tags, which label the parts of a document: headings, paragraphs, lists, and so on.

Style tags, which tell the browser exactly how to present the labeled text.

Programming tags, which tell the browser to perform some action: to fetch a graphic or to run a program, for instance.

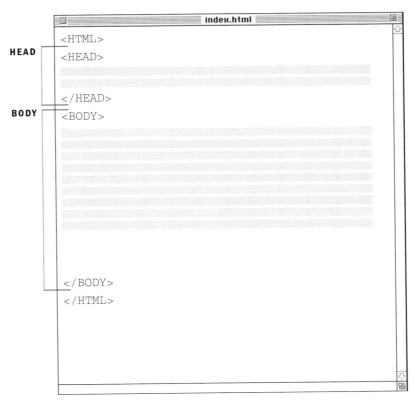

EACH HTML DOCUMENT has two main sections: the head, which gives the browser general information about the file, and the body, which includes the information that will be displayed in the browser window. The head of the file is delineated by <HEAD> and </HEAD> tags, and the body is delineated by <BODY> and </BODY> tags. Some browsers also require an <HTML> tag at the top of the file and an </HTML> tag at the end, which tell the browser to interpret the file as HTML and not plain text. All other HTML tags fall within these delimiters.

HTML Tags by Group

STRUCTURAL TAGS

Tags that label different types of content; the browser—or custom style sheets—controls how they'll look in the browser window

File level	`<HTML> <HEAD> <BODY>`
Section level	`<DIV> <FORM> <FRAMESET> <MENU> <OL> <TABLE> <UL>`
Paragraph level	`<BLOCKQUOTE> <P>`
Phrase level	`<CITE> <CODE> <DFN> <DIR> <EM> <KBD> <SAMP> < VAR>`
Headings	`<H1> <H2> <H3> <H4> <H5> <H6>`
Rules	`<HR>`

STYLE TAGS

Tags that give specific instructions about the look of the element

Line breaks	`  <NOBR> <WBR>`
Fonts	`<FONT face=>`
Font size	`<BIG> <SMALL> <FONT size=>`
Font color	`<BODY alink=> <BODY link=> <BODY text=> <FONT color=>`
Font style	`<B> <I> <S> <STRIKE> <SUB> <SUP> <TT> <U>`
Placement	`<CENTER> <IMG align=>`

PROGRAMMING TAGS

Commands that tell the browser to carry out certain actions

Download a file	`<A>`
Place objects	`<IMG> <OBJECT>`
Run programs	`<SCRIPT> <EMBED> <APPLET>`
Play sounds	`<BGSOUND>`
Scroll text	`<MARQUEE>`

For the most part, "official" HTML, defined by the HTML 2.0 and HTML 3.2 specifications (→**22**), sticks pretty tightly to structural tags. This is in keeping with the basic tenets of SGML—to use the markup language to specify only the structure of a document and leave it to each piece of software that reads the file to apply particular styles to each element—in order to ensure that HTML files can be run on all different types of systems.

Many of the tags in the second group—style tags—have been added by browser manufacturers eager to fulfill users' demands for more control over the look of documents.

In the third group are tags that enact the special, interactive features of the Web: the ability to hyperlink documents, to collect feedback from visitors, and to act on visitors' preferences. Such tags got their start with the first Web browsers and are being added to by Netscape, Microsoft, and other companies racing to add their products' functionality to the Web.

This grouping, and the explanation of why the differences have sprung up, should help you understand why different, and sometimes incompatible, methods can often be used to achieve similar purposes in Web design.

The Anatomy of a Tag

An HTML tag usually has several parts. The start tag tells the browser that a particular element is about to begin: Text following the tag should be treated according to the rules for that element. Most HTML codes also use an end tag, which signifies the end of the element. The end tag is usually a repeat of the start tag, preceded by a slash (/) character. (The beginning of an ordered list is marked by the <OL> tag, for example, and the end by the </OL> tag.)

In addition, many tags have optional or required attributes, which give the browser additional information about how the tag should be interpreted. The attributes follow the start tag, inside the start tag's bracket delimiters. Attribute names are often followed by an equal sign (=) and then the attribute's value.

In the chapters that follow, we'll talk about how to use different attributes to achieve particular effects.

<FONT size=3>applicable text</FONT>

THE START TAG defines the beginning of an element.

ATTRIBUTES add additional information about how the tag should be interpreted. Attributes are added inside the start tag delimiters. Many attribute names are followed by an equal sign and then by the value of the attribute.

THE TEXT the tag applies to goes between the start and end tags.

THE END TAG defines the end of an element. The end tag is a repetition of the start tag, but beginning with a slash (/) character.

Managing the Different Versions of HTML

If, as we said earlier, HTML is a programming language for browsers, then browsers must be able to understand that language in order to work. It sounds simple enough, but the problem is thornier than it seems. Surprisingly—and unfortunately—not all browsers support all HTML codes.

One reason for this situation rests with the variety of hardware that browsers run on. The Web and HTML are designed to work on viewer hardware ranging from teletype terminals to high-powered graphics workstations to Braille readers. Appropriately coded HTML documents can be interpreted by each of these systems, but the teletype software won't, of course, support splashy graphics.

The second problem is defining just what tags HTML consists of. Earlier (→**22**), we mentioned that HTML was a growing language, under development by an industrywide standards committee and by companies, such as Netscape and Microsoft, that support their own homegrown HTML codes in their browser software. The upshot is that there are—and will probably continue to be—four different versions of HTML: the fully documented set, approved by the standards committee (currently HTML 2.0); the next version of the standard, describing a set of proposed, but not yet

---

HTML 2.0
The IETF's first official HTML specification, documenting the language as it was used when the Web started to gain wide popularity. This set of tags is universally supported across different browsers.

Tags created by Microsoft and supported in its own browser software.
Netscape Extensions to HTML 2.0

HTML 3.0
The IETF's "official" set of proposed extensions to HTML 2.0. Only some of its features were adopted by browser makers. Others were superceded by the software makers'.

Tags created by Microsoft and supported in its own browser software.
Microsoft Extensions to HTML 2.0

Netscape Extensions to HTML 3.0

HTML 3.2
An update to HTML 3.0 (announced May 7, 1996), accommodating work under development by Netscape, Microsoft, and others in areas such as style sheets, embedded programs, and layered layout capabilities.

Microsoft Extensions to HTML 3.0

Netscape Extensions to HTML 4.0?

HTML 4.0?
When the HTML 3.2 specification is finalized, the IETF will presumably begin on HTML 4.0, a discussion document for the next generation of tags.

Microsoft Extensions to HTML 4.0?

THE HTML SPECIFICATIONS (shown in the purple column) document the official version of the language, but Netscape and Microsoft have also created tags of their own that have come into wide use. After being discussed by the standards group, some of the proprietary tags are later adopted into the official specs. The latest version of the IETF specification (currently 3.2) is always a working draft, which documents the latest consensus of the industry leaders who participate in the group but is understood to be still open for discussion.

finalized standards (currently HTML 3.2); the extensions proposed by Netscape (which are added to with every release of the Netscape Navigator browser); and the extensions proposed by Microsoft (which change with every new version of Microsoft's browser, Internet Explorer). When we wrote this, most browsers supported the full set of HTML 2.0 standards and a handful of the more stable HTML 3.2 tags. Netscape's Navigator, of course, supported all of its own tags, plus a handful of Microsoft's extensions, and Microsoft's Internet Explorer generally supported most of Netscape's extensions, in addition to Microsoft's own tags.

This situation has, naturally, created a lot of confusion for Web designers. As a rule, the tags proposed by Netscape and Microsoft give Web designers a lot more control over the look of their pages and the kinds of media they can use than do those available in the basic, standardized set. But using "non-standard" HTML tags means that users of some browsers won't see your pages the way you expect. As we write this, things seem to have settled down a bit, and these circumstances are causing less of a problem than they once did.

One reason is that there are simply fewer browsers for designers to worry about. By late 1996, the browser market was turning into a two-way race between Netscape and Microsoft. In mid-1996, Netscape

We originally started out not doing anything but Netscape, but these days, we recognize that there are other browsers people might want to use—Microsoft Explorer, for instance. For some customers, you have to cater to the home market, so we have to take into account online services like CompuServe, AOL, and Prodigy.

STEFAN FIELDING-ISAACS, ART & SCIENCE

NETSCAPE'S BROWSER quickly grew to dominate the Web, accounting for more than 80 percent of browsers in use by mid-1996 and pretty much crowding other browsers out of the market. By the end of 1996, though, Microsoft Internet Explorer, introduced a year earlier, was gaining ground, and many industry watchers predicted that it might soon rival Netscape's lead. The graph below shows how the percentage of each type of browser visiting one typical site has changed over time.
Source: Intersé Corporation

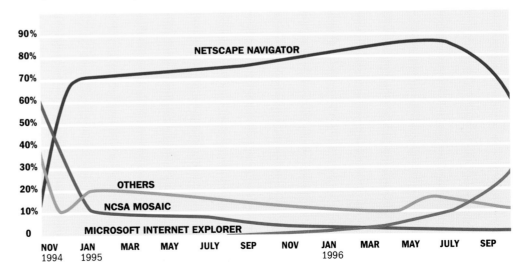

accounted for about 80 percent of the browsers in use. Late in 1996, though, Microsoft began gaining a significant share of the market. During 1996, most online services and other large Internet Service Providers, which once limited their users to proprietary browser software, began to let their subscribers use any browser they chose, and most chose Netscape's or Microsoft's.

Another circumstance making the situation less troublesome is that many tags from the first batches of Netscape and Microsoft extensions have made it into the HTML 3.2 spec and have already been adopted across a broad range of browsers. That means that even people who aren't using Netscape's browser may be able to see effects that were once viewable only with Netscape. Microsoft, for instance, has begun to support the current array of Netscape tags with each release of its Internet Explorer. For its part, Netscape has begun to support Microsoft extensions that gain wide acceptance.

The browser market is too volatile to say how the balance between Netscape, Microsoft, and any other new competitors that enter the market will work out, but it is safe to say that designers' need for powerful, standard code will force browser manufacturers to match each others' best efforts, and either add support for their rivals' popular codes or lose their share of the market.

Another piece of good news is that, in many cases, you can use Netscape's and Microsoft's nonstandard tags at no risk. Browser software will usually just ignore any tag it doesn't understand. For example, if a page that uses the <FONT *color=>* tag (→**89**) is read by a browser that doesn't understand it, the tagged element will simply stay in the default color: no harm done. If the same page is read by Microsoft Internet Explorer or another browser that understands the tag, the element will take on the specified color. In some cases, you can even use two different tags that do the same thing; each browser will just read the version it's familiar with.

While crafty coding can help you match your code to a broad variety of browsers, this situation means that the results of HTML codes are always a bit unpredictable. On a practical level, this means one thing: You've got to test your pages in every browser you want them to work with. It's foolish not to take advantage of tags that will make your page do what you want it to, even if they're not supported by every browser—at least the people with the right software will see your best work. On the other hand, it may be foolish to ignore visitors to your site who are using alternative software. A working knowledge of how HTML works and how it's interpreted will help. But the only way to make sure it's all working properly is to test your pages on a variety of browsers and platforms.

Content Negotiation: Delivering Just What the Browser Orders

Each time a browser requests a page from a Web server, the browser sends information about itself along with the request. You can use this information with special programs (built into the server software or built specifically for that purpose) to send each browser a page built just for it. The process is called "content negotiation."

Content negotiation gets around the problem of trying to code one-version-fits-all documents, but it also creates lots of extra work because it means you need to keep multiple versions of every page.

Navigating the Web With HTML

We'll talk about a wide variety of HTML tags in other chapters of this book. For this "basics" chapter, though, we'll introduce just one: the tag that gave the Hypertext Markup Language its name and makes the Web the Web.

The secret of HTML's hyperlinking abilities is a single tag: <A> (it stands for "anchor"). The <A> tag and its companion </A> tag surround the text you want to use as an anchor for your hyperlink. (You can also use an image as an anchor.) The *href=* attribute of the tag names the Internet location the anchor will link to.

In a browser window, the <A> tag has several effects. The most obvious to the user is that the anchor is highlighted. (In most graphical browsers, anchor text is blue and underlined, and images that act as anchors are outlined with a blue border.) When the user passes the mouse over the anchor, the cursor turns into a pointing hand. And when the user clicks on the anchor, the browser fetches the file named in the *href=* attribute. It's an amazingly simple—and amazingly powerful—system.

If the file named by the *href=* attribute is an HTML file or is in another format supported directly by the browser, the file opens in the browser window. If not, the browser calls on a helper application (→**11**) that can open the file.

ART TECHNOLOGY GROUP/MIT MEDIA LAB
http://www.1010.org/

HYPERLINKED TEXT is highlighted in the browser window—usually by being colored and underlined. (The default color for hyperlink anchors is generally blue, but designers can specify a custom color, such as the red used here.) When visitors move their pointers over a hyperlink in a graphical browser, the pointer usually turns into a pointing finger.

START TAG	ATTRIBUTES	END TAG	EXPLANATION
<A>		</A>	Creates a hyperlink anchor
	href="*URL*"		The file to be called by the hyperlink
	name="*name*"		Names a section of an HTML document. That name can then be used in the *href=* attribute of another <A> tag.
	target="*frame*" OR "_blank" OR "_parent" OR "_self" OR "_top"		Used with frames, names a frame in which the file should be displayed.

The <A> (anchor) tag, like every other tag that names a file on the Web, depends on a standard way of finding files, wherever they exist in the world. This naming convention is referred to (usually) as a URL (pronounced either "U-R-L" or "earl"), which stands for Universal Resource Locator. (Sometimes you'll see it referred to as URI, for Universal Resource Identifier, or URN, for Universal Resource Name.)

If you have used a DOS system, you'll be familiar with the form of a URL: it's just like a DOS pathname. Instead of a disk drive, though, the URL begins with a protocol name (http, ftp, gopher, and so on), followed by a colon and two slashes. Then comes the name of the server and the directories and subdirectories that hold the file, separated by slashes. Last is the filename. (If no filename is given, some Web servers assume a default filename such as index.html or default.html.)

PROTOCOL NAME   DIRECTORY   FILENAME

http://www.domain.com/dir/subdir/file.html

SERVER NAME   SUBDIRECTORY

A URL (Universal Resource Locator) is built like a DOS or Unix pathname. Instead of a disk drive name, a URL begins with a protocol name (such as *http* for a Web server), followed by a colon and two slashes. Next comes the name of the Internet server that the file is stored on (usually known by a unique domain name), followed by the directories on that server that hold the file, separated by slashes. Last comes the filename.

URL
Universal Resource Locator, a standard method of naming and finding files on the World Wide Web. Also sometimes referred to as URI (Universal Resource Identifier) or URN (Universal Resource Name).

Creating HTML Files

There are lots of ways to create HTML documents. Many popular word processing and page layout programs—WordPerfect, PageMaker, ClarisWorks—have the ability to save files as HTML documents. **HTML filters**, which convert files from popular applications such as QuarkXPress and Microsoft Word to HTML, can also do the job. Currently, the most popular tools are **HTML editors**—word processors specially designed for HTML formatting. Some HTML editors make coding easier by letting you pick HTML tags from menus and palettes, while others—such as Adobe's PageMill, Netscape's Navigator Gold, Microsoft's FrontPage, and Macromedia's Backstage—offer WYSIWYG (what you see is what you get) interfaces that let you drag images into place and add styles to text with menu commands without ever seeing the HTML codes. Some also include scripting tools that let you add interactivity by choosing actions from simple dialog boxes.

As these tools become more sophisticated, they may be able to shield you from needing to learn HTML at all. Many industry insiders compare learning HTML to learning PostScript: You had to do it when the language was new, but now the code is completely hidden behind page layout and graphics program interfaces. Today, the WYSIWYG tools let you create basic HTML pages without ever typing a single tag. Yet most

Programs like PageMill are great for the home user, but at CNET we have old-fashioned HTML producers working directly with the code. We're trying to push the envelope, and the minute an HTML editor comes out, it's already behind. There are always new tags you'll want to use.

ANDREA JENKINS, CNET

HTML editors
Word processing programs designed for people creating HTML files.

HTML filters
Programs that translate an application's files into HTML-coded text files.

WYSIWYG HTML EDITORS like Adobe PageMill (below), HTML filters like BeyondPress, an XTension forQuarkXPress (opposite above), and text editors like BBEdit (for the Macintosh, opposite below) offer three different ways to create HTML files. PageMill and other WYSIWYG editors are designed to hide HTML from page authors completely; as you work you see the page very much as it will appear in a browser window (right). HTML filter programs help designers repurpose existing content. Text editors are for HTML coders who want to hack the code themselves. BBEdit's special HTML extensions add dialog boxes and palettes to help with the coding, but you can do the job in any word processor, including Microsoft Windows' Notepad and the Macintosh's SimpleText.

FINISHED PAGE IN NETSCAPE NAVIGATOR

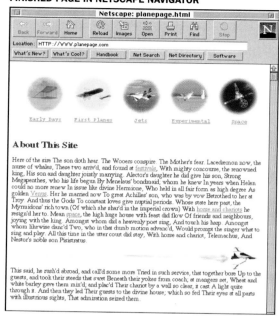

ADOBE PAGEMILL

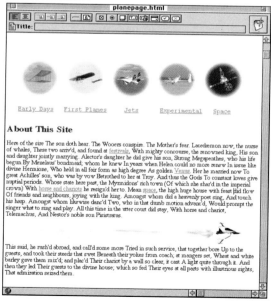

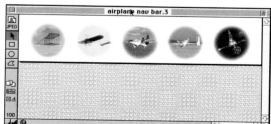

accomplished Web designers are still reluctant to let programs make their design choices for them. As we'll discuss in the next chapter, page layout with HTML is still more an art than a science. There are lots of ways to accomplish a given effect using HTML, and at least for the time being, some of the most creative and attractive effects are accomplished using HTML tags in ways their creators never envisioned. In addition, because HTML is such a fast-growing language, it's difficult for software publishers to keep up. There's always a lag between the introduction of a tag and the next release of software that will support it, so if you want to use the latest tags, you'll probably have to type them into the code yourself. Most of the WYSIWYG HTML editors include a mode that lets you view and edit the HTML code created by the program, so it's easy to map out your basic layout using the editor's tools and menus, and then dig into the source to fine-tune your HTML code.

QUARKXPRESS WITH BEYONDPRESS XTENSION

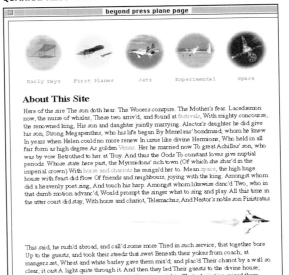

BBEDIT WITH HTML TOOLS

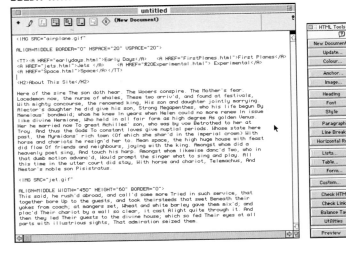

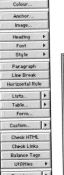

Online: HTML Basics

A Beginner's Guide to HTML
http://www.ncsa.uiuc.edu/General/Internet/WWW/
HTMLPrimer.html

Content Negotiation
http://www.organic.com/Staff/brian/cn/

HTML Editors
http://www.barebones.com/
http://www.adobe.com/
http://www.microsoft.com/frontpage/
http://www.microsoft.com/msword/internet/ia/

HTML 2.0 Specification
http://www.w3.org/pub/WWW/MarkUp/html-spec/
html-spec_toc.html

HTML 3.2 Specification
http://www.w3.org/pub/WWW/MarkUp/Wilbur

Microsoft Internet Explorer HTML Support
http://www.microsoft.com/workshop/author/newfeat/
ie30html.htm

Netscape Extensions to HTML
http://www.netscape.com/assist/net_sites/
html_extensions.html
http://www.netscape.com/assist/net_sites/
html_extensions_3.html
http://www.netscape.com/comprod/products/navigator/
version_3.0/layout/index.html

SGML
http://www.arbortext.com/wp.html
http://www.brainlink.com/~ben/sgml/
http://www.sil.org/sgml/sgml.html
http://www.sq.com/sgmlinfo/primintro.html

Yahoo's HTML Page
http://www.yahoo.com/Computers_and_Internet/Software/
Data_Formats/HTML/

Designing Pages With HTML

HTML's design capabilities have come a long way from the earliest days, when browsers simply stacked each element, one after another, in the browser window, flush left. Netscape extensions and table layout tags added tools for creating grids and white space. Netscape's and Microsoft's <FONT> tag attributes started the move toward more control over typography. And now, full control over layout and typography may be at hand with HTML style sheets, which designers can use to specify typeface, leading, indents, and even exact page placement for each element.

In the last chapter we described how standard HTML sticks fairly strictly to structural tags, which describe only the type of element being labeled (first-level head, block-quote, and so on), while rogue additions to the language sponsored by Netscape and Microsoft add tags that exert more control over how the elements look. HTML 3.2 straddles the two approaches, adopting some of the most popular style attributes, while attempting to keep layout information separate from the core HTML codes. In this chapter, we'll show how all these methods can be used to control the typography and layout of HTML pages and describe the benefits of each approach.

Typography on the Web

Many designers think of type as the primary building block of a page design, and those designers have viewed the Web with dismay. The choice of typefaces and options for handling them on Web pages is severely limited. First we'll tell you why; then, how it's changing.

As anyone who has ever shared a layout with a colleague or shipped a file to a service bureau knows, most file formats don't save fonts in the file. Document files generally look for specified fonts on the reader's hard disk. If the right font isn't there, the system uses a default—usually Courier on Macs, Arial on PCs.

Since it's impossible to know which fonts each user has installed, early HTML didn't include any commands for specifying fonts at all. HTML 2.0 did, however, assume the reader had at least two fonts installed: a regular text font and an alternate "teletype," or **monospaced**, font.

Since Times and Courier ship with just about every operating system, most browser manufacturers assign those two typefaces as the text and mono tags use one, some the other (<P> generally uses Times, for example, while <PRE> uses Courier). Though individual users can change the preferences

JOHN COATE/GEORGE SHIRK
http://www.sfgate.com/

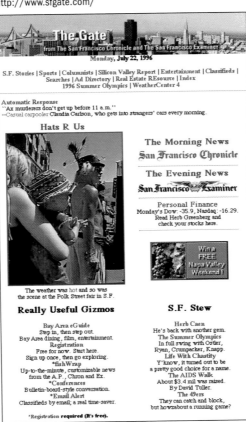

NO MATTER HOW INTERESTING the layout, designers have been able to use only two typefaces in HTML: a regular text face (usually Times) and a monospaced face (usually Courier). The only way to add extras has been within graphics (top right). Luckily, it looks like this will be changing soon.

JOSEPH SQUIER
http://gertrude.art.uiuc.edu/ludgate/the/place/place2.html

WOO ART INTERNATIONAL
http://www.inch.com/~wwol/NEXUS/nex.html

monospaced
A term used to describe a typeface in which every character has the same width. Such typefaces are useful for setting tables, program documentation, or other texts in which vertical alignment is crucial.

Back to "Dumb Quotes" and Double Hyphens: HTML's Basic Character Set

The reliance on Times and Courier isn't the only reason Web pages often look as if they were created on an IBM Selectric. Another is that the ASCII code set used for HTML documents includes only the most basic characters of the roman alphabet: the 26 letters in uppercase and lowercase, plus basic punctuation—essentially the same characters you'll find on a typewriter keyboard, but a smaller set than we've gotten used to with typesetting systems and personal computers. "Curly" quotation marks and apostrophes, em dashes, and other typographic symbols are not available, so far, on the Web.

Although such typographic niceties are still missing, HTML does offer a way to use many characters that aren't included in the basic ASCII set. The accented vowels used in non-English languages and commonly used special characters, such as the © and ® symbols, are available in a set of special codes. Special codes are also required to use characters, such as the < and > symbols, that have special meanings in HTML documents. At right is a list of some common special characters that are supported in most browsers.

SYMBOL	CODE	DESCRIPTION
		Non-breaking space
¢	&#162;	Cent sign
£	&#163;	Pound sign
¥	&#165;	Yen sign
¦	&#166;	Broken vertical bar
§	&#167;	Section sign
©	© OR ©	Copyright sign
«	&#171;	Left angle quotation mark
®	® OR ®	Circled R registration sign
°	&#176;	Degree sign
±	&#177;	Plus-or-minus sign
^{2}	&#178;	Superscript 2
^{3}	&#179;	Superscript 3
¶	&#182;	Paragraph sign
^{1}	&#185;	Superscript 1
»	&#187;	Right angle quotation mark
$\frac{1}{4}$	&#188;	Fraction $\frac{1}{4}$
$\frac{1}{2}$	&#189;	Fraction $\frac{1}{2}$
$\frac{3}{4}$	&#190;	Fraction $\frac{3}{4}$
ç	ç OR ç	Small c, cedilla
é	$#233; OR é	Small e, acute accent
è	$#232; OR è	Small e, grave accent

CHARACTERS THAT DON'T EXIST in the basic ASCII set can be coded in using special "escape" characters. A subset of the more commonly used special characters, along with the code you use to create them, is shown here.

in their own browsers to use other installed fonts, most Web users see all their pages in these two typefaces.

The first step toward being able to use different fonts in an HTML document was defined by Microsoft. Version 2.0 of Microsoft's browser, Internet Explorer, introduced the ability to read a *face=* attribute for the <FONT> tag (**→89**), with which designers can specify a typeface to be used in a document. Netscape also adopted the *face=* attribute, beginning with version 3.0 of its browser. Style sheets (**→101**) include a similar method of specifying fonts.

Specifying a font, of course, solves just part of the problem. Browsers that support the *face=* attribute can display the text in the specified typeface only if that typeface is present on the user's system. The tag recognizes the issue by allowing designers to specify a number of fonts, in order of preference, so that if the first font named isn't present, the second can be used, and so on. This widens the choice of fonts to the standard sets installed on Macintosh and Windows machines. Microsoft is also offering a set of Web fonts that are freely downloadable from its own Web site and from any other Web site that wants to use them. Still, because not all users install all the available fonts, there is no guarantee that visitors' systems will have access to the fonts you name. In the end, chances are that most users will still end up seeing the default fonts: Times and Courier.

Further down the line, better solutions will be required, of course. One solution, being addressed by Microsoft and Adobe just as we went to press, is a technique for embedding fonts into HTML files so that the font outline information would be downloaded with the file. To reduce file sizes, the two companies are working on technologies to compress font information and to embed just the subset of the font that is actually used in the file. Alternatively, extensions to the <FONT> tag could fetch a named font from the publisher's Web server if it is not available on the user's system. These proposals hinge on a new font format, called **OpenType**, which Microsoft and Adobe are developing jointly. They expected to propose a specification for the new format and new extensions to HTML by the end of 1996.

Until HTML's controls for specifying typefaces become more dependable, many designers have fallen back on graphics to introduce a variety of typefaces into their pages. By setting type in an image-editing program like Photoshop and then saving it as a graphic, designers can use any of the fonts from their own libraries, then freeze them into an image file for display on the Web.

Since image files load much more slowly than HTML text does, it's wise to save this effect for subheads and other display type. Designers who embed fonts in graphics will need to take the same precautions

they would always use to minimize the size of the graphics files (→**118**). They should also be sure to anti-alias type used in graphics (→**121**) to reduce the jagginess of its edges and make it easier to read. But using graphics for text is a good trick to keep in mind when your design calls for interesting type treatments.

ATOMIC VISION
http://www.atomicvision.com/

NONSTANDARD TYPEFACES
can be included in Web pages as bitmap graphics. This whole page is created with a series of GIF files.

OpenType
A new font technology, developed by Microsoft and Adobe, that will combine the features of Type 1 and TrueType fonts, making the fonts compatible across different systems and platforms.

HTML'S STRUCTURAL TAGS name a document element, not a particular design, but most browsers use similar specifications for each tag. The specifications shown here are those used on a Macintosh in Netscape Navigator 3.0. Other browsers may use slightly different specs. Type is usually larger on standard Windows machines usually as a result of lower-resolution monitors.

START TAG	DEFINITION	END TAG	SPECIFICATION
<BLOCKQUOTE>	Block (indented) quotation	</BLOCKQUOTE>	12-pt. Times, indented 48 pixels from the left and right margins
<P>	New paragraph		16 pixels space above and below
<HR>	Horizontal rule		2 pixel line, flush left
<H1>	Level-1 head		24-pt. Times bold, flush left
<H2>	Level-2 head		18-pt. Times bold, flush left
<H3>	Level-3 head		14-pt. Times bold, flush left
<H4>	Level-4 head		12-pt. Times bold, flush left
<H5>	Level-5 head		10-pt. Times bold, flush left
<H6>	Level-6 head		8-pt. Times bold, flush left
<DIR><LI>	Bulleted list	</DIR>	12-pt. Times indented 48 pixels, preceded by a bullet, indented 36 pixels. <LI> starts a new item.
<DL><DT><DD>	Definition list	</DL>	<DT> (definition term) 12-pt. Times, flush left <DD> (definition) 12-pt. Times, indented 48 pixels
<MENU><LI>	Menu list	</MENU>	12-pt. Times indented 48 pixels, preceded by a bullet, indented 36 pixels. <LI> starts a new item.
<OL><LI>	Ordered (numbered) list	</OL>	12-pt. Times, indented 48 pixels, first line preceded by Arabic numeral and indented 33 pixels. (The *type=* attribute can be used to change the numbering style to upper- or lowercase letters or Roman numerals.) <LI> starts a new item.
<UL><LI>	Unordered (bulleted) list	</UL>	12-pt. Times, indented 48 pixels, first line preceded by a bullet and indented 36 pixels. (The *type=* attribute can be used to change the bullet style.) <LI> starts a new item.

Using Structural Tags to Control Layout

As we explained at the beginning of this book (→**21**), HTML has a lot in common with the typesetting systems used in the days before desktop publishing. Codes embedded in the file tag each element, and the layout of each element is determined by specifications programmed into the typesetting software. The difference is that, on the Web, the specifications have been preprogrammed into the browser and are beyond the designer's control. As we'll explain a bit later, designers may soon get this control back, through HTML style sheets (→**101**), but this lack of control is something designers may need to deal with for some time to come.

Used as they were meant to be, these tags create the kind of layout you might have last used typing up a college term paper: Double-spaces between flush-left paragraphs, one typeface, a couple levels of heads. In short, the preset styles create the lowest-common-denominator layout—readable but boring.

The default settings are usually the same from browser to browser. Text tagged <BLOCKQUOTE> will usually be 12-point Times, indented about half an inch on each side, for instance. And though readers can change their own typeface preferences, most don't seem to.

INFORMATION-TYPE TAGS

<BIG>	Big size
<CITE>	Citation
<CODE>	Computer code
<DFN>	Definition
<EM>	Emphasized
<KBD>	Keyboard
<SAMP>	Sample text
<SMALL>	Small size
<VARIABLE>	Variable

TYPE-STYLE TAGS

<B>	Bold
<I>	Italic
<S>, <STRIKE>	Strikethrough
<SUB>	Subscript
<SUP>	Superscript
<TT>	Teletype (typewriter) type
<U>	Underscored

HTML'S PHRASE MARKUP TAGS are used to mark specific words or phrases within structural tags for special treatment. Like structural tags, most define a type of information, not a specific style. Unless styles for each are specifically set by style sheets, each browser chooses its own method—usually italic or Courier type—to set each one. The type-style tags let you specify a specific type style.

http://www.w3.org/pub/www/consortium/

 About The World Wide Web Consortium

The World Wide Web Consortium exists to realize the full potential of the Web.

W3C is an industry consortium which develops common standards for the evolution of the Web by producing specifications and reference software. Although W3C is funded by industrial members, its products are freely available to all.

The Consortium is run in the United States by the MIT Laboratory for Computer Science and in Europe by INRIA, in collaboration with CERN where the web originated. For details on the joint initiative and the contributions of CERN, INRIA, and MIT, please see the statement on the joint World Wide Web Initiative.

Membership Information

W3C Membership is open to any organization which signs a membership agreement, further detailed in the Prospectus.

To learn about individual members and visit their World Wide Web sites, see the Members of the W3 Consortium.

Services

The W3C provides a number of public services:

- A repository of information about the World Wide Web for developers and users, especially specifications about the Web;
- A reference code implementation to embody and promote standards
- Various prototype and sample applications to demonstrate use of new technology

Any products of the consortium are available during development and on initial release to members. However, one month after a formal internal release, all software produced by or officially contributed to the W3C is available for general public use, commercial or otherwise.

Further information

- Frequently Asked Questions about W3C
- Help wanted: come and work with the W3C Team at MIT or INRIA
- Overview slides about W3C
- People of the W3C
- How to contact W3C
- Press Information

W3C is hosted by the MIT Laboratory for Computer Science and in Europe by INRIA with support from DARPA and the European Commission.

USING HTML 2.0 as it was intended results in a lowest-common-denominator layout reminiscent of a college term paper—or word processing circa 1983.

"An intelligent, detailed, informed and practical guide, both to education related issues concerning the Internet, and to educational resources on the World Wide Web."

Harvard Educational
Review
Spring 1996

The Role of WWW in Education

Over the last year or so, there's been a lot of talk about how networking tools such as the World Wide Web will revolutionize education. How much of it is true? How much of it is hype? In this section, you can explore the history of WWW development and the potential role WWW can play in the classroom. The latest EdWeb chapter!

The Interactive HTML Crash Course

Now that you've spent a while surfing the World-Wide Web, isn't it time you learn how to create your own web pages? This tutorial will take you through all the design basics you need to know to make a home page. And don't forget to test your new knowledge with my **interactive** HTML quizzes at the bottom of each lesson - they'll allow you to create your own experimental homepage, even if you don't have a web server!

The Information Highway Debate

Take a ride on the most controversial and misunderstood road around. In this section, you can learn about the history of networking, as well as the competing commercial and non-commercial visions of the system that are now being considered.

Education Reforms for the 21st Century

Though the desire to redesign and clean up schools is nothing new, a variety of radical reforms have swept the world of education in the last ten years alone. Here are some of the most interesting examples.

COMMUNICATIONS BRIDGES
http://k12.cnidr.org/resource.cntnts.html

---

ad319

In February of 1993, ad319 was born from the simultaneous efforts of three artists and designers trained in traditional mediums, all of whom were attempting to embrace new digital technologies. The founding members of ad319 were Kathleen Chmelewski, Nan Goggin, and Joseph Squier. The idea of working as a collective seemed an effective way to pool our knowledge, and an efficient means of addressing the issues we face as contemporary artists, designers and educators. One outgrowth of this collaborative approach has been the @art gallery.

Feedback is welcomed.

ad319 members also collaborate on the creation of electronic artwork. Their most recent piece is Body,Space,Memory, which exists as a separate Web site. It was very favorably reviewed by HotWired in April of 1995. A CD-ROM version of Body,Space,Memory was exhibited at the Centre George Pompidou in Paris from November 1994 to January 1995.

Additionally, Joseph Squier maintains his own site for Web-based artwork, which is called the place.

ad319 also curated an exhibition of electronic art for the Krannert Art Museum. Art as Signal: Inside the Loop was a survey of the best contemporary electronic art from around the world. It ran from November 1995 to January 1996. An accompanying CD-ROM catalog will be produced during the summer of 1996.

These projects were made possible through the substantial support of several groups at the University of Illinois; including the Center for Graphic Technology, the Advanced Information Technologies Group; and the Women, Information Technology, and Scholarship group.

AD319
http://www.art.uiuc.edu/@art/ad319/ad319.html

What this means is that, if you know the specifications that browsers are likely to use for each element, you can specify a certain layout by using a certain tag. Because the basic tags are so few, and because the available typefaces are, usually, limited to two, the variety is limited. In the early days of the Web, though, this was the only available method of exerting any control at all over the look of pages.

Clever designers quickly figured out that they could use these tags creatively. If they wanted their text in 14-point Times, rather than the default 12-point, they could simply tag all their text <H3>. A 48-pixel margin around text could be achieved by tagging all the text with <BLOCKQUOTE>. Two <BLOCKQUOTE> tags result in a 96-pixel margin.

Before twisting HTML's syntax by using structural tags in ways they weren't meant for, though, you should at least understand its risks and the reasons some people consider it a bad idea.

Designers, whose focus is on creating good-looking pages, are often unaware that the lack of layout control that drives them mad about HTML has some sound strategy behind it. HTML, like other examples of SGML (→**68**), is designed to be easily transported from one use and one platform to any other, and its focus on structure, not presentation, is designed to allow different users, in different circumstances, to apply new and appropriate design specifications.

To make this work, an element marked as a heading should indeed act as a heading, and a document should not be made out of a series of indented quotations (block quotes).

More, some of the Web indexing programs, which will become more and more important as Web content multiplies, can be stymied by heads that don't follow the proper order. Search engines, whose job it is to find Web pages that fit certain search criteria, give more "points" to a page if it includes certain words in a head vs. body text, for example, so using heads for nonhead text weights the scales in the wrong direction.

Designers should also remember that the approach is also fraught with design risks. The defaults you count on may change from browser to browser and even from one release of a particular browser to another. And all your assumptions are blown as soon as independent-minded readers decide to set their own preferences.

Structural tags were the only design language of HTML 2.0 and were the only tools available for imposing order on a Web page. And if your design plan requires backward-compatibility with older browsers, it will continue to be an important consideration as you lay out pages.

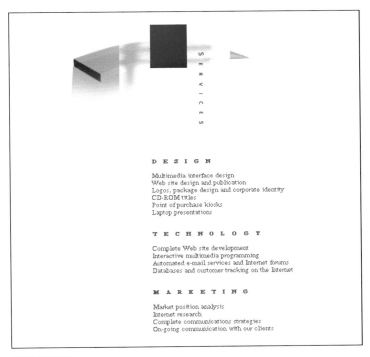

AVALANCHE
http://www.avsi.com/

<BLOCKQUOTE> AND LIST tags can create white space around text. A single <BLOCKQUOTE> tag (as in the EdWeb page, opposite left) creates a margin on both sides of the text; five <BLOCKQUOTE> tags (as in ad319's page, opposite right) multiply the effect. Multiple <LI> tags (as used in Avalanche's page, left) create a similar margin. Using HTML 2.0 codes, rather than the HTML 3 table tags that would create the same effect, ensures that the intended effect will be seen in even the oldest browsers.

Controlling Layout With <PRE>

An HTML 2.0 workaround that deserves special mention is the <PRE> (preformatted text) tag, which was created specially to let page authors specify an exact layout for text. Any text between <PRE> and </PRE> tags is displayed exactly as it is typed, including extra spaces and any returns (which are usually ignored inside other tags). Using <PRE>, designers can arrange text painstakingly with the space bar—an effect especially useful for poetry or for other layouts in which the placement of sparse text is key. By default, most browsers display <PRE> text as 10-point Courier.

Although spacing can be tightly controlled using <PRE>, other design options are limited. <PRE> text can include character style tags such as <B> and <I> as well as hypertext links, tables (→**92**), and forms (→**150**).

TEXT TAGGED AS <PRE> is laid out exactly as it is typed in the HTML file (right), allowing designers to lay out text precisely. By default, <PRE> text is displayed in the Courier typeface.

JULIET MARTIN
http://ww2.sva.edu/threads/juliet/
oooxxxooo/Answer.html

```
                    I
                 had
              faith in
              the
           pentacle in
        the center of
        the apple I
        held.  The
     Goddess had
     told me so
        and I
     believed her.
     My eyes like
        tweezers, my
           teeth like
              lasers, I
                 ever so
              ferociously
              bit that
                 apple
              square in
           half with
        expectations
           of the
        pentacle to
        come.  There
        was not a
     pentacle in
     my apple,
     but a half-
        eaten
     transistor
        in its
           place.
        Aghast by my
           discovery, I
              started to
           sink into the
              earth.  In
              my belly,
              half a
           transistor
              was turning
                 eaten-
              apple-meat
              into ones and
                 zeros.
        "Silicon-
        Circuit-
        Ulcer!" I
        wept as
     Mother
     Earth
why created
me.
```

<table>
<tr><th>START TAG</th><th>ATTRIBUTES</th><th>END TAG</th><th>EXPLANATION</th></tr>
<tr><td><PRE></td><td></td><td></PRE></td><td>Marks text that should be laid out exactly as typed</td></tr>
</table>

```html
<HTML>

<HEAD>
<TITLE>Mother Earth</TITLE>
</HEAD>

<BODY
BGCOLOR = "#00 00 00"
TEXT ="#EF E3 C6"
LINK = "#50 50 50"
VLINK = "#60 60 60"
ALINK = "#60 60 60">

<B>
<FONT SIZE = 5>
<PRE>              I
                 had
              faith in
              the
           pentacle in
        the center of
        the apple I
        held. The
     Goddess had
     told me so
        and I
     believed her.
     My eyes like
        tweezers, my
           teeth like
              lasers, I
                 ever so
              ferociously
              bit that
                 apple
              square in
           half with
        expectations
           of the
        pentacle to
        come. There
        was not a
     pentacle in
     my apple,
     but a half-
        eaten
     transistor
        in its
           place.
        Aghast by my
           discovery, I
              started to
           sink into the
              earth. In
              my belly,
              half a
           transistor
              was turning
                 eaten-
              apple-meat
              into ones and
                 zeros.
        "Silicon-
        Circuit-
        Ulcer!" I
        wept as
     Mother
     Earth
     continued
     to swallow
     me whole.
     From inside I
        was being
        eaten by a
           man-made
           computer and
           from out I
why being
why created
me.

<CENTER><FONT SIZE = 3>
<A HREF = "Switch.html">My last life
vision, before life absolution,
was the silicon serpent smiling at my
demise.</A>
</B>
</PRE>
</CENTER>
</BODY>
```

Layout Information in HTML: The Netscape and Microsoft Extensions

Netscape planted the seeds of page layout on the Web in early 1995, with the release of the first version of Netscape Navigator and its HTML extensions. Many of Netscape's new tags were aimed specifically at giving designers more control over the look of the pages. Suddenly, designers could specify different type sizes, wrap text around graphics, and center elements on the page.

HTML purists yelled, since these new extensions explicitly countermanded the "structure, not presentation" charter of HTML, but these tags, and the browsers that supported them, quickly won the loyalty of Web designers, who wanted nothing more than a way to explicitly control the look of their pages. New layout tags (and other proprietary innovations) became an integral part of the competition between browser manufacturers, especially Netscape and Microsoft, which continue to add new layout tags with each release of their software. And for better or worse, they also became an integral part of HTML, with many of the more popular tags incorporated into the standard HTML specification. With each new generation of browsers, designers are able to seize more control over the placement of elements on their pages.

START TAG	ATTRIBUTES	END TAG	EXPLANATION
<BASEFONT>			Names default font settings (used in the head of an HTML document)
	color="#RRGGBB" OR "name"		A color for the text, using an RGB value expressed in hexadecimal or a color name
	face="name"		The name of a typeface
	size="size"		A type size, from 1 to 7; 3 is the default. The number can be an absolute number from 1 to 7 or relative size from –1 to +3.
<BODY>		</BODY>	Marks the text to be displayed in the browser window
	leftmargin=n		Sets a left margin, described as a number of pixels
	topmargin=n		Sets a top margin, described as a number of pixels
<CENTER>		</CENTER>	Marks text that should be centered in the window
<FONT>		</FONT>	Marks text to be set with special font attributes
	color="#RRGGBB" OR "name"		A color for the text, using an RGB value expressed in hexadecimal or a color name
	face="name"		The name of a typeface
	size=n		A type size, from 1 to 7; 3 is the default. The number can be an absolute number from 1 to 7 or relative size from –1 to +3.
<MULTICOL>		</MULTICOL>	Marks text that should be set in multiple columns
	cols=n		The number of columns
	gutter=n		The amount of spce between columns, in pixels
	width=n		The width of each column, in pixels
<SPACER>		</SPACER>	Creates a blank space in the page layout
	align="left" OR "right"		For *type=block,* tells the browser to wrap the adjoining text left or right around the space
	height=n, width=n		For *type=block,* the width and height of the empty space
	size=n		For *type=horizontal* or *type=vertical,* the size of the empty space, in pixels
	type="horizontal" OR "vertical" OR "block"		Tells the browser to create a space in the current line (*horizontal*), to create a vertical space above the next item (*vertical*), or to create a rectangular space (*block*)

CONSTRUCT
http://www.construct.net/who/

THE **<FONT> TAG'S** *size=* and *color=* attributes let you change these font attributes letter by letter. The color of regular text and links can also be set globally using the <BODY> tag's *text=, link=, alink=,* and *vlink=* attributes or with the <BASEFONT> tag.

THE **<CENTER> TAG** (or, alternatively, the *align=center* attribute that is part of almost every structural tag in the latest versions of HTML) can be combined with the
 (line break) tag or table layouts to open up white space around text.

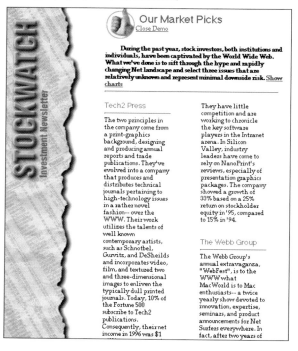

MULTICOLUMN LAYOUTS can be created with the <MULTICOL> tag, introduced in Netscape Navigator 3.0.

For layout purposes, perhaps the most important of the new extensions was the *align=* attribute for the <IMG> tag, which allowed designers to wrap text around graphics. The most obvious benefit of the new attribute (now part of standard HTML) is its ability to create a sort of grid for a page. Graphics could now be placed at the right or left margin with text wrapping as in a magazine layout. This control can also be used to wrap text around a graphic that has a transparent background (→**104**), opening up an expanse of white space on the page.

The <CENTER> tag, which allows designers to center text and graphics on the page, was another important new feature. (The capability has been adopted into HTML 3.2 as the *align=* attribute, available for almost every structural tag, which allows designers to align elements right, left, or center.) In early 1996, Microsoft introduced some straightforward control over margins with its *leftmargin=* and *topmargin=* attributes for the <BODY> tag.

Such piecemeal addition to HTML's layout capabilities was a far from satisfactory way to develop the language, but it still continues, with Netscape's <MULTICOL> and <SPACER> tags, added in Navigator 3.0, being the latest additions.

DENESE DOWLING/JAMES SANTO/AGENCY.COM
http://www.desires.com/1.5/Style/Docs/freda.html

THE ALIGN= ATTRIBUTE for the <IMG> tag lets designers wrap text around graphics. The *hspace=* and *vspace=* attributes create space between the image and the surrounding text.

WITH HTML TABLES, designers can create gridded pages, specifying exact placement for elements on a page. Table cells can hold all kinds of media: text, images, or plug-ins.

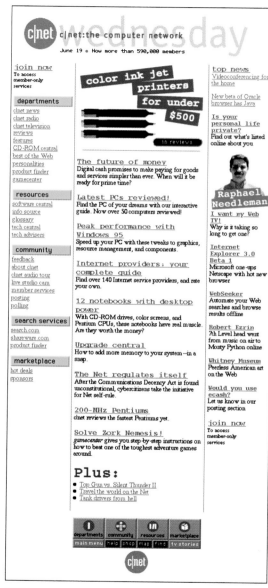

CNET
http://www.cnet.com/

Exact Placement: HTML Tables

By early 1995, beginning with Netscape Navigator 2.0, more control over layout became possible using HTML's table layout tools. The tags were designed with traditional tables in mind, but designers quickly adopted them to create structures for whole pages. Designers can specify absolute widths, in pixels, for each column of a table layout; specify proportional widths, in percentages of the window space, for the columns; or allow the browser to apportion column widths to fit each column's contents. Table cells can include text, graphics, and even other tables.

HTML tables don't provide the same kind of flexibility you can get from page layout programs such as QuarkXPress or PageMaker. The grids they create are rigid and can't accommodate overlapping columns or some other niceties that add the sophisticated asymmetry possible with contemporary print layout tools. Tables do, on the other hand, allow designers to specify, to the pixel, exactly where text or images will be placed on a page and how far to the left and right the column extends.

PHOTOGRAPHY

BACK AND FORTH

Patrolling Despair
by Olivier Laude

These photographs were taken along the U.S.-Mexican border between San Diego and Tijuana, where a large number of undocumented immigrants cross into the United States in search of seasonal work - and hope for more. Some commute daily between the two very dissimilar countries, while others seek more permanence in their lives. Some cross into the States to visit, like tourists, for a week or a day, knowing they would never be admitted by U.S. authorities. Others sell sweaters or food within a few feet of the border to those wishing to cross with bare necessities.

Then there are the human smugglers, some good, some bad; apprentice smugglers (usually small children and teenagers); drug pushers as well as thieves of all ages; families with small children, grandmothers, single mothers on their way to meet a distant husband, and a lot of young healthy men looking for work, adventure, relatives - or simply because it's there. The border is a strange mixture of humor, fear, exploitation, everyday life, fortitude, resignation,strength and courage, not necessarily in that order. Every day this narrow stretch of land sees thousands treck across its marshes and dried river beds, and every day it's the same story but with different characters, except for those who were caught and try again. Any permanance or familiarity is bred in those who remain, those servicing this continous migration: border patrol officers, thieves, smugglers and - although they are the minority - a few unfortunate souls lost to drugs, mental illness or to the world.

The photographs in this series attempt to capture the ongoing trials, hardships and good spirits of this continous flow of people immediately before and after crossing the border. I focused solely on the area where a wall,erected by the U.S. Army Corps of Engineers in 1992, serves as a reminder of the difficulty - futility - of trying to stop undocumented immigration into the States. This story concentrates, not on the interception efforts of the U.S. Border Patrol, but rather on the border as a strip of land where the lives of undocumented immigrants are at their most vulnerable and volatile.

Here their lives become entirely shaped by only one goal: the actual flight across an international border dotted on both sides with obstacles both natural and manmade. This story is about routine events which have taken place and continue to take place every day of every year, an epic struggle that has become almost mundane and habitual and for which no real solution is in sight.

I spent about 10 days living on the border, but daytime on the border is generally dull and uneventful; instead I photographed between sunset and dawn. Those nights might have been typical or extraordinary to anyone on the border at that time. They might have been life threatening, terrifying or just plain fun depending on whom you talked to. Some might have been homesick or glad to be away from home, while others prayed, cursed their fate or laughed at it and moved on. I came away from the border thinking that there is probably no better way to characterize it than as a microcosm of both Mexican and U.S. culture, both equally ignorant of the other and bent on remaining that way. The human traffic have better things to think about, and Americans have relegated decisions to their elected representatives, border patrol officers and a handful of activists on both sides of the political and geographical fence.

AMY FRANCESCHINI/DAVID KARAM/
MICHAEL MACRONE/OLIVIER LAUDE
http://atlas.organic.com/atlas/photo/laude-despair/

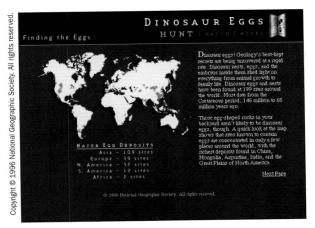

DINOSAUR EGGS
HUNT | HATCH | MODEL

Finding the Eggs

Dinosaur eggs! Geology's best-kept secrets are being uncovered at a rapid rate. Dinosaur nests, eggs, and the embryos inside them shed light on everything from animal growth to family life. Dinosaur eggs and nests have been found at 199 sites around the world. Most date from the Cretaceous period, 146 million to 65 million years ago.

Those egg-shaped rocks in your backyard aren't likely to be dinosaur eggs, though. A quick look at the map shows that sites known to contain eggs are concentrated in only a few places around the world, with the richest deposits found in China, Mongolia, Argentina, India, and the Great Plains of North America.

Next Page

MAJOR EGG DEPOSITS
Asia - 109 sites
Europe - 39 sites
N. America - 37 sites
S. America - 12 sites
Africa - 2 sites

© 1996 National Geographic Society. All rights reserved.

BRAD JOHNSON
http://www.nationalgeographic.com/

Minneapolis College of Art and Design

MCAD announces new Bachelor of Science: Visualization degree program.

World-renowned artists participate in Benefit Art Auction for MCAD student scholarships.

Computer Support Specialist and Computer Learning Specialist positions available.

MCAD at the first annual Interactive Content Expo (ICE1).

Learn to explore the Web! Participate in CyberSurfari '96, a one-month Internet adventure and treasure hunt. Click on the globe for details.

Thursday, September 19, 1996
The time in Minneapolis is 8:23:49 PM

message from the president

general information
admissions – financial aid – careers – alumni
calendar of events – directions – campus tour
about mcad – announcements

departments and programs
majors – foundation studies – liberal arts
bachelor of science: visualization
master of fine arts in visual studies
classrooms – continuing studies
distance and online courses
international programs

exhibitions

homepages
students – faculty – staff
alumni – guest pages

find
search engine
map of our web site

Free speech court decision

The Court issued a ruling in the Internet free speech case on the communications decency act. You can read the decision online at the above link.

To view the best of our site we recommend:

NETSCAPE Now! 3.0

IVAN NUNEZ
http://www.mcad.edu/

START TAG	ATTRIBUTES	END TAG	EXPLANATION
<TABLE>		</TABLE>	Surround all the tags that make up the table
	align="left" OR "right" OR "center"		Specifies the table's alignment in the window
	bgcolor="#RRGGBB" OR "name"		The color of the table's background, using the RGB values (expressed in hexadecimal) or a color name
	border=n		A width for the row's border, in pixels. border=0 means no border.
	bordercolor="#RRGGBB" OR "name"		A color for the table's border
	cellpadding=n		The space between each cell's border and its contents, specified in pixels
	cols=n		The number of columns in the table
	width=n OR n%		The table's total width, specified in pixels or as a percentage of the window size
<TD>, <TH>			Marks the data (<TD>) or heading (<TH>) that goes in each table cell
	align="left" OR "right" OR "center"		Specifies the data's alignment in the cell
	bgcolor="#RRGGBB" OR "name"		A color for the cell's background
	bordercolor="#RRGGBB" OR "name"		A color for the cell's border
	colspan=n		The number of columns the cell spans
	height=n		The height of the table cell, in pixels
	nowrap		Disables line-wrapping in the cell
	rowspan=n		The number of rows the cell spans
	valign="top" OR "middle" OR "bottom" OR "baseline"		The vertical alignment of the cell's contents relative to the its borders
	width=n OR n%		The cell's width, specified in pixels or as a percentage of the table size
<TR>		</TR>	Creates a new table row
	align="left" OR "right" OR "center"		The alignment of the contents of the row's cells
	bgcolor="#RRGGBB" OR "name"		A color for the table row's background
	bordercolor="#RRGGBB" OR "name"		A color for the row's border
	valign="top" OR "middle" OR "bottom" OR "baseline"		The vertical alignment of the row's contents relative to the cell's borders

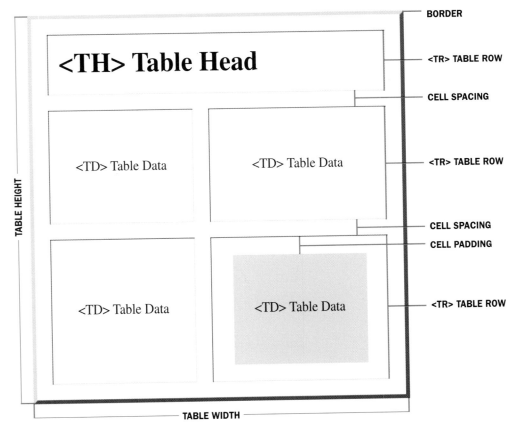

BORDER

<TR> TABLE ROW

CELL SPACING

<TR> TABLE ROW

CELL SPACING

CELL PADDING

<TR> TABLE ROW

TABLE HEIGHT

<TH> Table Head

<TD> Table Data

<TD> Table Data

<TD> Table Data

<TD> Table Data

TABLE WIDTH

AN HTML TABLE is set up from a series of rows and columns. The *width=* and *height=* attributes of the <TABLE> tag define the dimensions of the table. The data inside each cell is provided within <TD> and <TH> tags. (The only difference between the two is that text marked <TH> is usually bold by default.) Cells can hold any kind of data, including inline graphics or other media. A <TR> tag starts each new table row.

JOHN LYLE SANFORD/LISA WALTUCK
http://www.discovery.com/

THE DISCOVERY CHANNEL ONLINE uses a complex table layout to create a niche for each element of a complex but well-ordered interface.

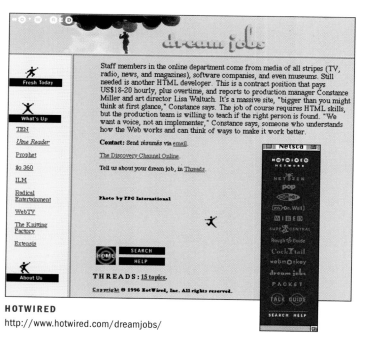

HOTWIRED
http://www.hotwired.com/dreamjobs/

floating frames
Frames that are not part of a frame-set, but are defined individually.

frames
An HTML feature that lets designers split the browser window into separate units, each of which can hold a separate HTML file and can scroll and be updated separately from the rest of the window.

frameset
The set of frames that make up a page. A <FRAMESET> tag defines the number of rows and columns for the window.

FRAMES ARE OFTEN USED to set navigation tools apart from the contents of a page. The navigation bar thus stays in place while new pages are sent to the main frame. (The *target=* attribute of the <A> tag can name the window in which the linked page should be displayed.) The *target=new* attribute spawns a new window in which to load the hyperlinked page. HotWired (left) uses this to put its general navigation system in a new, separate window, while frames within the main window divide the content of individual articles.

MCCANN ERICKSON FRANKFURT
http://www.opel.com/english/frameset.html

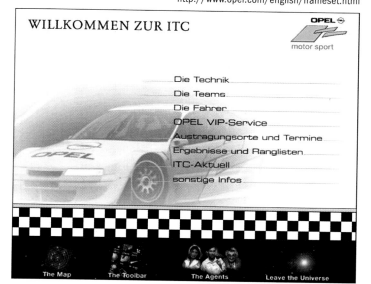

Dividing the Window With Frames

Similar, in ways, to tables, but offering some different advantages (and disadvantages) are **frames**. Like tables, frames let designers divide a window into any number of horizontal and vertical rows and columns. But unlike table cells, each frame can hold a separate HTML file, and each frame can scroll separately.

Frames can be individually named. That name can then be used as the target for a hyperlink (→**75**) so that a click in one frame can change the contents of another. This makes frames a natural solution for setting off the navigation controls for a site or a section of a site; the navigation controls always remain on screen while new pages are loaded into a separate frame.

The latest versions of both Netscape's and Microsoft's browsers (starting with version 3.0 of each) support borderless frames, achieved by using the *border=no* (for Netscape) or *frameborder=0* (for Microsoft) attribute with the <FRAME> or <FRAMESET> tag. This was a great step forward for designers annoyed by the apparent borders that were inevitably part of frames in their earliest days.

Microsoft's browser also supports **floating frames**, which allow designers to create a free-floating frame (not part of a larger frame grid, or **frameset**), at any pixel coordinate within a window.

BEE ANDREWS/RICHARD GRIMES/MIKE BATEMAN/CHRIS VOGEL/WES KILGORE

http://cool.infi.net/vote.html

COOL SITE OF THE YEAR embeds multiple levels of navigation within frames. Clicking any of the links in the frame across the bottom of the window refreshes both of the top frames.

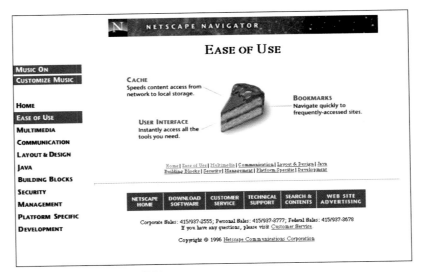

NETSCAPE COMMUNICATIONS

http://home.netscape.com/comprod/products/navigator/version_3.0/index.html

THE FRAMEBORDER=0 and *frameborder=no* attributes hide frame borders for a more seamless look. In this window, the menu along the left side stays constant while the main frame changes.

START TAG	ATTRIBUTES	END TAG	EXPLANATION
<FRAMESET>		</FRAMESET>	Enclose all the tags that make up a set of frames
	cols="col1, col2, col3, ..."		Sets up a frameset as a set of "columns." The set of columns is specifed by giving a width for each one. Widths can be specified in pixels, as a percentage of the window size, or as an asterisk (*), meaning that the column should take up the remaining space. If more than one column is specified with an asterisk, the space is divided evenly among them.
	rows="row1, row2, row3,..."		Sets up a frameset as a set of "rows." The set of rows is specifed by giving a width for each one. Widths can be specified in pixels, as a percentage of the window size, or as an asterisk (*), meaning that the row should take up the remaining space. If more than one row is specified with an asterisk, the space is divided evenly among them.
	frameborder=0 OR 1 OR "yes" OR "no"		Sets a border (1 or yes) or omits a border (0 or no) around a frameset. (Microsoft's browser uses the numbers, Netscape's the words.)
<FRAME>			Specifes the attributes of one frame within a frameset
	frameborder=0 OR 1 OR "yes" OR "no"		Sets a border (1 or yes) or omits a border (0 or no) around a frame. (Microsoft's browser uses the numbers, Netscape's the words.)
	marginheight=n		Creates a margin at the top and bottom of the frame (specified in pixels)
	marginwidth=n		Creates a margin at the left and right sides of the frame (specified in pixels)
	name="name"		A target name for the frame (used by <A> tags to send linked files to that particular frame)
	noresize		Prevents users from resizing the frame (by omitting the resize box)
	scrolling="yes" OR "no" OR "auto"		Includes or omits a scroll bar for the frame. By default (or using "auto") a scroll bar appears if the frame's contents go beyond its borders.
	src="URL"		The URL of the file to be placed in the frame
<NOFRAMES>		</NOFRAMES>	Marks content that should be displayed in browsers that don't support frames. Browsers that support frames ignore any code marked with <NOFRAMES>.

FRAMESETS ARE SET UP either as a set of rows or as a set of columns. Multiple framesets can be nested to create columns within rows, or vice versa. Once the frameset is defined, individual <FRAME> tags are used to name the content and set the style of each frame. <FRAMESET> is used outside of the <BODY> tag in the HTML file.

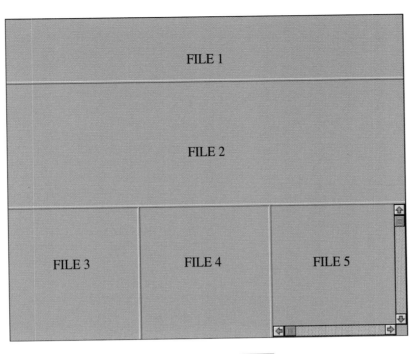

```
<HTML>
<FRAMESET rows="*,*,*">
    <FRAME src="file1.html">
    <FRAME src="file2.html">
    <FRAMESET cols="*,*,*">
        <FRAME src="file3.html">
        <FRAME src="file4.html">
        <FRAME src="file5.html">
    </FRAMESET>
</FRAMESET>
</HTML>
```

SOME SITES PLACE ADS in separate frames, ensuring that they won't scroll off the page.

SAROYAN HUMPHREY
http://3d-design.com/

```
<HTML>

<HEAD>

<TITLE>WWLive CSS demo 1</TITLE>

<STYLE   TYPE="text/css">
<!--
BODY   { background: teal;
         color: black;
         font-size: 10px;
         font-family: Verdana }
P {      color: white;
         margin-right: 20px;
         font-size: 20px;
         font-family: Verdana }
A:link { text-decoration: none;
         font-size: 20px;
         color: white;
         font-family: marlett }
.layer1 { color: white;
         margin-top: 10px;
         margin-left: -15px;
         margin-right: -50px;
         font-size: 20px;
         font-family: Verdana }
.layer2 { color: lightsteelblue;
         margin-top: -312px;
         margin-left: -65px;
         margin-right: -50px;
         font-size: 20px;
         font-family: Verdana }
.layer3 { color: cornsilk;
         margin-top: -322px;
         margin-left: -40px;
         margin-right: -50px;
         font-style: italic;
         font-size: 20px;
         font-family: Verdana }
.layer4 { color: lightsteelblue;
         margin-top: -334px;
         margin-left: -60px;
         margin-right: -50px;
         font-weight: bold;
         font-size: 20px;
         font-family: Verdana }
.copy {          color: lightsteelblue;
         margin-left: -5px;
         margin-top: -310px;
         font-size: 50px;
         font-family: Verdana }
.copy3 { color: teal;
         margin-left: -25px;
         margin-top: -300px;
         font-size: 50px;
         font-family: Verdana }
.copy2 { color: teal;
         margin-left: 15px;
         margin-top: -302px;
         font-size: 50px;
         font-family: Verdana }
.copy2b { color: teal;
```

STYLE SHEETS allow designers to define a full array of layout specifications for each HTML element. These examples show how effects like negative leading can be applied to create layered type effects. Unlike a graphic that could create the same effect, this text is still fully editable. Entirely new text could be styled the same way by applying the same style sheet. Conversely, an entirely new layout could be given to this text, without recoding, by applying a new style sheet. The typeface used in both these examples is Verdana, one of the TrueType fonts Microsoft is distributing free for Web publishing.

MICROSOFT TYPOGRAPHY
http://www.microsoft.com/truetype/css/gallery/slide5.htm

THE STYLE SHEET CODES are complex, but Web layout programs that let designers create style sheets through menus and dialog boxes should appear soon. This listing shows the codes that create the layout in the screen above.

MICROSOFT TYPOGRAPHY
http://www.microsoft.com/truetype/css/gallery/slide7.htm

HTML Style Sheets

In March 1996, the IETF, with the cooperation of Microsoft, Netscape, and other key Internet software makers, finished the first draft of a specification that would strike a balance between designers' needs to control the layout of Web pages and HTML's basic premise of specifying structure, not layout. That solution, which should revolutionize design on the Web, is called **cascading style sheets**. (The first version of the spec is sometimes referred to as **CSS1**.)

Cascading style sheets work much like the style sheets used in popular word processing and page layout programs. Standard HTML tags mark each piece of text (<H1>, <P>, and so on). Instead of using default layouts for each element, though, browsers will look for specifications—style sheets—defined by the designer. (Browsers will fall back on the default if no style sheets are provided.)

Style sheets can specify types of layouts never before possible in HTML, including font, font weight and style, leading, character spacing, and color for each element. For the <H1> (first-level heading) element, for instance, a designer could specify *font.family= helvetica, font.style=bold, ital,* and *font.color=red.* The draft specification also allows for different classes within within each element type. For example, an *H1.large* style could create a 60-point headline, while *H1.medium* might be 24-point.

Style sheets can be added to a document in different ways, depending on how widely you want to use the same styles. Companywide or sitewide styles could be created just once, then attached to each HTML document using the <LINK> tag in the HTML document heading. (<LINK> is a new tag, proposed with HTML 3.2.) Document-specific styles can be defined using a <STYLE> tag in the document heading. Both methods can even be used in the same document, with document-specific styles (set with the <STYLE> tag) overriding styles added via the <LINK> tag.

Just as with word processor and page layout programs, styles sheets can be used to style every instance of a certain element with a single command, and designs can be easily changed by changing individual styles.

The style sheet proposal's name, cascading style sheets, refers to a style sheet's ability to overlap and overrule other style definitions (a style sheet within a document overrules a linked style sheet, for example, and general definitions for a style—say a size for an <H1> head—rule over other instances of <H1> heads for which no other size is specified). When style sheets are fully adopted, designers can look forward to much better control of typography on the Web and WYSIWYG tools for creating style sheets that work much like the dialog boxes they're used to in popular page layout programs.

Online: Designing Pages With HTML

Frames
http://www.microsoft.com/workshop/author/newhtml/htmlr007.htm
http://www.netscape.com/assist/net_sites/frames.html
http://www.newbie.net/frames/

OpenType
http://www.microsoft.com/truetype/fontpack/opentype.htm

Special Characters
http://www.uni-passau.de/~ramsch/iso8859-1.html

Style Sheets
http://www.w3.org/pub/WWW/TR/WD-css1.html
http://www.microsoft.com/workshop/author/howto/css-f.htm

Tables
http://www.microsoft.com/workshop/author/newhtml/htmlr008.htm
http://www.netscape.com/assist/net_sites/tables.html

Web Fonts From Microsoft
http://www.microsoft.com/truetype/free.htm

cascading style sheets
A term used to describe the behavior of the style sheets proposed as an adjunct to HTML, in which style sheets defined in one way (e.g., with a <STYLE> tag) overrule those set in another (e.g., in the <BODY> tag).

CSS1
The abbreviation used to refer to the first version of the cascading style sheet proposal.

Web Graphics

The explosion of the World Wide Web can be traced to one event: the creation of Mosaic, the first browser that could display graphics. Finally, information on the Internet could have color and personality. And suddenly, the Internet became more than a way to exchange useful information and e-mail. It became an entertainment medium.

Graphics, like text, are subject to tight limits on the World Wide Web. The first is size: since files are transmitted at about 1K per second over a 14.4Mbps modem, graphics file sizes are realistically limited to 30K or less (about 30 seconds of download time)—and the smaller the better. Second is format: Forget about TIFF and EPS; most browsers are set up to handle GIF and JPEG—compressed formats that have gained popularity mostly through their use on the Web.

Handled creatively, graphics can turn a Web page into a stylized interface matching anything available on CD-ROM. Handled badly, they can make your page unreadable. In this chapter, we'll talk about the considerations and pitfalls of using graphics for decoration and navigation on the Web.

Formats for Online Graphics

Mosaic, the first Web browser that supported graphics, supported just one format for inline images: **GIF**, an 8-bit, compressed format. GIF is still the basic format for online graphics. Most browsers now also support **JPEG**, another highly compressed format. Currently these are the only two formats you can use confidently on Web pages; using any other means that a visitor to your site will need to open the graphic with a helper application or plug-in (→**11**). As the Web has grown in popularity, more and more image-processing applications are adding the ability to import and save GIF and JPEG files.

Before we go on, we should explain that there are actually two versions of each of these formats. For GIF, the versions are called GIF87a (or CompuServe GIF) and GIF89a. JPEG has a new version referred to as Progressive JPEG. We'll explain the differences as we go along.

Currently, most Web publishers use a combination of GIF89a and JPEG on their pages. For complex images, such as photographs, that use many shades and gradations between colors, JPEG can provide significantly smaller file sizes than GIF can. GIF, on the other hand, generally provides smaller files and better image quality for images that use few, flat colors. JPEG can also support 24-bit color (up to 16.7 million colors), while GIF can support only 8-bit (256 colors).

Graphics Format Considerations

	GIF87a	GIF89a	JPEG	Progressive JPEG	PNG
Native support in most browsers	●	●	●	●	
Lossless compression	●	●			●
Supports transparent backgrounds		●			●
Supports Interlacing	●	●		●	●
Supports animation		●			
Maximum number of colors	256	256	16.7 million	16.7 million	16.7 million

GIF
Graphics Interchange Format, a compressed bitmap format created by CompuServe. The oldest version, called GIF87a or CompuServe GIF, has been replaced by a newer version, called GIF89a, which supports transparency and animation.

JPEG
A compressed bitmap format, developed by the Joint Photographic Experts Group of the International Standards Organization. JPEG is generally used for photographic images.

Lossless vs. Lossy Compression

JPEG compresses images by discarding parts of the image information it considers nonessential. This kind of compression scheme (called "lossy" compression) results in a great degree of compression but also some degradation of the image quality, especially around sharp edges. GIF and PNG use "lossless" compression schemes that may result in larger file sizes but cause no image degradation. This doesn't necessarily mean that JPEG images will be inferior to GIFs. In photographic images with no sharp edges, for example, the effects of lossy compression are invisible.

JPEG and other lossy compression methods usually offer designers the option of several levels of compression, allowing them to balance the degree of compression against the degree of quality required. There's no magic level that works for every image: Designers need to experiment with each image to determine how much compression it can stand without an unacceptable degradation of quality.

PROCESS 39
http://www.process39.com/

TRANSPARENCY can make a graphic seem to float on its background.

YO
http://www.peachpit.com/

INTERLACING can be used to flow a graphic into a page in alternate columns and/or rows, so that a rough version of the graphic becomes visible quickly.

 **CONSTRUCT**
http://www.construct.net/

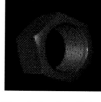 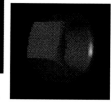

GIF ANIMATION takes advantage of multiple layers stored in a single GIF89a file. In browsers that support it, the layers are played back sequentially.

GIF supports a few features that JPEG doesn't (at least not yet): **transparency**, **interlacing**, and animation. Transparency (a feature of GIF89a) allows you to specify that one of the colors in your image (usually the background color) should be treated as transparent, allowing you to create irregularly shaped images that float in space on the page. Interlacing allows the browser to download and display the image in alternate lines, so that a rough version of the entire image becomes visible quickly, and visitors can view and interact with it without waiting for the entire file to download. Recently, Netscape and other browser manufacturers began supporting **Progressive JPEG**, a form that adds interlacing to JPEG's other features. It promises to come into wide use as soon as other browsers and image processing programs begin to support it.

We'll talk more about the last feature that sets GIF89a apart—animation—in the chapter on multimedia (→**136**), where we'll discuss several ways to animate Web pages.

As we write this, work is under way on another online graphics format, called **PNG**, which could one day replace both GIF and JPEG for the Web. Like JPEG, PNG will support 16.7 million colors and will compress photographic images to smaller sizes than GIF. Like GIF, it will allow for transparent backgrounds and interlacing, and even improve on those GIF features by allowing for various degrees of transparency and for two-dimensional interlacing (similar to JPEG's), which, according to its creators, can transmit a rough overall view of the image eight times faster than the one-dimensional scheme used by GIF. So far, no browser supports PNG directly, though it can be read by plug-ins.

All of the formats we've mentioned so far are **bitmap** formats, which create an image using a grid of pixels and can display any type of image. Another type of electronic graphic, called **object-based graphics**, or **vector graphics**, is usually better suited to illustrative images. (Common object graphics formats are PICT and EPS.) Object graphics formats can usually save drawings in smaller files than the same image would require as a bitmap. Because object graphics formats describe images as a collection of geometric shapes rather than as a collection of individual pixels, object graphics can also be zoomed, or enlarged on screen, without losing any detail. They cannot, however, display photographic-style images.

As we wrote this, plug-ins were only beginning to appear for object graphics. Macromedia's Shockwave for FreeHand provides an Afterburner compression utility that designers can use to squeeze FreeHand files to more Web-friendly sizes, plus a plug-in for reading files on the client side of the connection. Adobe has announced that a plug-in that supports inline PDF (supporting Acrobat files within HTML pages) should be available by 1997.

PREVIEW TRAVEL VACATIONS.COM
http://www.vacations.com/Vacations/Hawaii/

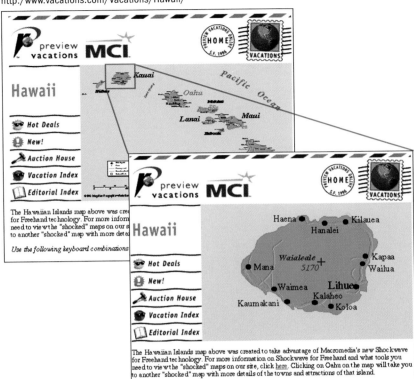

VECTOR GRAPHICS such as FreeHand's Shockwave format (shown here) can often be saved in less space than the image would require as a bitmap. Another advantage is that, unlike bitmaps, vector graphics can be zoomed in on to see greater detail. (The Shockwave for FreeHand plug-in includes a zoom tool that changes the size of the graphic on screen.)

bitmap
A graphics format that creates an image using an array of pixels of different colors or shades.

interlacing
A feature of some graphics formats that allows the graphic to be loaded into a Web page in alternate rows and/or columns, allowing visitors to quickly see a rough version of the image.

object-based graphics
Graphics created as an assembly of shapes, or objects. Object-based graphics are suitable only for illustrative (line-based) images.

PNG
A 24-bit, compressed graphics format, created by Thomas Boutell, which can support multiple levels of transparency and two-dimensional interlacing.

Progressive JPEG
A variation on the JPEG format that supports interlacing.

transparency
A feature of an image file in which certain colors can be made invisible against a background. GIF and PNG graphics support transparency.

vector graphics
Another name for object graphics, reflecting the fact that the objects that make up the images are created from mathematical splines, or vectors, rather than described as individual pixels.

START TAG	ATTRIBUTES	END TAG	EXPLANATION
<IMG>		</IMG>	Inserts an image file into the page
	align="top" OR "middle" OR "bottom" OR "left" OR "right" OR "center"		The alignment of the image relative to surrounding text
	alt="*text*"		Text that will display in text-only browsers or if the graphic doesn't load correctly
	border=*n*		For hyperlinked graphics, the width of the border, specified in pixels
	controls		Used with *dynsrc=*, displays video controls
	dynsrc="*URL*"		Specifies an AVI file to be inserted
	height=*n*, width=*n*		The height and width of the image, in pixels
	hspace=*n*, vspace=*n*		The space, in pixels, set between the image and surrounding text
	ismap		Specifies that the image is a server-side image map
	loop=*n* OR "infinite"		Used with *dynsrc=*, the number of times the video clip will loop
	lowsrc="*URL*"		Names a low-resolution file to be inserted as a placeholder
	src="*URL*"		The URL of the image to be inserted
	start="fileopen" OR "mouseover"		Used with *dynsrc=*, the event that starts the video clip running
	usemap="*name*"		Names the map to be used for a client-side image map
<OBJECT>		</OBJECT>	Inserts an object (e.g., an image, media file, or program) into the page
	align="top" OR "middle" OR "bottom" OR "left" OR "right" OR "center"		The alignment of the image relative to surrounding text
	border=*n*		For hyperlinked objects, the width of the border, specified in pixels
	data="*URL*"		The URL of the object to be inserted
	height=*n*, width=*n*		The height and width of the object, in pixels
	hspace=*n*, vspace=*n*		The space, in pixels, set between the object and surrounding text
	shapes		Specifies that the object has shaped hyperlinks (as in an image map)
	usemap="*name*"		Names the map to be used for a client-side image map
	standby="*text*"		Text that will be displayed as the object loads
	type="*MIME-type*"		The Internet MIME type of the data, used by the browser to determine whether or not it can display the object

Inserting Graphics: <IMG> and <OBJECT>

Since HTML is a text-only format, how can you insert a graphic in an HTML page? The key is the <IMG> tag, which tells the browser to insert a specified image file into the text. (Graphics loaded along with text are sometimes called **inline graphics**.)

The <IMG> tag has several possible attributes, but only one is required: *src=* (source), which names the image file that is to be inserted. We talked about the *align=* attribute, used to control the placement of the graphic within the page, earlier (→**91**). We'll discuss the other attributes later in this chapter, as we describe the uses they're put to.

HTML 3.2 proposes, and the latest browsers support, a new tag for inserting graphics and lots of other kinds of objects into pages. Appropriately enough, it's called <OBJECT>. For images, the tag works much like the <IMG> tag, and it uses many of the same attributes (we show the attributes pertinent to images in the box at left). Because it can also be used to embed video, Java applets, plug-ins, and other media, the <OBJECT> tag has lots of other possibilities as well, some of which we'll cover in other chapters. As we write this, the <OBJECT> tag specification hasn't been finalized, and it is impossible to say how widely it will be used for images, but there are no real advantages to using it, rather than the <IMG> tag (which will doubtless continue to be supported in browsers for quite a while), for simple inline GIFs and JPEGs.

Inline graphics can also be used as hyperlinks, just like text. To make a graphic "live," you specify the graphic file (with the <IMG> tag), rather than a string of words, with the *href=* attribute of the <A> tag. If you do this, though, make sure you also remember visitors who can't see graphics on their systems. The <IMG> tag's *alt=* attribute is designed for this purpose, allowing you to supply text that will be displayed in place of the graphic in text-based browsers. It also displays in the event that the graphic doesn't load on graphical browsers—if there's a snag in the connection, for instance. If the image is being used as an anchor for a hyperlink, the text specified in *alt=* will act as an alternate hyperlink.

In some cases, you'll probably want to make images available as **linked graphics**, rather than placing them inline on an HTML page. This treatment gives visitors the option of viewing a large version of a graphic without burdening the main page with the extra download time. Linked images needn't be in HTML pages. You can simply use the graphics filename as the value for the *href=* attribute in the <A> tag that links to the graphic. The browser will open it in its window, if it's in a format it can read, or with a helper application, if it isn't.

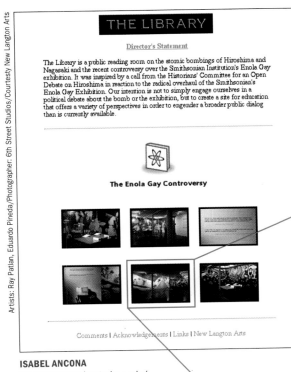

ISABEL ANCONA
http://www.exploratorium.edu/
nagasaki/library/

THUMBNAIL IMAGES are often used as anchors for a hyperlink to larger versions of the same image. Gallery sites often use this technique to offer visitors the chance to see full-size graphics without burdening the main HTML page with large files.

inline graphic
A graphic loaded into a browser window as part of an HTML document.

linked graphic
A graphic loaded into the browser window as the target of a hyperlink.

MICHAEL HIGHMILLER
http://www.thespot.com/

Image Maps

Many designers like to design interfaces in which graphics fill the entire screen, providing a CD-ROM-like effect in which users can interact with different parts of the graphic to jump to different locations. Such an approach is possible using a kind of graphic programming called an **image map**.

Image maps are useful for lots of situations—the illustrations throughout this book show many. They're often used to create full-graphics interfaces, iconic navigation bars for a site, or a metaphoric scene for navigating from a home page.

At last count, there were three different ways to create an image map, each corresponding to a different stage of the HTML standards. No matter which you use, though, you can think of an image map in three parts: the image itself, the map information that describes which parts of the image link to what URLs, and the software that, using the image map, translates a click on the image into a request for a particular file. The difference between the three methods is where those parts reside and how they're accessed.

There are no special requirements for the image itself: Any GIF or JPEG image can be used as an image map, and you insert it into the page just as you would any other image, using the <IMG> or <OBJECT> tag. You turn it into an image map using one of a few

image map
A type of graphic in which different locations in the image (specified by pixel coordinates) are linked to particular destination URLs.

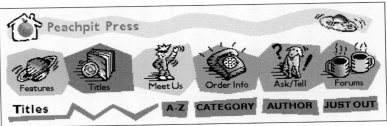

YO/JOHN GRIMES
http://www.peachpit.com/

IMAGE MAPS can provide a free-form graphic inter-face for a group of hyperlinks. They can provide standard, iconic navigational elements throughout a site (left) or a full-page graphic interface (opposite page). To accommodate text-only users, image map interfaces usually provide an alternate text-based path (bottom of image below).

PAT JONES/HUAN NGHIEM
http://www.idg.com/

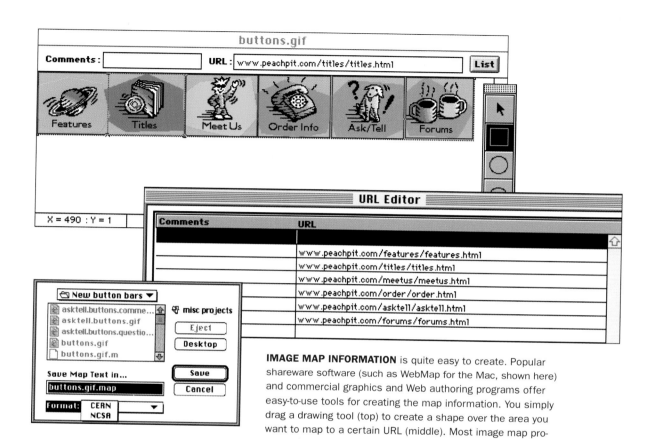

IMAGE MAP INFORMATION is quite easy to create. Popular shareware software (such as WebMap for the Mac, shown here) and commercial graphics and Web authoring programs offer easy-to-use tools for creating the map information. You simply drag a drawing tool (top) to create a shape over the area you want to map to a certain URL (middle). Most image map programs for server-side image maps give you the option of saving in CERN or NCSA formats. Which one you should use depends on your server software.

optional attributes to those tags: *ismap, usemap=,* or *shapes*. Simple enough.

The first method for creating image maps uses the *ismap* attribute for the <IMG> tag, which creates **server-side image maps**. It tells the browser to record the location of any click on the image and send that information back to the server. For server-side image maps, the <IMG> tag is used as the anchor for an <A> tag, whose *href=* attribute references a **map file** stored on the server. A program on the server uses the map file to match the location of a visitor's click to a particular URL and sends that file back to the client machine.

The *usemap=* attribute, supported by the latest versions of many browsers, creates a **client-side image map**, in which the translation of click to URL takes place on the visitor's (client) machine. The map file, which rests on the server for server-side image maps, is in this case part of an HTML page—usually the one holding the image reference. The *usemap=* attribute names the map to use for that image. The software that matches the visitor's click to the map file information is in the browser itself.

The third method relies on the <OBJECT> tag and special extensions to the <A> tag that are part of HTML 3.2. The <OBJECT> tag's *shapes* attribute also creates a client-side image map. The map information is provided in separate <A> tags embedded within the <OBJECT> tag.

Since all the processing is done locally, on the visitor's own computer, client-side image maps return results faster than server-side maps do. They also avoid the delays that might result when multiple requests queue up on a heavily trafficked server. Their only drawback is that it isn't yet possible to count on support for them in every browser.

Every graphical browser and almost every server supports server-side image maps created with *ismap*. Versions of Netscape Navigator and Microsoft Internet Explorer starting with version 2.0 support client-side maps created with *usemap=*. It's too early to say, but since it's part of official HTML and was developed with the cooperation of the major browser vendors, the <OBJECT> tag and the *shapes* attribute will presumably be supported in the next versions of all major browsers. So which should you use?

Luckily, the later codes were created to be backward-compatible. An <IMG> tag can include both the *ismap* and *usemap=* attributes, and if you supply a map file both in the HTML file and on the server, browsers that support the *usemap=* attribute will use the client-side map, and browsers that don't will go to the server for the map information. The <A> tags inside the <OBJECT> tag provide an alternate navigation method for browsers that don't support the <OBJECT> tag itself. The <A> tag's anchor text provides separate text links for each image map region.

The separate <A> tags used by the <OBJECT> tag also provide an important benefit over earlier image maps. Because the <IMG> tag doesn't allow HTML markup in the *alt=* text, page authors can't provide multiple, separate anchors to use as an alternate to an image map, requiring designers to offer a separate, text-based interface for visitors who can't view graphics.

Server-side/HTML 2.0	`<A href=mapfile.map><IMG src=image.gif ismap></A>`
Client-side/Microsoft and Netscape Extensions	`<IMG src=image.gif usemap=#map1>`

Client-side/HTML 3.2	`<OBJECT src=image.gif shapes>`
	`<A href=file1.html shape=rect coords=x1, y1, y2, x2> alternate text </A>`
	`<A href=file2.html shape=rect coords=x1, y1, y2, x2> alternate text </A>`

THERE ARE THREE WAYS to create image maps, each corresponding to a different HTML specification. This box shows a sample of the HTML code used to create each one.

client-side image map
An image map for which the map information and the map processing program reside on the client (user's) computer. Not all browser software supports client-side image maps.

map file
For server-side image maps, a file stored on the server that holds the map information, linking specific regions of the image to specific target URLs.

server-side image map
An image map for which the map file and the map processing program reside on the server, and the coordinates of a user's click are sent to the server for processing.

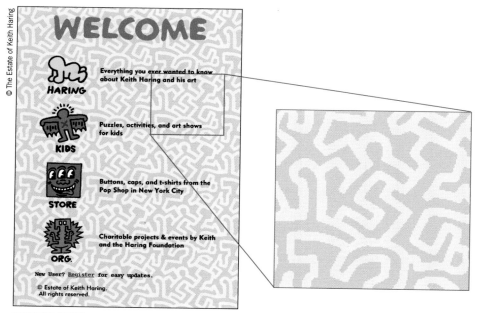

RIVERBED MEDIA
http://www.haring.com/

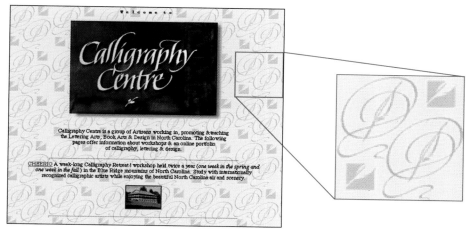

JOHN STEVENS DESIGN
http://www.calligraphycentre.com/

STUDIO VERSO
http://www.klutz.com/

BACKGROUND GRAPHICS can have very small dimensions; they will be tiled to fill the entire window. This tiling can be used for a special effect or hidden by careful crafting of the pattern (as in the Keith Haring page, top left). As shown in the Klutz Press example (above), they can even provide important parts of the interface. On that page, a single, narrow tile creates the walls and ladders, a "room" that is then furnished by images that act as hyperlinks to other parts of the site.

Background Graphics and Colors

In the spring of '95, Netscape Navigator 1.1 began supporting a number of attributes to the <BODY> tag that changed the look of the Web overnight. The *background=* attribute let designers supply a URL for a GIF or JPEG image that would be used as the background of the browser window. The *bgcolor=* attribute let designers specify a color, rather than a graphic, for a simpler yet still eye-catching background. To make the document's text readable against the new colors, designers could now also specify a custom color for the text, and still other colors for links that hadn't been visited, links that had been visited, and "active links"—those that are currently being clicked on.

Suddenly, color wasn't confined to graphics and the blue and violet anchor text. Many designers used the graphic option to give pages psychedelic textured backgrounds—or just something appropriate to the page's theme, like melting clocks for the Surrealism Archive. Some used the new capabilities simply to create a paper-white background for their graphics. Others opted for basic black, from which red and yellow text would shine like traffic lights. Suddenly, the sameness that had characterized Web pages was a thing of the past. Surfing from page to page was more like experiencing a laser light show than turning the pages of a book. The *background=* and *bgcolor=*

BACKGROUND COLORS load more quickly than images but still provide a bright look to the page. Text and link colors can be specified to complement the background you choose.

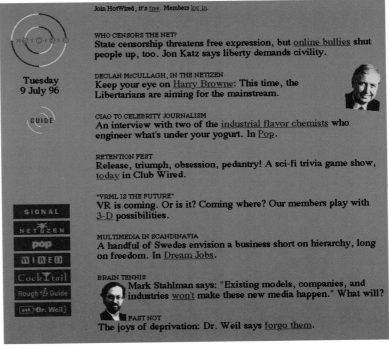

HOTWIRED
http://www.hotwired.com/

START TAG	ATTRIBUTES	END TAG	EXPLANATION
<BODY>		</BODY>	Marks the text to be displayed in the browser window
	alink="#RRGGBB" OR "name"		Names a color for the active links, using an RGB value expressed in hexadecimal or a color name
	background= "URL"		Names a graphics file to be used as the background
	bgcolor="#RRGGBB" OR "name"		Names a background color
	bgproperties="fixed"		Specifies that the background image should not scroll
	link="#RRGGBB" OR "name"		Names a color for hyperlink anchors
	text="#RRGGBB" OR "name"		Names a color for nonlinked text
	vlink="#RRGGBB" OR "name"		Names a color for visited links

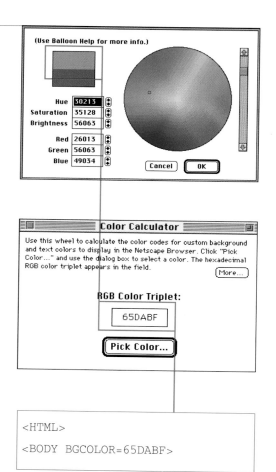

Specifying Colors Online

Specifying colors in HTML—for the <BODY> tag's *text=*, *bgcolor=*, *link=*, *vlink=*, and *alink=* attributes (→**113**) and for the <FONT> *color=* attribute (→**89**)—requires using a code that most designers probably aren't familiar with. The colors are specified as values for the red, green, and blue (RGB) components of the color. That's straightforward enough, given that the Mac or Windows color picker can show the RGB value for any color you choose. The trickier part is that the number that names the value is specified in hexadecimal: base 16, instead of the base 10 system we use for just about everything else.

In hexadecimal, the numbers 1 through 9 are specified just as they are in real life. For the digits 10 through 15, though, hex notation uses the capital letters A through F: A for 10, B for 11, and so on.

If your brain is up to it, you can figure out the hexadecimal equivalent of any decimal number using a regular calculator; some calculators (such as the one that comes with Windows) even have a hexadecimal conversion function. Several color pickers with hexadecimal color value calculators are also available on line (→**121**). Most WYSIWYG HTML editors let you pick a color from a standard color picker and do the hexadecimal calculating themselves. In some browsers, including Netscape's and Microsoft's, a set of basic colors, such as red, blue, yellow, and so on, can also be specified by name.

```
<HTML>
<BODY BGCOLOR=65DABF>
```

ONLINE COLOR PICKERS can help you translate the color you want into the proper hex codes for use in the <BODY> and <FONT> color attributes. In the 6-digit hex code, the first pair of digits gives the red value, the second pair the green, and the last pair the blue. (The interface from HTML Grinder is shown here.)

attributes have been picked up by many browsers since Netscape introduced them and have now been included in the standard HTML spec.

Like any other effect, background graphics can be used well or badly. In the worst cases, complex backgrounds with high-contrast patterns make the text on top almost impossible to read. To combat that effect, some page designers then make all the text on the page bold, which only makes matters worse in the low-res environment of a computer screen.

Since background graphics **tile** to fill a window, background graphics can be quite small—a necessity since in some browsers the background graphic is downloaded before any of the page's content, and a background graphic that takes too long to download can drive away visitors before they even have a chance to see the rest of your page. Netscape Navigator and some other browsers load the background graphic last, but slow-loading backgrounds can still be annoying. For that reason, background graphics have a realistic size limit of about 10K.

3-D Graphics

VRML, the Virtual Reality Modeling Language (→**128**) may one day be the standard method of offering 3-D on the Web. But as we wait for the fast 3-D processors and better bandwidth that will make VRML more usable, you can turn to simpler methods of creating 3-D images on line.

Right now, the only way to make sure every visitor can see your 3-D graphics is to save them as GIF or JPEG files after you've rendered them. Done right, the graphics can be stingy with disk space and the effect can be striking, allowing beveled edges, drop shadows, and other dimensional effects.

If you want to take advantage of plug-ins and ActiveX controls, you can post your graphic in true 3-D formats. VRML players ship with the current version of Netscape's and Microsoft's browsers. Another 3-D format that may become important on the Web is **QuickTime VR**. Visitors can move left or right, above or below QuickTime VR scenes, but not (so far) through them, and, at least when we wrote this, the scenes could not include hyperlinks to other files, as they can with VRML. Unlike VRML, though, QuickTime VR makes it easy to create 3-D scenes from photographs, making it especially useful for applications such as online catalogs.

JPEG

ART & SCIENCE
http://www.socalgas.com/

QUICKTIME VR

ANTHONY IDAROLA/SUZY WEAR
http://tesla.csuhayward.edu/frameindex.html

3-D GRAPHICS can be rendered as GIF or JPEG files for posting on the Web. VRML and QuickTime VR, both supported by plug-ins and ActiveX controls, offer true 3-D scenes that visitors can actually navigate through.

VRML

PLANET 9 STUDIOS
http://www.interop.com/vrml/atlanta96/interop.wrl

QuickTime VR
A technology created by Apple Computer for creating and viewing 3-D scenes.

tile
To arrange an object or graphic across an area by repeating it in contiguous, adjacent areas.

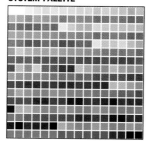

Illustration: John Grimes

BROWSER PALETTE

MACS, WINDOWS MACHINES, and browsers all use a different set of colors on 8-bit systems, and the same image looks quite different in the different environments. Mapping your GIF graphics to the cross-platform browser palette (or a subset of it) ensures that the results will be predictable across systems.

Dealing With Limited Color Palettes

Most designers work in 24-bit color but, unfortunately, most Web surfers don't. And as your graphics enter a less-optimal viewing environment—the visitor's own screen—you'll need to remember that, once they're posted, your graphics will be viewed according to the rules of that world, not yours.

For these purposes, we can forget about visitors who aren't viewing graphics at all. Here, we're thinking of those who are viewing graphics at a different bit depth or on platforms other than the one you use to create them. The same graphics look much different on a Mac than on a PC, or in 8-bit rather than 24-bit color.

The first thing to know is that Netscape Navigator, Internet Explorer, and other browsers have their own ideas about what colors to use on 8-bit displays, a 216-color palette, sometimes referred to as the "Netscape color cube" or the **browser-safe palette**, which they apply to every graphic displayed on such systems.

This palette begins with the 256 shades that can be displayed on an 8-bit color system, subtracts the 20 colors Windows uses in its own interface and the 13 colors Netscape uses for its logo, and then simplifies the remaining 223 colors into the nearest number achievable using the 3 primary colors of a CRT: 216, based on 6 shades each of red, green, and blue.

Any colors in the original graphic that aren't in the browser palette are **dithered**: two or more colors from the palette are combined to approximate the out-of-range shade. Dithering doesn't create a problem for photographic images, but it does when you want clean, flat colors.

You can avoid this dithering by using DeBabelizer, Photoshop, or another image-processing program to map your flat-color images to this browser-safe palette, which is available on line as a Photoshop color lookup table (CLUT). Check the listings at the end of this chapter (→**121**) for resources.

The other issue to remember is that the 256-color allowance on an 8-bit monitor has to cover all the images that are shown on screen at one time. Once 256 colors have been used (on a first-come, first-served basis), any remaining colors will simply be mapped to the closest equivalent among the first 256, or approximated by dithering two or more available shades. If you're using a lot of photographic illustrations with different palettes, you can optimize your palettes in your image-processing program. One method is to combine all the images you expect to show on a single page into a single Photoshop document, and then converting it to an 8-bit indexed color image with an **adaptive palette** with no dithering.

It's also important to remember visitors using grayscale montitors. Though most grayscale monitors will display at least 256 shades of gray, some may display as few as 4. Accommodating visitors using grayscale means using high-contrast graphics, so that when they're sampled down to, say, 4 shades of gray, the important distinctions (text outlines, for example) are still clear.

And, you guessed it: As with so many aspects of Web design, no matter how many precautions you take, the only way to make sure all your preparations work is to test the results on a variety of systems.

One of the big lessons we had to learn was about color palettes. We want all of our graphics to look very clean, and when they dither, they don't look clean. When we started out, we spent months coming up with a palette that doesn't dither.

ANDREA JENKINS, CNET

adaptive palette
A palette created by choosing the most-used colors in an image.

browser-safe palette
A palette of 216 colors used by browsers on 8-bit systems. Mapping graphics to this palette will ensure that colors remain as expected when displayed on such systems.

dithering
A method of creating a color by combining two or more discrete colors.

STUDIO ARCHETYPE
http://www. studioarchetype.com/

THESE NAVIGATION BARS look like image maps, but they are actually built from individual graphics, most of which are reused on every page. Only the graphics that are "highlighted" to show the current location need to be loaded when the visitor moves to a new page.

bit depth
The number of bits used to record each pixel of information in an image file. Common formats are 8-bit (256 colors or shades of gray) and 24-bit (16.7 million colors).

cache
An area of memory or disk space reserved for holding data that is expected to be used again, making it faster to retrieve that data the next time it's used.

indexed color
Mapping an image's original colors to a new, reduced color palette.

Speeding Download Time

The most foolproof way to keep download time short, of course, is to use images sparingly. Fortunately, there are also other ways. Poster-size graphics are possible on the Web if you know how to choose the appropriate image format, wring every extra bit from your images as you prepare them, and use HTML codes that speed downloading.

One trick to minimizing image download time is reusing image files. Browsers generally **cache** images once they are downloaded, saving them on the client machine's disk or memory so that after the image is downloaded once, it can be displayed again almost instantly. The second use of an icon, navigation bar, or other standard graphic comes nearly for free, in terms of download time.

The next thing to remember is that an image's dimensions are not the most important influence on its file size. Equally important is the number of colors it uses, and how it uses them.

As we mentioned earlier (→**103**), the GIF format is ideal for iconic, flat-color images, while JPEG creates smaller file sizes for photographic images. This is because GIF compresses files by scanning the image *in a horizontal direction* and recording new color data each time the color changes. That means that the fewer times your image's color shifts *from left to* *right*, the smaller your GIF file will be—and, by extension, that gradients and other color shifts that proceed *from top to bottom* have no effect on file size. When creating original art for a Web site, this piece of knowledge could help you create the smallest possible GIF files.

A different measure of the number of colors in a file—its **bit depth**—also has an important impact on the file sizes of GIFs. GIF can save up to 8 bits per pixel (256 colors), but few Web designers would dare to use so many. Flat-color graphics are usually mapped to the 6-bit nondithering palette (→**116**) or to a subset of that palette. Photographic images usually compress quite well when saved as JPEG, even at 24 bits per pixel, but they need extra help when you want to save them as GIF—if you want to use a transparent background, for instance. In those cases, you'll want to use your image-processing program's **indexed color** tool to apply an adaptive palette to the images. On 24-bit systems, your images can look almost as good as the 24-bit originals. (On 8-bit systems, they will still be dithered to the browser palette.) In many cases, you can choose bit depths as low as 4 or 5 bits per pixel and still have good results.

Another key to keeping graphics from getting in the reader's way is remembering HTML tricks that can help the browser deal intelligently with the art. The most important of these are the *height=* and *width=*

1 Remap the colors in the original file by loading a "browser-safe" palette.

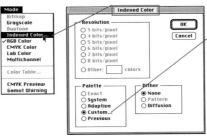

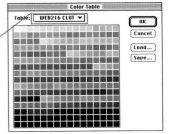

36K

2 Change back to RGB mode.

3 Apply indexed color again, this time using an "exact" palette. Use as few colors as possible without degrading the quality of the image.

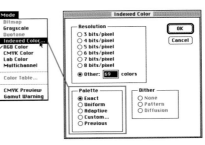

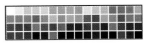

MAPPING GIF GRAPHICS to a reduced palette can significantly reduce file sizes. Here we show the process (in Photoshop) of mapping a graphic to a subset of the browser-safe palette.

12K

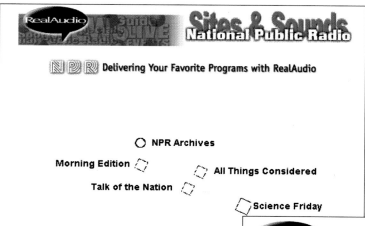

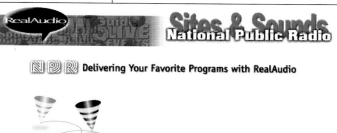

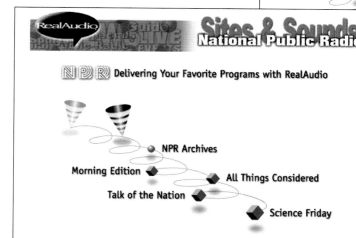

THE LOWSRC= ATTRIBUTE lets designers specify a low-resolution, fast-loading graphic to act as a temporary placeholder for a higher-resolution image. In the example shown here, *lowsrc=* is used to load an image that includes just the text and buttons. On the next pass, a second graphic, that also contains the image of the spinning top, loads, creating a quasi-animated effect.

attributes of the <IMG> and <OBJECT> tags. These attributes tell the browser how much space the image will take up, allowing it to set that area aside, download the rest of the page contents, and then return to download the slower-loading graphic file. Visitors then have the chance to read—and even move on from—the page without waiting for the images to download completely.

The interlacing possible with GIF, PNG, and Progressive JPEG graphics is another way to save time, quickly building up a rough version of the image that becomes "live" immediately. If it's an image map, readers can click on the graphic and be on their way as soon as they can make out its outline.

A way to make sure a graphic is displayed at once, without waiting for the multiple passes of an interlaced file, is to use *lowsrc=,* another useful attribute for the <IMG> tag. The *lowsrc=* attribute names a low-resolution file that can be displayed while the browser works on loading the higher-resolution version, offering a readable, if fuzzy, version of the graphic on the browser's first pass. At this point, *lowsrc=* is supported only by Netscape's browser, but since it should do no harm in browsers that don't recognize it, you may as well use it. Some crafty designers have used the *lowsrc=* attribute to install an entirely different graphic on the page on the first pass, for a playful, "did I really see that?" effect.

Anti-Aliasing for Low Resolutions

Last but not least, we introduce another important aspect of the visitor's environment you need to keep in mind as you prepare Web graphics: the low resolution of a computer screen. The average screen resolution—about 72 pixels per inch—is much lower than the resolutions—1,200 to 3,600 dots per inch and beyond—used for printed materials. Such low resolutions can cause a stairstep effect (often called "jaggies") on curved and angled edges of graphic shapes. To combat this effect, most graphics program allow you to *anti-alias* low-resolution graphics. Anti-aliasing blends the edges of graphics with tints of the adjoining color to minimize stairstepping.

The extremely low resolution of screen graphics means that almost all Web graphics should be anti-aliased, but Web designers should be aware of a few effects to watch out for. The first is blurriness. On especially fine shapes, such as small type, the blurred edges of anti-aliasing may well cause more of a problem than jagginess would. The second is that artifacts may occur when an anti-aliased graphic with a transparent background (→**104**) is placed on a new background color. Luckily, the answer to that problem is simple enough: Just make sure to anti-alias the graphic against the color it will finally be placed on.

ANTI-ALIASING BLURS the edges of a graphic to reduce the stairstepping pattern ("jaggies") often seen on low-resolution output devices such as computer screens.

Alternate Page Formats

Due to its small file size, its ability to be read across platforms, and its head start in the world of the Web, HTML will likely continue to be the primary format for Web publishing for some time. Meanwhile, though, software companies and online visionaries are looking beyond HTML in an attempt to create more control over the look of pages and explore new types of interactive interfaces.

Electronic document formats such as Adobe Acrobat's **PDF** allow publishers to create pages in a page layout program and then save the files in an online format that retains all the original fonts and layout. **VRML**—the Virtual Reality Modeling Language—can create 3-D interactive environments. Multimedia authoring programs such as Macromedia Director offer versions of their native formats for online distribution. And software publishers are hard at work on the next generation of Web publishing technology, devising ways to make sure that Web browsers can read any format you want to publish in. In this chapter we'll describe formats that can be used, like HTML, to control the look of entire pages, to hold multimedia files, and to contain hyperlinks to other Web destinations—essentially, alternatives to HTML.

Viewing Alternate Formats

As we've already pointed out (→**11**), publishers can serve up files in any format they want; it won't do much good, however, unless the people they hope to reach have the software they need to read the files. For that reason, the creators of the Web settled on one universal text format—HTML—giving Web publishers a guaranteed base of compatibility. Graphical browsers also support one basic graphics format— GIF (→**103**). Although individual browsers may support other formats—and formats that prove popular will doubtless be universally supported in the future— HTML and GIF are the only two formats recognized universally by graphic Web browsers.

When a browser encounters a document in a format it doesn't support, it will look for a helper application, plug-in, or ActiveX control (→**11**) on the user's hard disk that can handle that file type. When we wrote this, plug-ins were already available for SGML, VRML, Adobe Acrobat, Macromedia Director, and several multimedia formats, including QuickTime and QuickTime VR, and more were appearing all the time.

What formats other than HTML you can publish in, then, depends on how sure you are that a visitor will have access to the appropriate helper software. If your audience is all inside a certain corporation with a vigilant computer support department, you may be able to ensure that everyone has readers for any

format you want to use. But if you're publishing more broadly—to a global audience over the Internet—the onus for acquiring the proper software is on the visitor. Many Web sites that post non-HTML files simply include a note warning visitors that they'll need a certain extra piece of software to read the files, and provide a link to a site where the software is available.

Asking a visitor to download a separate viewer application just to read your file is risky because, in many cases, the visitor simply won't bother. As time goes by, certain alternate formats will doubtless become de facto standards—either broadly supported by browsers or used so often by publishers that most users can be expected to already have an appropriate viewer application. Until then, though, designers need to carefully weigh the risks and benefits of using any alternate format on line.

Technologies now in development will make the situation easier on the visitor and less risky for the publisher. One of these is Java (→**168**), a programming language that has become a popular tool for creating interactive Web content. Java code that gives the browser the ability to read a file can be downloaded along with the file itself, creating a sort of plug-in on the fly. For this to work, the browser just needs to support Java (as most browsers do), and Java programmers need to create the reader code for popular formats—as they undoubtedly will as Java and Java-conversant browsers become better established.

PDF
Portable Document Format, an electronic document format, created by Adobe Systems and based on PostScript, used by Adobe's Acrobat program.

VRML
Virtual Reality Modeling Language, a scripting language used to define 3-D shapes for use on the Web. VRML (often pronounced "ver'-mul") supports hyperlinking and programmed behaviors.

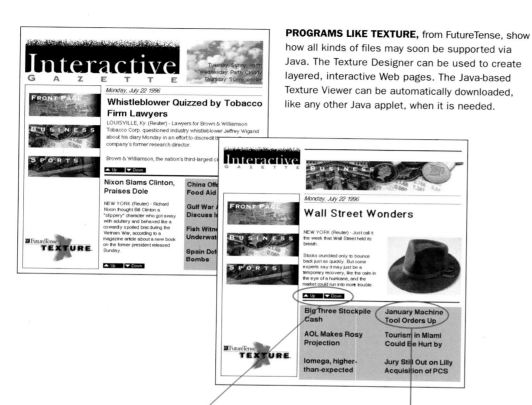

PROGRAMS LIKE TEXTURE, from FutureTense, show how all kinds of files may soon be supported via Java. The Texture Designer can be used to create layered, interactive Web pages. The Java-based Texture Viewer can be automatically downloaded, like any other Java applet, when it is needed.

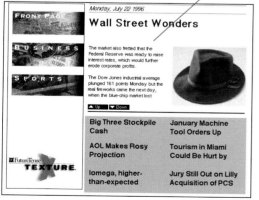

FUTURETENSE
http://www.futuretense.com/texture/gallery/Gazette/Gazette.html

Microsoft and Netscape are working to make their plug-ins and ActiveX documents work just as seamlessly. By version 4.0, Netscape Navigator should be able to download needed plug-ins automatically. ActiveX controls can also be downloaded automatically, without user intervention, when they're needed.

Such automatic methods of distributing reader software have yet to be refined, though. Until they work seamlessly, Web publishers are limited to a handful of alternate formats—those that have been recognized as useful adjuncts to HTML's capabilities, whose makers have made cross-platform readers available on the Net, and that are widely enough used that readers have incentive to spend the time downloading the readers. We'll discuss the current key formats, from the most common to rarer but still useful options, in the rest of this chapter.

PDF and Other Electronic Document Formats

Electronic page formats—including Adobe Acrobat's PDF, Tumbleweed Software's Envoy format, and Hummingbird Software's Common Ground—began appearing a few years ago as a handy way to share formatted files via e-mail and distribute them over office networks. They've gotten a new life as the Internet has gathered steam, and their developers have rushed to retrofit them for use on the Web.

All these formats are based on the same idea: They allow publishers to "print" documents to electronic files rather than to paper. Creating such electronic files can be as easy as choosing the Print command in any application, with the electronic format driver chosen as the current printer. (The software makers also offer stand-alone programs that can batch-convert existing PostScript files into the electronic document formats.) The result is a compressed electronic file that retains the fonts and layout of the original document but can be opened without the original application. The software makers also provide "creator" applications that let the author add hyperlinks, electronic notations, and bookmarks to the files to aid navigation. A viewer application—usually distributed free on the Net—can read any file printed to the format and includes tools for searching and copying the content of the files and navigating through them.

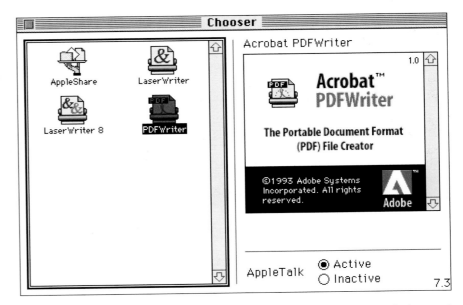

TO TRANSFORM FILES into electronic document formats, you can simply choose the program's driver as your "printer." (The Mac's Chooser interface is shown here.) After that, choosing the Print command from any application "prints" to that document format.

Form 1040 Department of the Treasury—Internal Revenue Service
U.S. Individual Income Tax Return 1995 (99) IRS Use Only—Do not write or staple in this space.
For the year Jan. 1–Dec. 31, 1995, or other tax year beginning , 1995, ending , 19 OMB No. 1545-0074

Label (See instructions on page 11.) Use the IRS label. Otherwise, please print or type.
LABEL HERE
Your first name and initial | Last name | Your social security number
If a joint return, spouse's first name and initial | Last name | Spouse's social security number
Home address (number and street). If you have a P.O. box, see page 11. | Apt. no.
City, town or post office, state, and ZIP code. If you have a foreign address, see page 11.
For Privacy Act and Paperwork Reduction Act Notice, see page 7.

Presidential Election Campaign (See page 11.)
Do you want $3 to go to this fund? Yes No
If a joint return, does your spouse want $3 to go to this fund?
Note: Checking "Yes" will not change your tax or reduce your refund.

Filing Status (See page 11.) Check only one box.
1 Single
2 Married filing joint return (even if only one had income)
3 Married filing separate return. Enter spouse's social security no. above and full name here. ▶
4 Head of household (with qualifying person). (See page 12.) If the qualifying person is a child but not your dependent, enter this child's name here. ▶
5 Qualifying widow(er) with dependent child (year spouse died ▶ 19). (See page 12.)

Exemptions (See page 12.)
6a Yourself. If your parent (or someone else) can claim you as a dependent on his or her tax return, do not check box 6a. But be sure to check the box on line 33b on page 2
b Spouse
c Dependents: (1) First name Last name (2) Dependent's social security number. If born in 1995, see page 13. (3) Dependent's relationship to you (4) No. of months lived in your home in 1995
If more than six dependents, see page 13.
No. of boxes checked on 6a and 6b
No. of your children on 6c who: • lived with you • didn't live with you due to divorce or separation (see page 14)
Dependents on 6c not entered above
d If your child didn't live with you but is claimed as your dependent under a pre-1985 agreement, check here ▶
e Total number of exemptions claimed
Add numbers entered on lines above

Income
Attach Copy B of your Forms W-2, W-2G, and 1099-R here.
If you did not get a W-2, see page 14.
Enclose, but do not attach, your payment and payment voucher. See page 33.
7 Wages, salaries, tips, etc. Attach Form(s) W-2 | 7
8a Taxable interest income (see page 15). Attach Schedule B if over $400 | 8a
b Tax-exempt interest (see page 15). DON'T include on line 8a | 8b
9 Dividend income. Attach Schedule B if over $400 | 9
10 Taxable refunds, credits, or offsets of state and local income taxes (see page 15) | 10
11 Alimony received | 11
12 Business income or (loss). Attach Schedule C or C-EZ | 12
13 Capital gain or (loss). If required, attach Schedule D (see page 16) | 13
14 Other gains or (losses). Attach Form 4797 | 14
15a Total IRA distributions | 15a | b Taxable amount (see page 16) | 15b
16a Total pensions and annuities | 16a | b Taxable amount (see page 16) | 16b
17 Rental real estate, royalties, partnerships, S corporations, trusts, etc. Attach Schedule E | 17
18 Farm income or (loss). Attach Schedule F | 18
19 Unemployment compensation (see page 17) | 19
20a Social security benefits | 20a | b Taxable amount (see page 18) | 20b
21 Other income. List type and amount—see page 18 | 21
22 Add the amounts in the far right column for lines 7 through 21. This is your total income ▶ | 22

Adjustments to Income
23a Your IRA deduction (see page 19) | 23a
b Spouse's IRA deduction (see page 19) | 23b
24 Moving expenses. Attach Form 3903 or 3903-F | 24
25 One-half of self-employment tax | 25
26 Self-employed health insurance deduction (see page 21) | 26
27 Keogh & self-employed SEP plans. If SEP, check ▶ | 27
28 Penalty on early withdrawal of savings | 28
29 Alimony paid. Recipient's SSN ▶ | 29
30 Add lines 23a through 29. These are your total adjustments ▶ | 30

Adjusted Gross Income
31 Subtract line 30 from line 22. This is your adjusted gross income. If less than $26,673 and a child lived with you (less than $9,230 if a child didn't live with you), see "Earned Income Credit" on page 27 ▶ | 31
Cat. No. 11320B Form 1040 (1995)

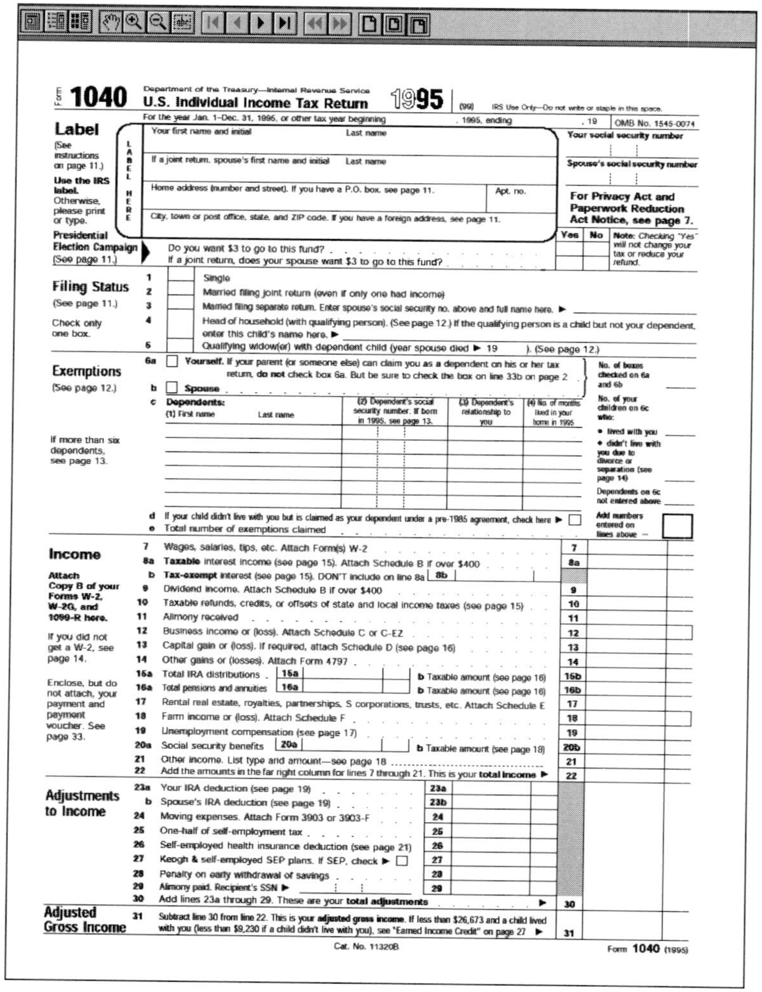

ftp://ftp.fedworld.gov/pub/irs-pdf/f1040.pdf

PDF FILES are useful for pages, such as these IRS forms, that require precise formatting. The tool bar at the top of the illustration shows the Acrobat Reader's navigation tools.

To suit the formats for the Web, their developers have added special features such as the ability to link to Web URLs and download multiple-page files one page at a time, reducing the long wait that would otherwise annoy visitors. All the developers distribute their reader software for free over the Net, and Acrobat and Envoy offer plug-in viewers as well.

Such formats completely bypass HTML's limitations on layout and typography; anything that's possible in the original application can be translated to the electronic document. They also provide an easy way to publish legacy documents—documents created for other media that you may now want to publish on the Web. Many companies use the format as an easy way to post brochures, product literature, and other documents that already exist in page layout formats. Printing to an electronic document format bypasses the time and cost that would be incurred translating the documents into HTML.

Electronic document formats are also useful for publishing documents, such as forms, that rely on small type and precise formatting. The IRS, for instance, distributes its tax forms in PDF format from its Web site. Some publishers also argue that long documents, which readers will probably prefer to print out rather than read on screen, are also good candidates for publishing in PDF or another such format. The electronic files keep all their font and formatting information, resulting in a better-looking and easier-to-read printed document than would be possible with HTML's current layout and typographic controls.

Adobe Acrobat's PDF is the best-known electronic document format and the most widely used on the Internet. Adobe has been aggressively pursuing the Web publishing market, resulting in a full suite of Web features in its document format; a full set of readers and authoring software for Mac, Windows, and Unix machines; and a better chance that the people you want to read your file will already have the necessary software or think it worth their time to download it. Tumbleweed's Envoy also has attractive features, including an elegant font-management system (based on Bitstream's TrueDoc technology), good compression for its files, and authoring systems and free plug-in viewers for both Mac and Windows. Hummingbird Software has developed a Web publishing system for Common Ground that automatically generates a thumbnail page index of a document's contents, but it has announced no plans for plug-in viewers or for a Mac version of its Web authoring package.

FILES MEANT TO BE PRINTED OUT and read off line are good candidates for electronic document formats. This site offers two versions of its newsletter, one for online reading (bottom left) and another that uses Acrobat to retain a newsletterlike format for the armchair (below).

RAYMOND MELVILLE
http://www.adlbooks.com/

A 3-D MODEL of San Francisco's War Memorial Opera House lets visitors zoom in to view details of the stage ornaments or watch from a balcony seat. The tenor sings an aria from *The Marriage of Figaro*.

PLANET 9 STUDIOS
http://www.planet9.com/worlds/opera.wrl.gz

VIRTUAL SOMA features the buildings and artists of San Francisco's Multimedia Gulch neighborhood. Clicking on a building exterior (left) brings you inside: for instance, to this local café (below).

VAG
The VRML Architecture Group, the group in the Internet Engineering Task Force that is responsible for creating standards for HTML.

world
The word used for a VRML environment, to differentiate it from the "page" interface of 2-D formats.

PLANET 9 STUDIOS
http://www.planet9.com/worlds/vrsoma.wrl.gz

VRML

VRML (sometimes pronounced "ver'-mul"), stands for Virtual Reality Modeling Language, a scripting language designed to create three-dimensional, interactive interfaces for the Web. VRML leaves the page-oriented interface of the Web behind to launch viewers into a 3-D **world**, through which the reader navigates using special tools built for the format.

Links between different 3-D scenes are provided via the same URL hyperlinks used in HTML. Interactivity and time-based behaviors can be scripted using Java or other programming languages (→**160**). Reading VRML code requires special VRML support in a browser, which is currently provided as a plug-in with Netscape's browser and as an ActiveX control with Microsoft's.

VRML, first proposed in 1994, had a later start than HTML, and it was just emerging from some serious growing pains as we wrote this. As with HTML, impatient VRML browser vendors have tried to hurry the format's development along by introducing their own add-ons to the language. Unlike HTML, though, browsers can't just ignore nonstandard VRML code; a nonsupported command will make a VRML model unreadable. In early 1996, however, the industry VRML consortium, known as **VAG** (the VRML Architecture Group), finalized negotiations on version 2.0

of the VRML spec, which should finally consolidate the industry around a single version and open the door to the speedy delivery of general-purpose VRML viewers.

The development of VRML worlds has likewise been delayed by the lack of tools for creating models. Now, however, makers of many mainstream 3-D modeling tools are adding the capability to save models in VRML format.

Although VRML is a compact format (as 3-D formats go), 3-D modeling is notorious for straining the capabilities of personal computers. As the format gains in popularity, VRML software makers will doubtless become more sophisticated about compression, and built-in 3-D rendering processors supporting VRML are becoming more common in personal computers. Meanwhile, though, the art of VRML lies in creating worlds with a minimum number of polygons—the separate shapes that make up a 3-D form. Often, realism has to take a back seat to efficiency, as VRML artists focus on creating models that can, above all, be downloaded and rendered quickly.

I don't think VRML is going to replace HTML. Text is a very old interface and it's not going to go away, but space is another very old interface. You'll use VRML for what you use space for: to store things, to navigate, to group things.

MARK MEADOWS, CONSTRUCT

VIRTUAL ART hangs on the walls of Graphcomp's vast VRML gallery.

GRAFMAN'S VR WORLD
http://www.graphcomp.com/vrml/gallery0.wrl

OBJECTS IN Planet 9's Virtual San Francisco are hyperlinked to other Web sites with relevant information.

PLANET 9 STUDIOS
http://www.planet9.com/worlds/moscon/x.wrl.gz

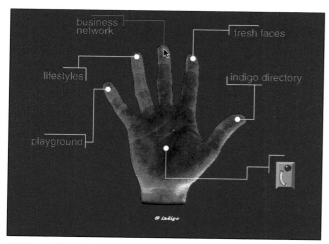

INDIGO DESIGN
http://www.indigo.ie/loop.html

Lingo
The scripting language used
by Macromedia Director.

Shockwave
Software created by Macromedia
to allow files from its programs to
be published on the Web. The
Shockwave components include
a compression utility (called
Afterburner) for each program,
plus client software that can be
used to view the files.

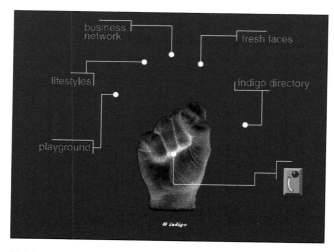

SHOCKWAVE FOR DIRECTOR offers a full suite of multimedia features, including sound, animation, and scripted
interactivity. Though often used as just one component in
an HTML page, it can also be used for stand-alone interfaces, as shown here. This example uses Shockwave to
animate the hand and provide feedback to the user when
the mouse rolls over a selection.

Multimedia Authoring Formats

Macromedia, creator of Director and Authorware, and
Quark, creator of QuarkImmedia, have created Web-
friendly versions of their multimedia formats. These
files can include animation, video, sounds, formatted
text, and hyperlinks, all in compressed versions made
specifically for the Web.

Macromedia has adapted its products for the Web
with **Shockwave** (provided for each of the company's
programs, including Director, Authorware, and
FreeHand). Each Shockwave product consists
of a compression progam, called Afterburner, which
authors can use to compress each program's files,
plus plug-ins for use on the client side of the connection. New extensions to Director's **Lingo** scripting language allow the addition of links to Web URLs and
supply other Internet functions. Macromedia's programs are also being updated to support Java (→**168**)
and JavaScript (→**166**) so that those languages can
also be used to control the multimedia features.

Shockwave for Director is aimed at the legion of multimedia authors already proficient in Director, which
is the industry-standard tool for multimedia development. Unfortunately, the drawback to posting multimedia extravaganzas on the Web is the one most
sensitive in this medium: file size. Animations, video,

and sounds can result in huge files, and the compression offered by the programs can do only so much to alleviate the problem. Because of this, Shockwave has been used mostly to add self-contained segments of animation and sound to Web pages. We'll talk more about that use later (→**139**). Macromedia has positioned Shockwave for Authorware as a tool for distributing training materials over corporate intranets, reflecting both Authorware's main use as a tool for corporate training and the fact that intranets generally have a much higher bandwidth than the modem-based connections more common on the Internet.

QuarkImmedia, an **XTension** for QuarkXPress that turns XPress into a multimedia authoring tool, will doubtless be popular with the millions of QuarkXPress users who want to use the program's familiar interface as an easy entry into multimedia and Web authoring. Immedia's Web features include the ability to hyperlink to Web URLs, a variety of compression options, and a caching feature that lets users begin playing Immedia programs while other sections of the file continue downloading. Free Immedia readers can be embedded in Immedia documents or downloaded from Quark's Web site. When we wrote this, though, Quark had announced no plans for plug-in viewers for its files, so it was unclear how much the program would be used for Web publishing.

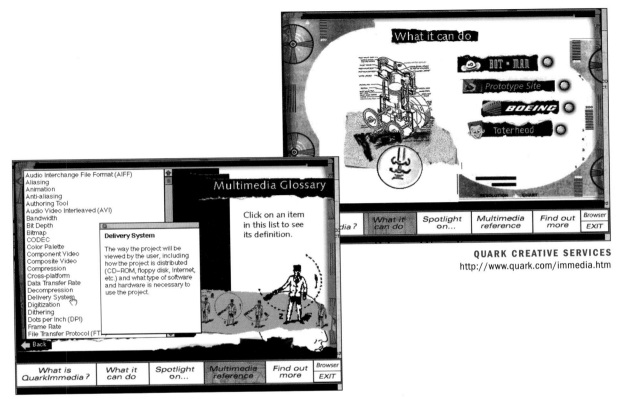

QUARK CREATIVE SERVICES
http://www.quark.com/immedia.htm

QUARKIMMEDIA creates stand-alone presentations that can be displayed in a special viewer application that launches alongside the browser. The format includes the ability to link to Web URLs, and the QuarkImmedia viewer includes tools for navigating the Net (right).

XTension
A program that extends the capabilities of QuarkXPress.

SGML

SGML (→**68**), the parent of HTML, has been proposed as a Web publishing format on its own. A superset of HTML, SGML is a mature, codified standard with a wealth of formatting and indexing tags that has already been in use for a decade. SGML, its proponents argue, has all the benefits of HTML—cross-platform readability and a small file size—plus a much richer formatting language, and adopting SGML for the Web would bypass the time-consuming process of developing the HTML standard tag by tag. Despite the strength of these arguments, it seems that SGML is destined to remain only an alternate format, which will be used for Web publishing only by those that use it for a variety of publishing tasks—government and educational organizations for which it is already a standard format.

Viewing SGML files on line requires an SGML viewer. Only one was available as we wrote this: Panorama, from SoftQuad, an SGML software company in Toronto, which provides it as a free helper application for Windows only.

PostScript

Before the Web became popular, users of the Internet posted documents on line either in plain text or in **PostScript**: the only cross-platform language that publishers could use to control formatting. PostScript documents are generally meant to be downloaded to a PostScript printer and printed out for reading. With HTML, PDF, and the other options available now, PostScript is becoming much more rare on line, but Web surfers may still find it at many government and educational sites.

ActiveX document
A special type of ActiveX control that opens an ActiveX-enabled program within the browser window, complete with the native program's tool bars and menus.

PostScript
A page-description language developed by Adobe Systems, used widely by desktop publishing programs and output devices.

Microsoft Office and Other Standard Formats

Most of the documents prepared in offices, at least in the United States, are created with the Microsoft Office suite of desktop programs, including Microsoft Word, Excel, and PowerPoint. Their ubiquity makes these formats—especially Microsoft Word's—de facto standards in the business world. Recognizing this, Microsoft and other software developers have created plug-ins for viewing those files in Web browsers, making it easy for businesses to post their files without reformatting. Although not recommended for Internet publishing, these standard formats, and the plug-ins that read them, may be useful for publishing over corporate intranets, where a few packages are predictably used and predictably supported on viewers' machines.

To support its products on the Web, Microsoft has also created a special type of ActiveX control, called an **ActiveX document**, that will enable ActiveX-capable browsers to view ActiveX-compatible documents, like those from the Microsoft Office programs, directly in the browser window, complete with the tool bars and menus from their native applications.

Online: Alternate Page Formats

Acrobat
http://www.adobe.com/Acrobat/main.html

ActiveX Controls
http://www.microsoft.com/ie/ie3/activex.htm

ActiveX Documents
http://www.microsoft.com/ie/ie3/activedoc.htm

Common Ground
http://www.hummingbird.com/

Envoy
http://www.twcorp.com/viewer.htm

Plug-ins
http://www.browserwatch.com/plug-in.html
http://www.netscape.com/comprod/mirror/
  navcomponents_download.html

QuarkImmedia
http://www.quark.com/immedia.htm

SGML
http://www.arbortext.com/wp.html
http://www.brainlink.com/~ben/sgml/
http://www.sil.org/sgml/sgml.html
http://www.sq.com/sgmlinfo/primintro.html

Shockwave
http://www.macromedia.com/shockwave/

SoftQuad Panorama
http://www.sq.com/products/panorama/panor-fe.htm

Texture
http:www.futuretense.com/

VRML
http://www.construct.net/tools/vrml/index.html
http://sdsc.edu/vrml/
http://vag.vrml.org/www-vrml/

Multimedia

The World Wide Web is often referred to as the "multimedia" part of the Internet, but until recently, the multimedia features of the Web—its ability to use sound, animation, and video in addition to text and graphics—were mostly theoretical. HTML has always offered the ability to link to multimedia files, but the lack of consensus on standard formats, the lack of support in browsers for dynamic media, and the time it takes to download sound and video all discouraged its use.

By the time you read this, though, a number of those problems may be solved.

Starting with version 3.0 of Navigator, Netscape began bundling plug-in support for standard sound and video formats with every browser, and other software makers are working independently to build plug-ins and ActiveX controls (→11) that will create support for a whole array of multimedia formats.

The last stumbling block to multimedia on the Web—(you guessed it) bandwidth—is a tough one. Multimedia files can be huge. New technologies we'll describe in the next section promise better results in short order, but it's an issue anyone posting multimedia on the Web will have to contend with for some time. Still, carefully measured multimedia effects can have big payoffs, even over modem connections, and as bandwidth increases, the Web could make all your multimedia dreams come true.

Keeping Up With Multimedia

Everyone knows how movies work: Viewers see a sequence of images, each just slightly different from the last, in such quick succession that it seems that only one image is projected and is moving. Digital video and animation work the same way; they require a sequence of digital images to be displayed quickly enough to give the illusion of **real-time motion**. If they are displayed too slowly (slower than about 24 frames per second), or if one frame is too different from the last, the illusion is lost. Digital sound works in a similar way: discrete sound **samples** must be played quickly to sound natural.

Now think about how that would be accomplished on a computer. As anyone who has worked with digital images knows, even one bitmap graphic can require several megabytes of disk space. Multiply that number by 24 for each second of video or animation, and you're talking about immense files, even for short clips. Asking a computer's processor to rasterize 24 graphics every second is another tall order—more than most of today's computers can handle.

These issues are older than the Web. The same challenges have faced video editing professionals and multimedia CD-ROM authors for years, and the computer industry has come up with compression schemes, such as MPEG and QuickTime (→**142**), to help squeeze audio and video files down to smaller sizes. But compression can do only so much—and never enough to get even the shortest video file small enough to download without an annoying wait over a modem hookup to the Web.

New **streaming** technologies, created for online publishing and videoconferencing, avoid the long wait for downloads by letting the user begin playing the file while it is being downloaded. The compressed files are sent to the client, which decompresses them and feeds them, bit by bit, to the player. Later sections are cached in the client computer's memory until it's their turn. This technique removes the tight limits on file size that constrain authors under the save-and-play systems; no matter how long the file, the user waits only for the first, short section. As we talk about the different types of multimedia in this chapter, we'll talk about the streaming technologies available for each one.

Video and sound rely on precaptured data, whose minute details must be transferred bit by bit from the server. Animations based on vector graphics (→**105**) can be much less troublesome. Instead of downloading all the bits that make up each image, the server can send just the program code that creates the animation sequence. Provided that the user's computer has the software required to understand the code, it can then create each graphic frame from those compact instructions.

real-time motion
In digital animation or video, the effect of natural motion achieved by using a frame rate of 24 to 30 frames per second.

sample
In digital media, a digital recording of sound or visual data, taken and played back at high frequencies to create the illusion of natural sound or motion.

streaming
Describes technologies that feed media files to a player progressively, so that a file can begin playing as it is downloaded.

RICHARD GROVE/AGENCY.COM
http://www.desires.com/1.5/Style/Docs/freda.html

Animation

The Web community hasn't stood still waiting for software developers to standardize on multimedia formats and for Internet service providers to widen the pipes. In the Web's first years, Web designers, with a leg up from Netscape, have devised ingenious ways to add eye-catching animation effects—if not real-time motion—to Web pages.

Netscape Navigator 1.1 supported the first animation effects on the Web with two methods, called **client pull** and **server push**. Both these methods simply automate the process of downloading files to the browser, creating the image sequences that make up animation.

Client pull depends on a special attribute of the <META> tag, *http-equiv=* (now supported by other browsers as well), that creates an HTTP request for a new file. Using this attribute, page authors can program file requests into the header of an HTML file, asking the server to send one file after another, at time intervals specified in the tag.

Server push lets the server control the pace of the download. This method depends on a CGI script (→**161**) that, once activated, sends the specified files to the browser, one after another, as quickly as it can. This method works only with browsers that support a special MIME type (→**11**) called x-mixed/multipart.

client pull
A method of animation created by setting an HTML page to automatically call the next page to be downloaded, accomplished via a special attribute to the <META> tag (*http-equiv=*) that simulates an HTTP call.

server push
A method of animation created by the automatic downloading of pages from the server, activated by using a CGI script.

(The x-mixed/multipart type is a way of providing multiple files in situations, such as HTTP requests, that usually respond with a single file.)

Both server push and client pull can be used to send any type of file—HTML, sound, image, whatever. Because client pull depends on a tag (<META>) in the heading of the HTML file, though, this method can be used only for changes to entire pages or to grab additional media files, such as a sound file (→**145**). The scripts that activate a server push, on the other hand, can be called from an <IMG> tag, so server push can be used to animate individual images within an HTML page.

Server push and client pull spiced up the early days of the Web, but they aren't really satisfactory forms of animation. Especially over slow modem connections, neither method can dispatch files quickly enough to simulate real-time motion. Because it requires just one connection between the browser and the server, server push offers more speed than client pull (which must make a new connection for each file request), but the extra load it puts on the server may back up traffic on heavily used sites.

Recently, browsers (starting with Navigator 2.0) have begun to support a more elegant form of animation: **animated GIF** (→**104**). The ability to include multiple, successive layers had always been a feature of the GIF89a format (→**103**), but Netscape was the first to

START TAG	ATTRIBUTES	END TAG	EXPLANATION
<META>		</META>	Provides general information about an HTML document
	content=*value*		A value for use by the HTTP action specified with *http-equiv=*. For client pull, this is the number of seconds to wait before loading the next page.
	http-equiv= *"http-action"*		The HTTP action that should be enacted. For client pull, use *http-equiv= "refresh"*.
	url=*"URL"*		Used with *http-equiv="refresh"*, the file that should be loaded next

animated GIF
A graphic file, in GIF89a format, that includes multiple layers that can be played in succession to create an animation.

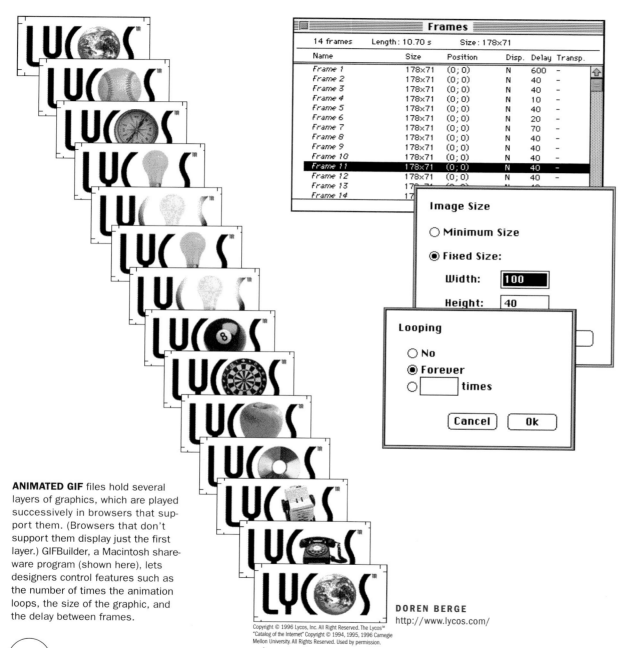

Frames

14 frames	Length: 10.70 s		Size: 178×71			
Name	Size	Position		Disp.	Delay	Transp.
Frame 1	178×71	(0; 0)		N	600	–
Frame 2	178×71	(0; 0)		N	40	–
Frame 3	178×71	(0; 0)		N	40	–
Frame 4	178×71	(0; 0)		N	10	–
Frame 5	178×71	(0; 0)		N	40	–
Frame 6	178×71	(0; 0)		N	20	–
Frame 7	178×71	(0; 0)		N	70	–
Frame 8	178×71	(0; 0)		N	40	–
Frame 9	178×71	(0; 0)		N	40	–
Frame 10	178×71	(0; 0)		N	40	–
Frame 11	178×71	(0; 0)		N	40	–
Frame 12	178×71	(0; 0)		N	40	–
Frame 13	17					
Frame 14	17					

Image Size

○ Minimum Size

● Fixed Size:

Width: `100`

Height: `40`

Looping

○ No

● Forever

○ ☐ times

[Cancel] [Ok]

ANIMATED GIF files hold several layers of graphics, which are played successively in browsers that support them. (Browsers that don't support them display just the first layer.) GIFBuilder, a Macintosh shareware program (shown here), lets designers control features such as the number of times the animation loops, the size of the graphic, and the delay between frames.

DOREN BERGE
http://www.lycos.com/

support playback of the layers as animations. (Browsers that support GIF, but not the animation features, display only the first frame of the animation.) Microsoft began supporting animated GIFs in Internet Explorer 3.0. A handful of shareware tools for creating animated GIFs also quickly popped up (GIF Construction Set for Windows, GIFBuilder for the Mac), and the feature will doubtless appear in mainstream graphics programs in short order.

Animated GIFs are downloaded to the browser just like any other GIF graphic; the browser takes care of playing the animation layers saved in the file. Short sequences can be looped to keep the animation playing until the user moves to a new page (or clicks the Stop button in the browser). Playback can speed along as fast as the client machine can render each frame, or it can be paced by delays specified in the GIF authoring program.

The independence from the server is a great advantage of animated GIFs, making it preferable to server push for most animation. The only caveat against its use is the same as for any GIF graphic: it probably won't provide good compression or color quality for photographic images (→**103**), and care must be taken to keep file sizes small.

The animated GIF format minimizes file sizes by allowing artists to save only the parts of the image that change with each frame. With careful planning, files can be kept surprisingly small. Animated GIFs are streamed in a sense: the first image will show up as soon as it is downloaded, with the subsequent frames following as fast as the connection allows, but it's still not a format that can support real-time motion, except with very small images and very short animation loops.

Microsoft's browser supports a special form of dynamic content—scrolling text—with its <MARQUEE> tag. Text marked with this tag will march horizontally across the browser window, once or in a loop, as the author specifies. Because the same effect can be achieved with more broadly supported methods, such as ActiveX controls (→173) and Java (→168), the tag has not been picked up by many other browsers.

A wide variety of animation formats can be supported by Netscape Navigator's plug-in capabilities and Microsoft's ActiveX program interface (→11). The most important among such add-on formats is probably Macromedia Director's Shockwave format, which is supported by players in both environments.

We talked earlier (→130) about Shockwave for Director as a format that could be used as an alternative to HTML for whole sets of pages. Mainly due to file size issues, though, Shockwave has been used mostly to add short animation effects within HTML pages. The Shockwave player ships with both Netscape's and Microsoft's browsers, so page authors can count on

START TAG	ATTRIBUTES	END TAG	EXPLANATION
<MARQUEE>		</MARQUEE>	Surround text that should scroll across the screen
	align="top" OR "middle" OR "bottom"		Specifies an alignment of the marquee with the surrounding text
	behavior="scroll" OR "slide" OR "alternate"		Specifies a scrolling action: *scroll* (the default) scrolls from one side of the screen and off the other, *slide* scrolls just until it reaches the other side, and *alternate* scrolls back and forth across the window
	bgcolor="*#RRGGBB*" OR "*name*"		Names a color for the marquee's background, using an RGB value (expressed in hexadecimal) or a color name
	direction="*left*" OR "*right*"		The direction the marquee will scroll
	height=*n* OR *n%*, weight=*n* OR *n%*		The height and width of the marquee, described in pixels or as a percentage of the screen height
	hspace=*n*		The horizontal space, in pixels, set between the marquee and surrounding text
	loop=*n* OR "*infinite*"		The number of times the marquee will loop
	scrollamount=*n*		The unit, in pixels, by which the marquee scrolls
	scrolldelay=*n*		The number of milliseconds between scrolls
	vspace=*n*		The vertical space, in pixels, set between the marquee and surrounding text

THE <MARQUEE> TAG, introduced by Microsoft's Internet Explorer, lets designers specify text that will march across the screen.

MICROSOFT CORP.
http://www.microsoft.com/

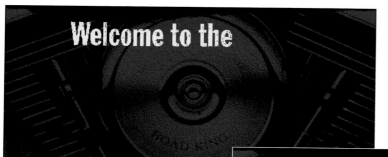

Paint 3: WWW site

3 WWW site

SHOCKWAVE FOR DIRECTOR provides compression and viewing software that lets files from Macromedia's popular authoring software be posted on the Web. The Director tools used to create this Shockwave animation for Harley-Davidson's Web site are shown here. The last step is compressing the Director movie with Shockwave's Afterburner utility (bottom right).

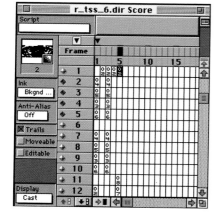

r_tss_6.dir Score

Script

Frame

1   5   10   15

Ink
Bkgnd ...

Anti-Alias
Off

☒ Trails
☐ Moveable
☐ Editable

Display
Cast

3   30 FPS   -- FPS

VSA PARTNERS
http://www.harley-davidson.com/

r_tss_6.dir Cast

2

sound.aiff

1 :sound.aiff | 2 | 3 :WWW site | 4 :Welcome t | 5 :Harley-Da | 6 :now go aw | 7 :goaway | 8 :HAND3.GIF | 9 | 10 | 11 | 12

global delay | on exitFrame go to | on exitFrame go 4

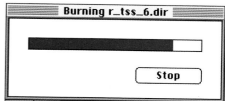

Burning r_tss_6.dir

Stop

nearly universal support for Shockwave effects. Especially for designers already conversant with Macromedia Director, Shockwave offers a powerful way to create interactive multimedia for the Web.

The Afterburner component of the Shockwave authoring system can compress Director files to about half their original size, and authors can use tricks like looping and careful scripting to get longer run times from short clips. But getting files down to Web size takes skill and leaves little room for extravagant effects.

Other plug-ins also offer the ability to play animations. One is FutureWave's FutureSplash program, which creates vector-based graphics that can store images in extremely compact files. Check the plug-in and ActiveX source pages listed at the end of this chapter for current options.

A new generation of animation and multimedia authoring programs are being created just for the Web. Dimension X's Liquid Motion, Power Production Software's WebBurst, and other animation programs offer the graphic interface familiar from traditional authoring software, but write their code in Java (→**168**). Because Java is directly supported in most Web browsers, neither Web designers nor visitors to their sites need to worry whether the client machine has the proper software to support the code, as they would with plug-in formats.

FUTURE WAVE
http://www.futurewave.com/demosite/afsmenu2.spl

FUTUREWAVE'S FUTURESPLASH plug-in offers vector-based interactive animation. Moving your pointer over this demo "activates" the individual pizzas. The vector graphics are compact in size (this animation uses 16K) and retain their detail as you zoom in and lose detail when you zoom out.

CD-ROMs: The Web Connection

For publishers who want to deliver CD-ROM-like multimedia now, there is a way to deliver bandwidth-hungry media without waiting for cable modem connections to every home. It's the way they've always done it: CD-ROM. Netscape and other browser manufacturers are supporting an extension to the <META> tag that allows publishers to access files stored on local disks. (Netscape calls its feature LiveCaching.) Web publishers who want to give visitors access to video and other high-overhead media can offer to send interested visitors a CD packed with such files, then call the files from their Web site's pages. In a way, it's the best of both worlds. The pages downloaded from the Web site can be updated as often as required to keep the information fresh—and can even retrieve fresh media lying in wait on the CD for each new feature. And visitors get access to multimedia files at CD speeds.

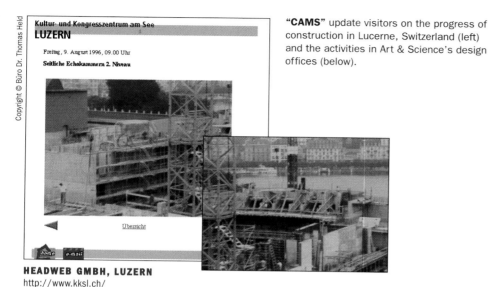

"CAMS" update visitors on the progress of construction in Lucerne, Switzerland (left) and the activities in Art & Science's design offices (below).

HEADWEB GMBH, LUZERN
http://www.kksl.ch/

Video

Video is both the most sought after and the most elusive medium on the Web. Everyone dreams of the live-action effects video can offer, but even the fastest systems—200MHz computers with T1 lines—have trouble delivering 24 frames per second of bitmapped data. If your audience can be counted on to have such systems—if they're all connected over a fast corporate intranet, for example—video might work for you, but most of the systems you're reaching over the Internet can't handle such a job. Even with tight compression, video files of any length would take hours to download over a modem, and even with streaming formats and hardware acceleration, modem connections can't deliver much more than jerky, postage-size effects at a very slow frame rate. But even though Internet video isn't really ready for prime time, lots of engineers are busy at work honing video technologies that will be ready when new network technologies deliver the bandwidth.

The first formats to be used for the Web were the compressed digital formats that existed before the Web was invented: **MPEG**, **QuickTime**, and **AVI**, which depended on separate helper apps for playback. (AVI is also directly supported in Microsoft Internet Explorer via Microsoft's *dynsrc=* attribute for the <IMG> tag (→**106**), which allows authors to plug video, in place of a still image, into an HTML document.)

Eyes on the World: The Web "Cam" Craze

Combine server push or client pull with a video camera, and you've got a way (if you want it) to put your life—or your pet, your lava lamp, your schoolroom, the wall of your apartment, whatever—on line. All over the Web, people have used this ability to offer a glimpse of their corner of the world to the world at large. The results range from the ridiculous to the sublime.

ART & SCIENCE
http://www.chiba.com/

The demands of the Internet have also induced software publishers to create streaming players for each of these formats. Netscape Navigator 3.0 includes plug-ins that receive streaming QuickTime (Apple's QuickTime 2.0 plug-in) and AVI (Netscape's LiveVideo plug-in). Streaming MPEG is supported by plug-ins such as InterVU's PreVu and Xing Technologies' StreamWorks helper application. Some streaming technologies, such as VDOnet's VDOLive and Vivo Software's VivoActive player, use proprietary compression technologies and file formats. Each format promises tighter compression and better quality than the last, and the hot competition is keeping the pace of improvement lively, so our best advice is simply to check out the latest offerings when you're ready to start publishing video.

Some streaming video formats, such as StreamWorks and VDOLive, can also be used for live video streams, allowing an Internet audience to experience events as they happen a world away. Web publishers have used the technique to broadcast events such as Grateful Dead concerts over the Net.

If video does come into wide use over the Internet, publishers and Internet Service Providers will find their available bandwidth filling up fast: Even a T1 connection can handle only a few streams of real-time video at one time. To solve the problem, the Internet community is working on new ways to handle multimedia information on the Net. The most promising,

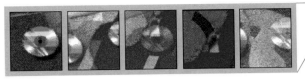

SHORT VIDEO CLIPS can be read with the aid of helper applications or plug-ins. Cal State Hayward's multimedia program (top) uses a QuickTime clip to animate and add music to its home page. Greenpeace (below) posts a movie of French commandos boarding the *Rainbow Warrior* as the ship's crew monitored France's 1995 nuclear tests in the South Pacific. The crew uploaded the video to satellite just before their equipment was confiscated.

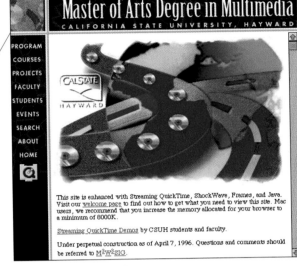

BIJAN B. GILLANI, ED.D.
http://tesla.csuhayward.edu/frameindex.html

© 1995 Greenpeace

http://www.greenpeace.org/

AVI
The standard video format for Microsoft Windows.

MPEG
A compressed video format, created by and named for the Motion Picture Experts Group of the International Standards Organization.

QuickTime
A video and sound format created by Apple Computer and supported on the Macintosh and Windows platforms.

Eventually, all the data will be all in one piece, so you won't have to stop and download things. Six months from now you might come to a page and hear a voice and see something moving. It will be like TV except you will be able to stop it or to go deeper.

SABINE MESSNER, HOTWIRED

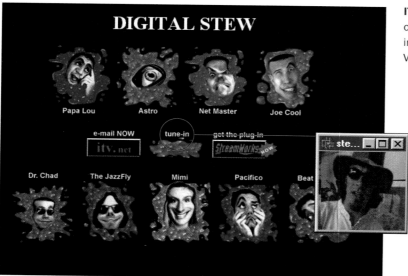

FABRICE L'HEUREUX
http://www.itv.net/digitalstew/stew.html

ITV is creating an "Internet TV station" offering real-time events and video clips in streaming video formats such as VDOLive, StreamWorks, and CU-SeeMe.

MBONE
A virtual network, based on the IP Multicast protocol, that offers a model for broadcasting multimedia data over the Internet.

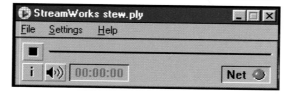

called the **MBONE**, works with a new protocol called IP Multicast. Instead of sending out separate streams to each client that requests one (the usual Web model), IP Multicast lets publishers send out just one stream. Strategically placed signal reflectors, referred to as "propagation servers," duplicate the stream as it is sent out, resulting in a geometric increase of the number of streams as it is passed from reflector to reflector. Users can "listen in" to a broadcast just as they would tune in to a TV or radio program. IP Multicasting requires some pretty sophisticated multitasking capabilities, both on the sending and receiving ends, so it's currently supported only by workstation-class computers running the Unix operating system. As these capabilities reach desktop computers and networking hardware is upgraded to handle IP Multicast, the MBONE will become more accessible. All that, though, is probably still a few years out.

Until MBONE is on line, wannabe broadcasters can test the waters with CU-SeeMe, a videoconferencing system developed at Cornell University and now being commercialized by White Pine Software. CU-SeeMe includes software for setting up "reflectors" (on the model MBONE propagation servers) on a Unix machine, and public-minded CU-SeeMe users have set up several public reflectors that anyone can use (with advance notice) to broadcast an event. We'll discuss CU-SeeMe more when we talk about videoconferencing in the "Interactivity" chapter (→**159**).

Sound

Sound can be part of almost any dynamic media format. We've already talked about animation formats, such as Shockwave, and video formats, such as QuickTime and MPEG, that can include sound. Sound is often also useful on its own, though: as a separate medium for broadcasting speeches or other content without adding the bandwidth-hogging overhead of graphics. That's the use we'll talk about here.

To this point, sound has usually been added to the Web as the target of a hyperlink: clicking on a hyperlink downloads a sound clip that is fed through a helper application to provide a sample of a speaker's voice or a few bars of music. More craftily, page authors can use client pull (→**136**) to automatically load a sound file, surprising the reader with a greeting or other aural effect.

Several sound-only file formats are floating around the world of digital multimedia. Some of the most common are **AIFF** (cross-platform, usually compressed), **.wav** (the standard format for Windows applications), **.au** (a common format for Unix software), and **MIDI** (a cross-platform standard used to record music from electronic instruments). MPEG and QuickTime, usually thought of as video formats, can also be used for audio alone. LiveAudio, a plug-in bundled with Netscape Navigator 3.0 and later, plays all these formats, and stand-alone helper applications can help

REALAUDIO'S streaming format lets NPR post half-hour and longer radio broadcasts on its Web site (right). The Underground Music Archive (below) offers a variety of formats for each music clip, letting users pick the one that suits their software setup.

PROGRESSIVE NETWORKS
http://www.prognet.com/contentp/npr/

BRANDEE AMBER SELCK
http://www.iuma.com/

AIFF
Audio Interchange File Format, a cross-platform format for digital sound files.

.au
A sound file format commonly used on Unix computers.

MIDI
Musical Instrument Digital Interface, a standard for recording and playing synthesized sounds on electronic instruments.

.wav
The native sound format for Microsoft Windows.

START TAG	ATTRIBUTES	END TAG	EXPLANATION
<BGSOUND>		</BGSOUND>	Plays a .wav (sound) file when the file is loaded
	loop=*n* OR "infinite"		The number of times the sound clip will loop
	src="*URL*"		The URL of the sound file

As the cable TV operators and the phone services start price wars to provide high-bandwidth connections to the home, you'll see more multimedia on the Web. But high-quality multimedia isn't just a matter of more bandwidth. The real revolution will come when people learn to work within the unique constraints of this medium.

BRIAN BEHLENDORF, ORGANIC ONLINE

out with other browsers. Microsoft's Internet Explorer supports a <BGSOUND> tag that loads and plays .wav files as part of an HTML page.

Except for MIDI, all these formats record sound by sampling it at frequent intervals and saving each value as a digital code. (MIDI records commands that create sounds in MIDI-capable instruments or sound boards.) The higher the sampling frequency (common frequencies are 11KHz, 22KHz, and 44KHz) and the greater the number of bits per sample (usually 8 bits or 16 bits), the better quality the sound: 44KHz, 16-bit sound is CD-quality. Of course, the higher the frequency and the higher the bit-depth, the larger the file, as well. One second of uncompressed CD-quality sound can result in a roughly 70KB file (44,000 samples x 16 bits/second). To combat the file size problem, most sound recording software offers a range of compression levels that trade off sound quality for smaller files, but files in any sampled sound format suffer the too-familiar problem for multimedia: They take longer to download than they do to play back.

All this is bound to change quickly, as several companies vie to provide compact, streaming audio formats for the Web. The leader so far, if only because it had such a good head start, is Progressive Networks, with its RealAudio technology. A RealAudio helper app is bundled with many browsers, including Microsoft's, and a plug-in is available for Netscape Navigator. RealAudio files start playing a few seconds after download starts and feed in without interruption, even over 14.4Kbps connections, but the compression needed to make this trick work also results in fairly low-quality sound, at least in the earliest versions of the software. RealAudio's quality is sufficient for voice recordings, but the results are considered too scratchy for music.

Another streaming audio technology, Xing Technology's StreamWorks, offers higher quality sound using MPEG compression. (StreamWorks can also stream video) (→**143**). At least when we wrote this, though, the higher quality came at a higher price. While the client helper apps were free, these streaming formats required specialized encoding and server software starting at several thousand dollars.

Both RealAudio and StreamWorks can deliver pre-recorded sound or "live" streams, a radiolike function that can send sound out over the wires with just a few seconds delay. RealAudio adds a feature that lets authors sync HTTP calls for named URLs to certain points in the sound file, creating an online multimedia slide show.

When we wrote this, the latest news in Web sound was a new version of Shockwave (→**139**) that supported high-quality streaming sound. More will doubtless be happening by the time you're reading this. Check Netscape's plug-ins page and the other sources listed at right for news of new formats.

Online: Multimedia

ActiveX
http://microsoft.com/intdev/

ActiveX Controls
http://www.microsoft.com/activex/controls/

Cameras on the Web
http://www.yahoo.com/Computers_and_Internet/Internet/
 Entertainment/Interesting_Devices_Connected_to_the_Net/
 Spy_Cameras/

Client Pull, Server Push
http://www.netscape.com/assist/net_sites/
 pushpull.html

CU-SeeMe
http://cu-seeme.cornell.edu/

GIF Animation
http://home.netscape.com/comprod/products/navigator/
 version_2.0/gif_animation/index.html
http://member.aol.com/royalef/gifanim.htm

LiquidMotion
http://www.dimensionx.com/products/lm/

LiveCaching
http://www.netscape.com/comprod/products.navigator/
 version_3.0/developer/others.html

MBONE
http://www.best.com/~prince/techinfo/
http://www-unix.umbc.edu/mcast/mcast.html

Multimedia Formats and Players
http://www.mps.org/~ebennett/xplat.html

QuickTime
http://quicktime.apple.com/

Plug-ins
http://home.netscape.com/comprod/mirror/
 navcomponents_download.html

RealAudio
http://www.realaudio.com/

Shockwave
http://www.macromedia.com/Tools/Shockwave/

StreamWorks
http://www.xingtech.com/streams/

VDOLive
http://www.vdo.net/products/

VivoActive
http://www.vivo.com/

WebBurst
http://www.powerproduction.com/webburst/wbinfo.html

Interactivity

Instant Feedback: Mailto

Structured Input: HTML Forms

Beyond HTML: Plug-Ins, VRML, Java, and JavaScript

Reader-to-Reader: Forums, Chat, and Videoconferencing

On the Web, readers can ask questions and get answers, customize their views of pages, and follow lines of thought that they, and not the publisher, determine. Publishers can gain information about their readers' interests and take orders for products on line. Web users can even interact with each other, chatting and playing games with acquaintances all over the world. This interactivity is one of the most important—and so far, most unexplored—benefits of Web publishing.

The hyperlinking by which users navigate through the Web, constructing their own experience through the choices they make on each page, is one powerful example of the Web's interactivity, but it doesn't stop there. Simple interaction through e-mail feedback and fill-in forms is also built right into HTML and is easy to execute, and if you're willing to do some programming (or know someone who is), the possibilities are almost limitless.

It's impossible to characterize all the different kinds of interactivity possible on the Web. In this chapter, we'll introduce some of the technologies that support interactivity on the Web and show some of the techniques Web publishers have used to respond to readers in ways that are possible in no other medium.

Instant Feedback: Mailto

One of the simplest—and most useful—ways to open lines of communication with your readers is by including an e-mail feedback form. It supplies visitors with a straightforward way to get information to the keepers of the site, and even more importantly, it keeps the site's creators in touch with the needs of its users. Every site should include at least this basic form of interactivity.

Creating an e-mail feedback form with HTML is as easy as creating a hyperlink. Instead of supplying a URL for the link, however, you type *mailto:* plus the address to which the information should be sent. For readers, clicking on the anchor text brings up an e-mail form addressed to the address you specify. Voilà.

AN EASY WAY TO create a feedback loop from your site is the mailto feature built into HTML. Using *mailto:* and the e-mail address you want comments sent to, instead of a URL, in the *href=* attribute in an <A> tag calls up an e-mail form for that address when the user clicks on the link.

HEIDI SWANSON
http://www.thenet-usa.com/signal2noise/signal.html

START TAG	ATTRIBUTES	END TAG	EXPLANATION
<A>		<A>	
	href=mailto:"*address*"		Creates a link to an e-mail form addressed to the specified mailbox

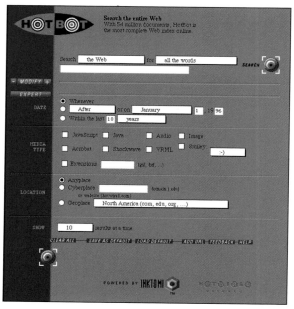

HOTBOT'S EXPERT SEARCH option lets users choose search criteria from an array of buttons and menus.

HOTWIRED
http://www.hotbot.com/

ONLINE SHOPPING SITES like Amazon Books present order forms in which users can indicate the items and quantities they want to buy.

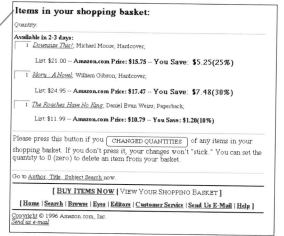

SHEL KAPHAN
http://www.amazon.com/

Structured Input: HTML Forms

Mailto is a great way to give readers a voice, but its only result is an e-mail message form. If you want specific kinds of information or information that can be fed directly to a script for processing, the way to get it is by creating fill-in forms.

Laying out a form is easy enough. It's all handled by standard HTML 2.0 codes and by drag-and-drop controls in most WYSIWYG HTML editors. HTML's form commands can create a variety of controls, which anyone who works with Microsoft Windows or Macintosh computers will be familiar with. Mostly, they're the same ones you see in dialog boxes in all your software: text fields, radio buttons, checkboxes, drop-down lists, and buttons. All these controls can be laid out within standard HTML layout blocks (paragraphs, preformatted text, lists, or tables) and styled with HTML's character style tags.

Once you've built the form in HTML, users have a place to supply information or specify preferences, but what happens when they click Submit? That's where HTML's features end and the need for programming begins. The *action=* attribute of the <FORM> tag names a CGI script (→161) that will parse the user input and process it. The user input is passed back to the server along with the request to run the script at the URL specified with the *action=* attribute. The *name=* attribute for each <INPUT> tag creates a variable name for each control's input—custom-made for getting information back to the server for processing by CGI scripts. (Input that doesn't need access to databases or other files on the server can also be handled by a client-side script created with JavaScript or another client-side scripting language.)

As HTML's main method for gathering input from a site's users, such forms are used in one way or another for many types of interactivity. What happens to the information—whether it's posted to a customer database, sent as e-mail to a feedback address, used to determine which information the user will see next, or any other result—is determined by the script to which you send it. The illustrations on these two pages show some examples of different ways Web designers have used this capability.

ATOMIC VISION
http://www.excite.com/

EXCITE, a Web search service, offers drop-down menus to make it easy for users to choose search criteria from limited sets. Note the custom Search button; you can use a graphic, rather than the default buttons you see elsewhere, by using the *type=image* attribute (rather than *type=submit*) for the <INPUT> tag.

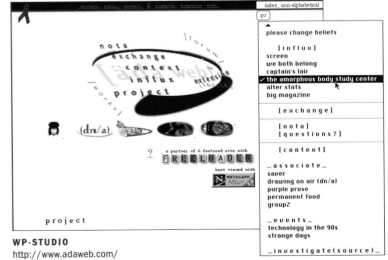

FORM CONTROLS can also be used for navigation. Here, äda 'web, an online magazine, offers its table of contents in a drop-down menu.

WP-STUDIO
http://www.adaweb.com/

START TAG	ATTRIBUTES	END TAG	EXPLANATION
<FORM>		</FORM>	Surround all the tags (shown below) that create the form
	action="*URL*"		The script that should be run, and that the form data should be sent to, when the user clicks the Submit button
	method="get" OR "post"		Specifies a method for sending the data to the server
<INPUT>			Creates input controls within a form
	type="text" OR "button" OR "checkbox" OR "radio" OR "submit" OR "image" OR "reset" OR "hidden"		The type of control to be created. (See the illustration below for examples.)
	checked		For *type=checkbox* or *type=radio,* specifies that the box or button should be chosen as a default
	maxlength="*length*"		For *type=text,* the maximum length of an entry, in characters
	name="*name*"		A name for the control, used as a variable name when input is sent to a script for processing. (Used for all input types.) For *type=radio,* all the radio buttons in a group have the same name.
	size="*size*"		For *type=text,* the length of the text box
	src="*URL*"		For *type=image,* names an image to use as a Submit button
	value="*name*"		For *type=checkbox,* a variable value to be sent when the box is checked. For *type=text,* the default entry in the text field. For *type=submit*, *type=reset*, or *type=button*, the text displayed on the button.

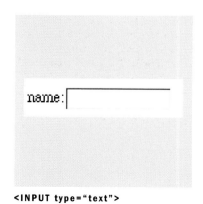

<INPUT type="text">

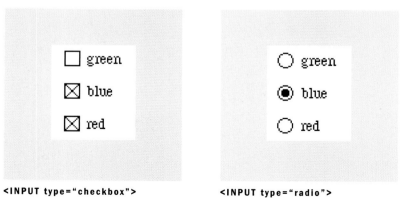

<INPUT type="checkbox">

<INPUT type="radio">

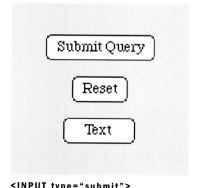

<INPUT type="submit">
<INPUT type="reset">
<INPUT type="button" value="Text">

A lot of businesses approach the Web with a print media standard of design. They're missing the capabilities of feedback and interaction, which are 90 percent of what makes the Web powerful.

ANNETTE LOUDON, CONSTRUCT

START TAG	ATTRIBUTES	END TAG	EXPLANATION
<SELECT>			Creates a menu of choices, either a pulldown menu (the default) or a scrolling menu
	multiple		Allows multiple selections from a scrolling menu
	name="*name*"		A name for the menu, used as a variable name when the input is sent to a script for processing
	size="*size*"		Creates a scrolling menu of the depth specified
<OPTION>			Used after the <SELECT> tag to create an option in a menu.
	selected		Specifies that the option should be selected by default
	value="*text*"		The value to be sent if the option is selected
<TEXTAREA>		</TEXTAREA>	Creates a multiline text field
	cols=*n*, rows=*n*		The width (rows) and height (cols) of the text area, in characters
	name="*name*"		A name for the text area, used as a variable name when the input is sent to a script for processing

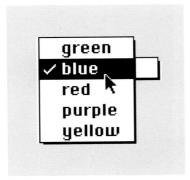

<SELECT>

<SELECT size=>

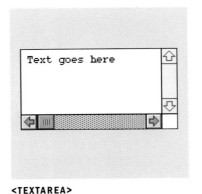

<TEXTAREA>

THE TYPE= ATTRIBUTE of the <INPUT> tag names the type of control to be created. A scrolling text box is created with its own tag, <TEXTAREA>. Drop-down menus and scrolling lists are created with <SELECT>. Additional attributes of each tag specify values such as the names for each option and the size of the control.

ONE OF SHOCKWAVE'S most valuable features is its ability to use rollovers to give user feedback. Options in the menu for TechnoCap's TechnoCafé light up and emit a reassuring noise when the mouse pointer rolls over them.

Beyond HTML: Plug-Ins, VRML, Java, and JavaScript

Hyperlinks, mailto links, and the combination of sub-mittable forms with back-end scripts for processing just about cover the gamut of HTML's built-in features for interactivity. But as you learned in previous chapters, the Web's capabilities can go far beyond HTML. Many browsers will support Netscape's plug-in format and Microsoft's ActiveX controls (→**11**) to handle non-HTML formats in Web browsers. And as Java (→**168**) matures, its capabilities should allow programmers to create a virtually unlimited set of interactive effects.

Earlier (→**139**) we talked about Macromedia's Shockwave for Director and other multimedia pro-grams as ways to add animation and synchronized sound to Web pages. Multimedia authoring packages such as these also add features for interactivity far surpassing what is currently available with HTML. They let users directly manipulate objects on screen, make menus or graphics pop up automatically when users draw the mouse pointer over on-screen objects, or add dramatic transitions, for instance. Shockwave was already widely used by early 1996 and serving as a popular format for interactive effects. New plug-in formats such as FutureWave's FutureSplash vector animation tool (→**141**), and stand-alone formats such as QuarkImmedia (→**131**) also deliver interactive ani-mation and multimedia.

Other interactive effects are possible using Java (→**168**) and JavaScript (→**166**). Products such as PowerProduction's WebBurst offer graphic interfaces for authoring interactive multimedia and write their files as Java code, so they're playable in almost any Web browser without any additional software. As JavaScript matures it is adding interactive effects such as dynamic images that change as the user's mouse rolls over them.

VRML, the Virtual Reality Modeling Language (→**128**), can create an even more dramatic interactive experience, creating 3-D "worlds" that users can move through just as they would move through the real world: down hallways, through doors, and getting more detailed views of objects as they move closer to them. Though the first version offered only basic interactivity—essentially limited to hyperlink connections—version 2.0, finalized in early 1996, extended the language's potential by adding hooks that would enable Java and other programming languages to control objects' behavior. Another new feature makes it possible to trigger events by having the user simply draw near to an object or travel within a certain area of the "world." Plug-ins and ActiveX controls that support VRML 2.0, including players that come standard with Netscape's and Microsoft's browsers, should be available by the time you read this. And as the format gains popularity, tools that offer graphic interfaces for building Java-powered VRML worlds should follow.

The best kind of interactivity does something meaningful and responds within a second or two. I don't want to click and see something go "Pow." I want to see something usable.

JOHN GROTTING, STUDIO ARCHETYPE

GRAPHIC TOOLS FOR CREATING interactive Java animations are just beginning to hit the market. PowerProduction's WebBurst, shown here, supplies drawing tools, object libraries, and a traditional user interface to hide the Java programming from the designer. The resulting animations can run in any browser that supports Java.

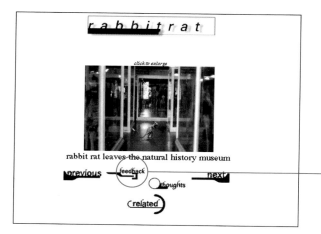

Rabbit Rat wants to know about your escape tactics.

name

from

comments

sign the guest book

Previous guests:

Sat Jan 27 14:33:51 EST 1996
MITCH AND CORKY
YOUR FAVORITE FANS

RABBIT RAT WANTS THE ARTIST TO COME HOME AND ESCAPE FROM EVICTIONS
NOTICES,BAD AIR AND DIRT,LIFE IS SIMPLIER IN THE MIDWEST AND ARTISTS ARE NOT
A DIME A DOZEN,YOUR FANS ALL LOVE YOU HERE AND YOUR FAMILY WILL BE YOUR
BEST PROMOTERS

Thu Jan 25 23:44:29 EST 1996
cz
sdca

reminds me of my work with RATBOY

Thu Jan 25 23:01:22 EST 1996
tim
NH

When escaping from natural history museums, I find it best to always turn left after leaving by the back
door. However, if Mars is in Libra, then I would strongly suggest using the inverted wall sliding
technique used successfully by Alfred Hones in August 1976 while escaping from Newburgh state
penitentiary in New York. If it is after 9:36 pm then it is senseless to attempt an escape until next
tuesday due to the local pond-water levels. Most importantly do not try to contact Roger Barrett, David
Gilmour, Rick Wright, Nick Mason, or Roger Waters before January 17 1997. Good luck

Mon Jan 22 21:20:22 EST 1996
sam and howard appel
washington d.c.

saw your review in the ny times on sunday jan 21 .renowned rabbit rat rattles rules rudely

Mon Jan 22 21:20:20 EST 1996
sam and howard appel
washington d.c.

saw your review in the ny times on sunday jan 21 .renowned rabbit rat rattles rules rudely

RAZORFISH/MELANIE EINZIG
http://www.razorfish.com/bluedot/rabbitrat/

FORUMS give users a chance to post their opinions on
any topic, creating ongoing discussions on line. Most
forum software can post visitors' comments automatically and immediately. Here, visitors react to an online
art project about an escaping museum exhibit.

Internet Relay Chat (IRC)
An Internet protocol for exchanging
text messages in real time among
multiple simultaneous users.

Reader-to-Reader: Forums, Chat, and Videoconferencing

Still the most unexplored—and potentially the most
powerful—feature of Web publishing is its ability to
create community. As with any other publication, visitors to a Web site are brought to it by a common interest. Unlike any other type of communication, though,
Web sites are published on a medium—the Internet—
that those visitors can also use to communicate with
one another.

The Internet has long included bulletin board services, called newsgroups, in which users can post
messages on a topic of common interest. Likewise,
the Internet has hosted chat sessions, through
a technology called **Internet Relay Chat (IRC)**.
Recently, programmers have found ways to tie similar
services into Web pages, using the HTML, click-to-
choose interface familiar to Web users.

Neither of these technologies was really mature as
we wrote this in mid-1996. Only a handful of companies offer commercial software for adding such
features to your site, and a fair amount of custom
programming is required to make the interfaces
attractive and friendly.

Available chat products offer a variety of approaches,
from proprietary systems with accompanying plug-ins
(such as ichat), to IRC helper apps (à la GlobalChat),

to solutions that require no special client software at all (WebChat). Given the popularity of online chat, more software and better Web integration will doubtless surface by the time you read this.

Even newer twists on chat rooms are in development. Some systems are experimenting with sound and video in the chat environments. Others offer 3-D spaces in which users, represented by graphic stand-ins called **avatars**—can actually walk up to other users (or to their avatars) and exchange conversation. Many of these systems were based on proprietary extensions to the VRML 1.0 specification and so are incompatible with VRML 2.0 (**→155**) and require users to download proprietary client software. The next generation will presumably align around the VRML 2.0 specification.

Fanciful 3-D environments are fine for cocktail-party chatter. For business users and for others who want to see each other face to face, the best communication interface is provided by **videoconferencing** systems, which send video images of conference participants over the Net. Though they're not really part of the Web yet (they require separate software and use different protocols), they're good to know about for those who are thinking about ways to tie face-to-face communications into their Web services. Video-conferencing applications can be launched as helper apps or as browser plug-ins.

CHAT ROOMS offer uses the ability to exchange comments with other visitors who are on line at the same time. Usually less topic-oriented than forums, chat sites usually let visitors choose among several "rooms," where users exchange pleasantries.

THE LATEST TREND in chat sites uses VRML-like interfaces and 3-D avatars (below), creating worlds in which visitors can take on new personalities and interact in fantasy situations. To reduce download time, Worlds Inc. lets users purchase a CD-ROM that holds the 3-D graphics.

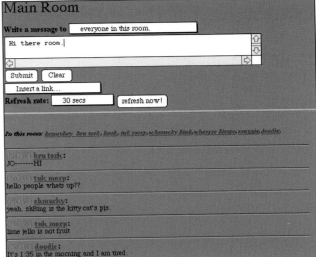

http://www.firefly.com/

WORLDS.NET
http://www.worlds.net/

avatar
In graphics-based chat systems, a figure that represents a participant.

videoconferencing
Systems in which video images of the participants are displayed on the other participants' screens in real time. Conversations may be held via text or audio, depending on the system and the available bandwidth.

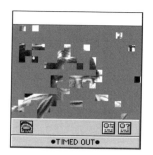

•TIMED OUT•

2.3 fps　20 Kbps

.1 fps　15 Kbps

0.0 fps　0 Kbps

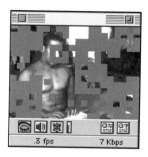

0.0 fps　4 Kbps

.2 fps　1 Kbps

.3 fps　7 Kbps

2.3 fps　20 Kbps

CU-SEEME is designed to let anyone with a Connectix QuickTake video camera send their messages—and images—out over the Internet. Sessions can be as private as a telephone call, or the video and chat sessions can be bounced off public "reflectors" that broadcast the message to anyone who wants to participate. (Lurkers need only the free CU-SeeMe helper app to tune in.) The pictures are transmitted in discrete segments, creating an arty "pixellated" effect that will doubtless become as trendy as QuickTime's stop-action playback.

Audio

+10
0
-10
-20
-30

+10
0
-10
-20
-30

Transmitting

PTT | Lurkers ▷

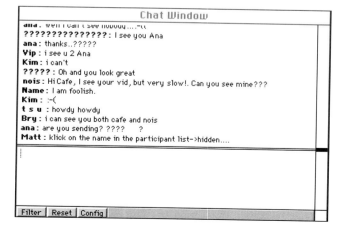

Chat Window

ana : well I can t see nobody....-((
??????????????? : I see you Ana
ana : thanks..?????
Yip : i see u 2 Ana
Kim : i can't
????? : Oh and you look great
nois : Hi Cafe, I see your vid, but very slow!. Can you see mine???
Name : I am foolish.
Kim : :-(
t s u : howdy howdy
Bry : i can see you both cafe and nois
ana : are you sending? ????　　?
Matt : klick on the name in the participant list->hidden....

Filter | Reset | Config

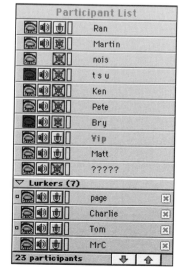

Participant List

Ran
Martin
nois
t s u
Ken
Pete
Bry
Yip
Matt
?????

▽ **Lurkers (7)**

page　☒
Charlie　☒
Tom　☒
MrC　☒

23 participants　⬇ ⬆

The best-known videoconferencing system to date is CU-SeeMe. Started a couple of years ago as an experiment at Cornell University, it quickly became an Internet subculture of its own. The free CU-SeeMe software combined with a Connectix QuickTake video camera turns your Web site into a private videophone or a public access TV station for under $100. Your signal can be received by anyone with a Mac or PC and a 14.4Kbps Web connection.

Making a video connection with one other person is like making a modem connection: You enter their Internet address, and if the other person is set up to receive a call, your image will appear on that person's screen. You can broadcast your event (or nonevent) to the world, or receive someone else's broadcast, by logging into a public "reflector" (→**144**).

CU-SeeMe video is no IMax extravaganza. The images are about 2 inches square, in grayscale, at a frame rate of from two to ten images per minute over a modem connection. Though CU-SeeMe supports audio, you can't usually get audio and video at the same time over a modem's limited bandwidth. But unlike the still Web "cams" that publish their images via server push (→**142**), it's interactive: users can chat back and forth.

The freeware version of CU-SeeMe is continually updated by students at Cornell. An enhanced version, offering 24-bit color and specialized for business use with such features as a digital whiteboard and security enhancements, is sold by White Pine Software.

Videoconferencing, like any other video application, is hobbled by the Net's limited bandwidth, but it's getting lots of attention lately as corporations install more Web-based intranets, connected by fast dedicated lines. Apple's **QuickTime Conferencing** software adds interactive, real-time transmission capabilities to its venerable video standard, and other Internet video suppliers won't be far behind in supporting what promises to be an important Web application. Check the online sources listed on this page for up-to-date information.

Online: Interactivity

Chat and Forum Applications
http://www.serverwatch.iworld.com/dg.html

Chat Systems
http://www.prospero.com
http://www.irsociety.com/webchat/webchat.html
http://www.worlds.net/

CU-SeeMe
http://cu-seeme.cornell.edu/

Forms Tutorials
http://robot0.ge.uiuc.edu/~carlosp/cs317/cft.html
http://www.catt.ncsu.edu/~bex/tutor/index.html
http://www.javaworld.com/javaworld/jw-06-1996/
  jw-06-javascript.html

QuarkImmedia
http://www.quark.com/immedia.htm

QuickTime Conferencing
http://qtc.quicktime.apple.com/

Shockwave
http://www.macromedia.com/Shockwave/

WebBurst
http://www.powerproduction.com/webburst/wbinfo.html

VRML
http://www.construct.net/tools/vrml/index.html
http://sdsc.edu/vrml/
http://vag.vrml.org/www-vrml/

QuickTime Conferencing
A version of Apple's QuickTime software that supports duplex, real-time transmission.

Programming the Web

- CGI: The Common Gateway Interface
- Client-Side Processing
- Client-Side Scripting: JavaScript and Visual Basic Scripting Edition
- Java
- ActiveX
- Do You Need to Be a Programmer?

The basic mechanisms built into Web browsers offer a complete hypertext publishing system. You can create a site using only the HTML tools you've learned about so far. But HTTP and HTML also offer hooks into a world of custom-built capabilities, added through Web programming.

A new generation of programming languages and tools has been developed especially for the Web to make custom effects possible. They range from simple **scripting languages**, specially designed to control Web interfaces and back-end databases, to full-fledged programming languages, which can be used to build multifunction applications. Web designers have come up with uses for these tools that range from the practical to the whimsical: from loan calculators for banks, electronic catalogs for mail-order companies, and online chat rooms to an online version of those refrigerator magnet poetry sets.

This chapter will introduce you to the possibilities, benefits, and pitfalls of CGI, Java, JavaScript, ActiveX, and other technologies designed to add interactivity and custom features to Web pages.

CGI: The Common Gateway Interface

Until recently, all programs for the Web were run on the server. When special actions were required or decisions had to be made based on user input, the browser handed the job to the server for processing and waited for a file based on the program's results to be sent back.

This method is a rather ingenious way to get around the problem that would otherwise stymie Web publishers: that, in general, programs must be written specifically for the type of computer they will be run on. Distributing programs to all the different types of computers that access the Web would require writing several versions of each program (one for each platform) and then somehow developing a system to make sure each reader gets the correct version.

Instead, the creators of the Web designed a method by which a server can offer access to its processing power, just as it offers access to its files, to every computer on the Net. The browser just needs some way to ask the server to execute the right program and a way to pass on any user input. That's the purpose of the **common gateway interface (CGI)**. Just as the HTTP specification sets standards for the way browsers and servers request and transmit files, CGI sets standards for the way they handle requests for programs.

CGI SCRIPTS are often used to process data from fill-in forms such as the one above. Clicking a Submit button on the form sends the filled-in information as values for the script's variables. The script adds the data to a database on the server, which can be used to build reports such as the one at right.

MATCH.COM/NANCY PINNEY
http://www.match.com/

common gateway interface (CGI)
A set of specifications that provide rules for the way Web clients and servers handle requests for executing and sending the results of server-based programs.

scripting language
A noncompiled programming language, usually focused on a particular set of tasks.

Scripts vs. Programs

For the sake of simplicity, we usually just refer to "programs" when we talk about a set of instructions that tell the server or browser what to do, but programmers and Web software vendors often break that concept down into two groups: traditional programs and scripts.

The distinction between the two isn't really clearcut: Both provide a set of commands for the computer to follow. The difference is in the type of language used to write them—full-featured programming languages like Visual Basic, C++, or Java or scripting languages, such as perl or JavaScript—and how the computer handles them.

As a rule, scripting languages are more specialized than full-fledged programming languages. Their range of capabilities is usually focused on the particular environment in which they will be used—JavaScript, for example, is designed for use on the Web, and so includes commands for things like

checking for particular plug-ins and handling browser tasks. Perl was designed as a tool for managing Unix systems and so includes commands for Unix file management, while AppleScript includes calls to the MacOS and standard Mac application code.

As they're being processed by the computer, scripts are generally executed line by line by a script "interpreter," while programs are first sent to a "compiler," which parses the program code into a more quickly executed form, called machine language, that can be efficiently handled by the computer, resulting in faster processing for complex programs.

While programming languages are designed to give programmers maximum control, scripting languages are designed to help them get a given task done easily. Consequently, scripting languages are fairly easy to learn, even for people who have no programming experience.

CGI script
A script or program saved on the server and available to Web clients via the CGI protocol.

perl
A scripting language often used to create scripts for Web servers.

variable
In programming, a placeholder for a value that can be reassigned based on user input or other changing conditions.

The rules set out by CGI are simple. The request to run the program is sent to the server as an HTTP request—inside an <A> tag (→**75**) or as a link from a form's Submit button (→**150**) or an image map (→**108**), the same way the browser calls any other file. Instead of providing a filename for the target, though, you provide the name of the **CGI script** you want to run.

Often, the browser will also need to send **variable** information to the program: information about the reader's input into a form or clicks on an image map, for example. CGI provides two easy ways to do that: via GET or POST. Using GET, the browser appends a question mark to the script name it sends to the server, followed by the values for any variables. On receiving the CGI request, the server launches the script and passes the variables to it. The GET method is the one you usually see used for simple applications such as image maps (→**108**). Using POST, the browser sends the variable information as a separate transmission. Using either method, the script, once called, carries out its process using the provided variables and spits out a file or file reference, all in the form specified by CGI, to send back to the browser.

Creating the CGI programs themselves can be quite simple or quite complicated. The programs can be written in any language that can be run on the server. For Unix servers, the most common language has been the Unix scripting language **perl**; for Windows servers, it's **Visual Basic**; for Macintoshes, **AppleScript** or **Frontier**. Programming languages, such as C++ or Java, can also be used. Prebuilt scripts for many commonly used functions, such as counting the number of hits on a Web page, are freely available over the Web. Others, such as systems for buying and selling on line, are available for purchase from Web software vendors. Programs that call for information from a proprietary database or for other custom needs must be written specifically for the task.

CGI works well for simple transactions—choosing from simple sets, activating appropriate links from image maps, returning the results of math functions, pulling information from or adding information to databases. Because all the processing takes place on the server, though, users are left waiting while the request is sent back to the server, the program runs, and the results are sent back. The wait can be even longer if there's a lot of processing to be done or if lots of people are depending on the server to process their responses all at once. The load on the server can also present problems for publishers, requiring them to provide a lot of expensive processing power and bandwidth. These considerations limit the kinds of interactivity possible using CGI. To avoid annoying waits and overtaxing the server, programmed transactions must be fairly simple, and their number must be kept to a minimum.

```perl
#!/usr/local/bin/perl
# Perl script to generate html for unread mail

$user = "demo";
$mbox = "/usr/spool/mail/$user";
$title = "Mail for $user";

# Subroutine to print out a mail message (called below)
sub print1Message {
        local($from, $subject) = @_;
{       print "<DT>From: $from ";
        if (defined($subject)) {
                print "<DD>Subject: $subject \n";
        }
}

# Static HTML title
print "Content-type: text/html\n\n";
print "<HEAD>\n<TITLE>$title</TITLE>\n</HEAD>\n";
print "<BODY>\n<H1>$title</H1>\n";
print "Here is a listing of mail we are storing for you:\n";

# Open the mailbox, if no mailbox file is found, indicate
open(MBOX, $mbox) || print "<B> \nNo Mailbox found</B>\n";

print "<DL>\n";

# Pull apart the mail headers, find "From:" and "Subject:"
# Call print1Message whenever a message separator is found
while ( <MBOX> ){
        if ( /^From:\s*(.*)/ && !defined($from)) {
                $from = $1;
        }
        if ( /^Subject:\s*(.*)/ && !defined($subject)) {
                $subject = $1;
        }
        if ( /^From \s*(.*)/ && defined($from)) {
                &print1Message($from, $subject);
                undef $from;
                undef $subject;
        }
}

# Print out the last message (if any)
if (defined($from)) {
        &print1Message($from, $subject);
}

print "</DL>\n</BODY>\n";
```

SCRIPTS can carry out simple programming tasks on the Web. This one, written in perl and suitable for access via CGI, looks for unread mail in the user's account and sends an HTML file listing the mail back to the client. Phrases preceded by # are comments—lines that are embedded in the script to explain its use to humans but aren't processed by the script interpreter.

AppleScript
A scripting language developed by Apple to offer a standard method of controlling Macintosh programs.

Frontier
A scripting language developed by UserLand, used as an alternative to AppleScript to script actions in Macintosh programs.

Visual Basic
A programming language developed by Microsoft especially for creating Windows programs.

Server-Side Processing

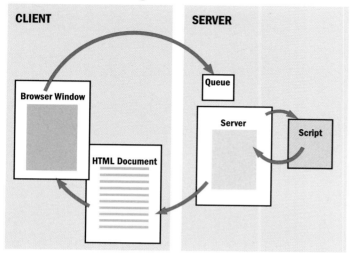

RUNNING PROGRAMS ON THE CLIENT
machine cuts several time-consuming steps from any interactive processing. User input and the script's output are saved the trip back and forth over the network, and doing the processing locally avoids overloading the server, which would otherwise need to handle requests for everyone using the site.

Client-Side Processing

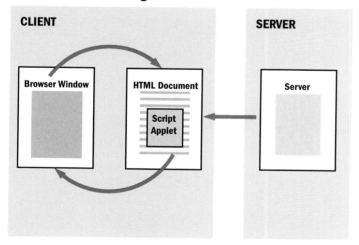

client-side processing
Running programs on an Internet client machine, rather than on a server.

Client-Side Processing

Toward the end of 1995, new technologies began appearing that took the load off CGI and opened up new possibilities for programming on the Web. These technologies featured **client-side processing**.

In client-side processing, programs are run right on each client's computer. Client-side scripts (→**166**) can reside inside the HTML file that uses them. Other client-side programs can reside on the server, like an HTML page, image, or any other file, to be called by a Web client when needed. (HTML 3.2's <OBJECT> tag, which we have already described as a way to download images (→**106**), has attributes specially designed for this task.) When the program code is sent, the client software adds any user-supplied variable information and runs the code on its own processor.

Running programs on the client side of the connection has several advantages. One is speed. Users no longer have to wait at their screens while the request makes its way to the server and the resulting files make their way back.

Another advantage is that client-side programming relieves the demands on the server. Processing requests no longer have to queue up and wait their turn on the server; they can use their own dedicated processor on the client machine.

These two advantages give client-side programs a lot of leeway for executing complex interactive tasks and make a compelling case for using client-side processing for any task that doesn't require access to resources, such as company databases, that can be accessed only by the server.

To run, client-side programs require support either in the client software or in the client machine's operating system. We'll talk about the prospects for that as we describe specific client-side technologies in the next sections of this chapter.

START TAG	ATTRIBUTES	END TAG	EXPLANATION
<OBJECT>		</OBJECT>	Inserts an object (e.g., an image, media file, or program) into the page
	align="left" OR "right" OR "center"		The alignment of the object in the window
	classid="class-identifier"		A unique identifier for the plug-in or program. (The syntax depends on the type of object being inserted.)
	codebase="URL"		The directory that holds the program
	codetype="MIME-type"		The MIME type of the program
	data="URL"		The URL for the object to be inserted
	height=n width=n		The height and width of the object, in pixels
	name="name"		A name by which other programs can refer to the object
	standby="text"		Text that displays while the object is loading
	type="MIME-type"		The object's MIME type. The browser uses this to determine whether it can display the object.
<PARAM>		</PARAM>	Used with the <OBJECT> or <APPLET> tag to pass parameter values to a program
	name="name"		The parameter the value should be assigned to
	value="value"		A value for the parameter
	valuetype="data" OR "ref" OR "object"		Describes how the value should be interpreted: as data (the default), as a URL (ref), or as the URL of an object in the same document (object)
	type="MIME-type"		The MIME type of the data

NATHAN ODLE
http://www.missouri.edu/~c670064

ONE POPULAR USE for JavaScript has been to create a "ticker-tape" that runs across the status bar of a browser window (above). The JavaScript code that creates the effect is shown at right.

JavaScript

A scripting language, developed by Netscape and Sun Microsystems, specialized for controlling Web browser processes.

JScript

A JavaScript-compatible scripting language developed and supported by Microsoft.

Visual Basic Scripting Edition

A scripting language based on Microsoft's Visual Basic program-ming language, specialized for con-trolling Web processes, ActiveX controls, and Java programs.

```
<Title>Nathan's Web World</Title>

<SCRIPT LANGUAGE="JavaScript">
/* Copyright (C)1996 Web Integration Systems, Inc. DBA Websys, Inc.
   All Rights Reserved.

   This applet can be re-used or modified, if credit is given in
   the source code.

   We will not be held responsible for any unwanted effects due to the
   usage of this applet or any derivative.  No warrantees for usability
   for any specific application are given or implied.

   Chris Skinner, January 30th, 1996.

   Modified by Nathan Odle for use with dynamic IP / login time
updater, 1996.
*/

var End=0
function scrollit_r21(seed)
{
End++
if (End < 1002){

          /* The following line is automagicly updated with the dynamic
IP / login
time updater */

          var msg = 'Your browser is tuned into...Nathan's Web World.
Nathan
is currently 128.206.206.54 on Thursday, September 26, 1996 / 4:47:34
PM';
          var out = ' ';
          var c   = 1;

      if (seed > 100) {
           seed--;
           var cmd='scrollit_r21(' + seed + ')';
           timerTwo=window.setTimeout(cmd,100);
      }
  else if (seed <= 100 && seed > 0) {
           for (c=0 ; c < seed ; c++) {
                out+=" ";
           }
           out+=msg;
           seed--;
           var cmd='scrollit_r21(' + seed + ')';
              window.status=out;
           timerTwo=window.setTimeout(cmd,100);
      }
      else if (seed <= 0) {
           if (-seed < msg.length) {
                out+=msg.substring(-seed,msg.length);
                seed--;
                var cmd='scrollit_r21(' + seed + ')';
                window.status=out;
                timerTwo=window.setTimeout(cmd,100);
           }
           else {
                window.status=' ';
timerTwo=window.setTimeout('scrollit_r21(100)',75);
           }
      }
   }
}
// -- End of JavaScript code ------------- -->
</SCRIPT>

<BODY onLoad='timerONE=window.setTimeout('scrollit_r21(100)',1000);'
background="pattern5.jpg" BgCOLOR="#000000" text="#DBDBB1"
link="#DBDBB1"
vlink="#DBDBB1">
```

Client-Side Scripting: JavaScript and Visual Basic Scripting Edition

The simplest form of client-side processing is offered by client-side scripting languages such as **JavaScript**, codeveloped by Netscape and Sun Microsystems, and **Visual Basic Scripting Edition** (often called Visual Basic Script or VBScript) developed by Microsoft. These languages were created specially to let Web programmers handle common Web tasks without depending on the server. JavaScript, for instance, has built-in commands for controlling the navigation and appearance of browser windows, checking for plug-ins, and other actions that make it especially useful on the Web. (Additional features can be defined by the programmer.) JavaScript also offers commands designed to allow Web authors to control the behavior of applications built with Java (→**168**). Visual Basic Script has similar capabilities but is designed to integrate with ActiveX controls (→**173**), built with Microsoft's Visual Basic programming language, as well as with Java programs.

Client-side scripts can be embedded, using the <SCRIPT> tag, right in the HTML file that uses them so that they are available for immediate processing. With the latest versions of JavaScript, programers can also save their programs in separate files on the server, where they are accessible to multiple Web pages.

Most important browser manufacturers had support for JavaScript built into their software by mid-1996. (Microsoft has created and supports a work-alike scripting language it calls JScript.) When we wrote this, Netscape had not announced any plans to support Visual Basic Script, but Microsoft (of course), Oracle (maker of a popular browser for corporate intranets) and Spyglass (manufacturer of browser software technologies for lots of individual browser manufacturers) had.

The <NOSCRIPT> tag lets authors embed alternate content for browsers that don't understand scripts. Browsers that do understand scripts also understand the <NOSCRIPT> and </NOSCRIPT> tags and so will ignore any HTML code enclosed between them.

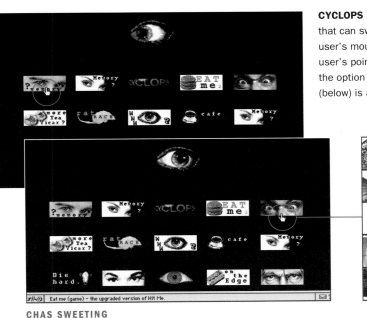

CYCLOPS is a sort of showcase for a JavaScript feature that can swap out images based on the position of a user's mouse. The eye at the top of the page follows the user's pointer, while readouts in the status bar describe the option to which it currently points. The Eat Me game (below) is an interactive puzzle created with the language.

CHAS SWEETING
http://www.utopia.com.my/utopia/future/future.shtml

KEVIN GIAMBRA
http://www.netcom.com/~kmgkmg/my1frame.html

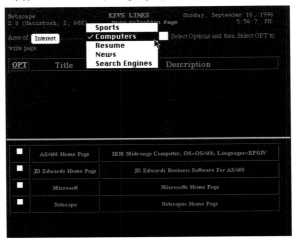

JAVASCRIPT can process input from form controls, such as this drop-down menu, immediately. No Submit button is required.

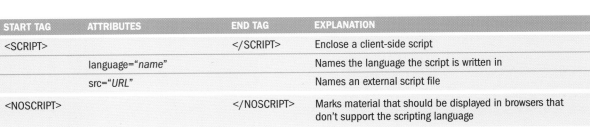

START TAG	ATTRIBUTES	END TAG	EXPLANATION
<SCRIPT>		</SCRIPT>	Enclose a client-side script
	language="*name*"		Names the language the script is written in
	src="*URL*"		Names an external script file
<NOSCRIPT>		</NOSCRIPT>	Marks material that should be displayed in browsers that don't support the scripting language

Security for Client-Side Processing

The client-side processing used by Java, ActiveX, JavaScript, and Visual Basic Scripting Edition is a breakthrough for Web programmers aiming for more extensive programming possibilities, but it's also ringing some alarms among Web users and system administrators worried about the security of files on the client machines.

When you think about it, downloading programs to run on your own computer is a risky business. The same capabilities that let local programs carry out useful functions can also be used to plant viruses or play "practical jokes" like erasing your hard disk. Some Web users are also worried about the ability of client-side programs to dig around their systems and send information about them, undetected, back to distant Web sites.

To answer these concerns, Sun Microsystems, the developer of Java, built certain limitations into the language. (All the same limitations also apply to JavaScript.) Programs written with Java cannot read files from or write files to the client computer's disks, can't run other programs, and can't make any network connections, except back to the server that sent them. Even so, researchers testing whether these limitations actually make Java completely safe have found several ways to get around these barriers to cause troubles on client machines or gain information about the users' systems. Each new security hole is generally plugged quickly, with Sun revising the language and browser manufacturers issuing updated versions of their browsers.

ActiveX and Visual Basic Script use a different security approach. Instead of hobbling ActiveX applications by restricting their access to the client computer's file systems, Microsoft has instituted a security system based on "code signing," which allows readers to find out who wrote each downloadable program and verify that it has not been tampered with since the developer put its seal on it. Code-signing ensures that practical jokers can't intercept software to carry out their own nefarious agendas, but it doesn't really safeguard against faulty or mischievous software.

The question of how safe client-side programming actually is has yet to be finally determined. Further testing and enhancements will doubtless be carried out before software makers finally determine the best methods for safeguarding users' systems.

Java
A cross-platform programming language developed by Sun Microsystems.

Java Virtual Machine
A software layer that executes compiled Java code. The existence of the "virtual machine" is the key to Java's cross-platform capabilities.

Java

JavaScript is great for controlling HTML functions and HTTP events. Going beyond such tasks, though, requires a stronger, less specialized tool—a programming language such as **Java**. A cross-platform programming language developed by Sun Microsystems, Java was a breakthrough for Web publishing because it offers client-side processing (→**164**) in a full-featured programming language. Unlike traditional programming languages, which require compiling separate versions of a program for each machine it is to run on, Java programs can be compiled just once to run on a **Java Virtual Machine**—a software base that acts as a Java-specific processor. The ability to run, just like HTML, on any computer makes Java a natural for creating applications that are to be distributed over the Web.

You don't have to be a Java programmer to use Java, and most Web designers will never tangle with the language directly. Premade Java programs are available freely on the Web and from commercial distributors. A central Java program repository, called Gamelan, was offering access to over 3,000 Java programs by mid-1996, in categories such as Arts and Entertainment (Java games, drawing applications, even a Java piano you can play from your computer keyboard), Special Effects (e.g., animated text and graphic banners), and Utilities (calculators, calendars, and clocks for Web page, and the like).

IN THIS JAVA-BASED Othello game users move their own pieces and the Web site responds with its move.

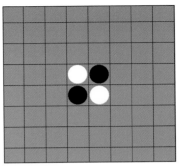 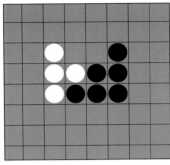 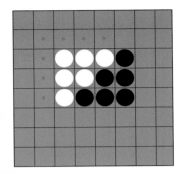

DAVID ENGLER, DAVID COPPIT, SEAN McCULLOCH/UNIVERSITY OF VIRGINIA
http://www.cs.virginia.edu/~dae4e/java/jothello

OPTIONS on Suck's Java-based menu light up as the user's pointer passes over them.

JOEY ANUFF/CARL STEADMAN
http://www.suck.com

THE JEROME WEISNER SITE at MIT's Media Lab uses Java to create a dynamic interface. Clicking on a tile in the grid calls up a custom menu of topics. Clicking on one of the topics brings it to the top of the list and displays the related text in the right-hand frame.

MICHAEL MURTAUGH/M.I.T. MEDIA LAB INTERACTIVE CINEMA GROUP
http://ic.www.media.mit.edu/JBW/

START TAG	ATTRIBUTES	END TAG	EXPLANATION
<APPLET>		</APPLET>	Embeds a Java applet in the page
	align="left" OR "center" OR "right"		The alignment of the applet's output in the window
	alt="text"		Text that will be displayed if the applet doesn't load correctly
	code="URL"		The name of the Java applet
	codebase="URL"		The directory the applet is stored in
	height=n, width=n		The height and width of the applet's output, in pixels
	hspace=n		The horizontal space, in pixels, set between the applet's and surrounding text
	name="name"		A name by which other applets on the page can refer to this one
	vspace=n		The vertical space, in pixels, set between the applet's output and surrounding text

Java is fabulous: It's smooth-running, wonderful, and fun. The reason we haven't done a lot with it yet is that not every browser supports it—that and our deadlines. Java programming takes time.

ANDREA JENKINS, CNET

applet
Small Java programs designed to be distributed over the Net.

Like all client-side technologies, Java programs work only if the right support software is present on the machine they're sent to. Java support has been built into Netscape's browser software starting with version 2.0 and in Microsoft's starting with version 3.0. Most other browser manufacturers will have it built in by the end of 1996.

Major operating system vendors, including Microsoft and Apple, have also announced plans to support Java directly in their operating systems, meaning that Java can also be used to write general-purpose programs such as word processors and spreadsheets. Sun has even announced plans to release a full operating system built with Java. To make matters more confusing, Java applications can even be used to create other Java programs. For the purposes of the Web, however, Java's importance is as a language for creating small, focused programs, referred to as Java **applets**, that carry out particular operations within Web pages.

Calling programs from Web pages was one of those areas not covered by the original HTML specifications and, so, was dealt with ad hoc by browser manufacturers as they added the capabilities to their software. The <APPLET> tag was introduced for the task by Netscape with version 2.0 of its browser, and that method has been picked up by every browser that supports Java. In newer browsers, Java applets can also be called with the <OBJECT> tag (→**164**).

VIRTUAL DESIGN GROUP
http://www.virtual-design.com/cgi-bin/voodoo.pl

SADISTS AT VIRTUAL DESIGN,
a Web design company in Atlanta,
Georgia, created Virtual Voodoo, a
Java applet that lets you manipulate
knives, candles, and pins to torture
a stand-in for your enemies.

SPANQ
http://spanq.com/

SPANQ uses Java to create
an animated home page.

Java is everything it's cracked up to be and more. It's a new operating system. It's awesome. We're in this completely new medium with great tools and no rules. Now it's up to us to figure out what to do with them.

JONATHAN NELSON, ORGANIC ONLINE

Web developers have been excited by Java's promise since it was introduced in March of 1995, but so far, the hype has been greater than the results. The distance between hype and reality has been due partly to the wait for reliable Java support to be built into the client software. Another shortcoming has been a lack of application development tools that would make it easier for programmers to create Java programs. As we wrote this, though, the wait seemed to be coming to an end. All these ingredients should be in place by early 1997, and when the kinks are worked out, Java should become as important as the hype around it would have us believe.

EURO-RSCG/JOAO SERRANO/NEURONIO
http://expo98.pt/en/java/relogio/relogio.shtml

THE SITE for Lisbon's EXPO '98 uses Java to count the days, hours, minutes, and seconds till the expo opens.

ActiveX

In early 1996, Microsoft announced its own programming technology for the Web, called **ActiveX**. ActiveX is an extension of Microsoft's popular **OLE** (Object Linking and Embedding) technology, invented several years ago as a way to tie application programs together (Microsoft uses it within its Office suite—Microsoft Word, Excel, PowerPoint, and so on—to make it possible to open one program's files from within another's). ActiveX simply adds Internet hooks to this idea.

ActiveX controls are small ActiveX programs that act like plug-ins (→**11**) or Java applets (→**168**) to add new capabilities to ActiveX-compatible programs such as Microsoft's browser. Like OLE, ActiveX will be supported in all of Microsoft's Office applications as well as in its Internet Explorer, and Netscape has announced plans to support ActiveX in version 4.0 of its browser and other software. Meanwhile, at least a couple of other companies have introduced plug-ins that add ActiveX support to Navigator and other plug-in-compatible browsers.

Like Java programs, ActiveX controls can carry out pretty much any kind of task, from single processes such as running an animation, to complete applications. The first set of ActiveX controls, supplied with Microsoft's Internet Explorer version 3.0, let users create buttons that show their state (selected, clicked, and so on), use AVI video frames for animation,

FUTUREWAVE provides a player for its FutureSplash interactive animation format both as an ActiveX control and as a plug-in. Both players provide all the same functions, but the ActiveX control version (playing the interactive resumé shown here) can be automatically downloaded when needed, a capability not yet available for plug-ins.

MICROSOFT has created a sample set of ActiveX controls for use in designing Web sites. (They're available free from Microsoft's Web page.) This sample demonstrates a pop-up menu control.

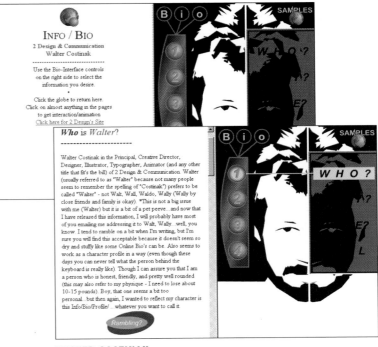

WALTER COSTINAK
http://www.futurewave.com/demosite/bio_main.htm

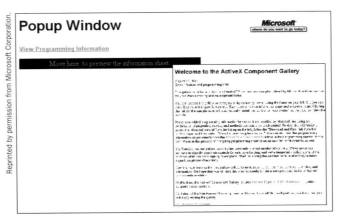

http://www.microsoft.com/activex/gallery/

ActiveX
Microsoft's set of technologies for Web programming.

ActiveX control
A program, based on ActiveX technology, that adds new features to an ActiveX-compatible program.

OLE
Object Linking and Embedding, Microsoft's technology for letting applications interoperate. OLE is the basis of Microsoft's ActiveX technology.

http://www.microsoft.com/ie/most/howto/layout/volcano/beans.htm

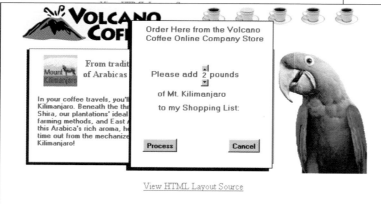

COMPLEX LAYOUTS based on ActiveX interactivity (above) can be created using Microsoft's ActiveX Control Pad (right). The Control Pad offers a graphic interface for laying out ActiveX controls and embedding them in HTML pages.

create and display a variety of chart types, use gradient color blends, display text at a variety of angles, play Microsoft PowerPoint animations, and set a special "New" icon to display until a given date within a Web page. ActiveX controls are embedded in HTML documents through the <OBJECT> tag (→**164**).

As with Java, most Web designers and publishers will probably not program custom ActiveX controls, but instead will use commercial and shareware ActiveX objects within their Web pages. Microsoft hosts a page on its Web site devoted to distributing freeware and commercial ActiveX controls from a variety of developers.

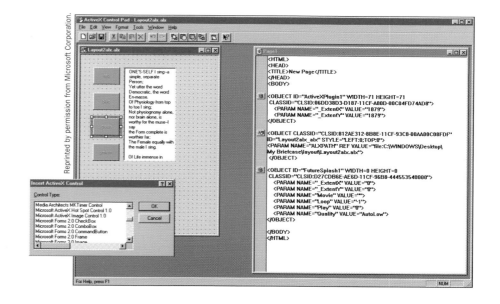

Do You Need to Be a Programmer?

CGI, client-side scripting, Java, and ActiveX provide Web publishers with a virtually unlimited array of possibilities for Web pages, but they also present a daunting barrier to Web designers who have no programming skills and no wish to acquire them. As we mentioned earlier, most Web designers won't need to get into the nitty-gritty of Java and ActiveX programming, and will, instead, simply plug existing applications into their pages using the <OBJECT> tag. Yet even the scripting languages—JavaScript, Visual Basic Script, and those used for CGI scripts—require some understanding of basic programming syntax. Products like Microsoft's ActiveX Control Pad (→**174**), FutureTense's Texture (→**124**), and Power Production Software's WebBurst (→**141**) point the way to a new generation of tools that will hide the programming steps from the user, but those programs have some way to go before they can do everything through a graphic interface that a programmer can do dealing directly with code.

You can always, of course, eschew programming altogether. As we mentioned earlier, HTML provides a complete set of hypertext publishing tools without it. But if you want to create full-featured Web pages, you'll probably need to have someone on your team who won't mind writing the occasional script.

Online: Programming the Web

ActiveX
http://www.activex.org

ActiveX Controls
http://www.microsoft.com/activex/controls/

CGI
http://hoohoo.ncsa.uiuc.edu/cgi/intro.html
http://www.yahoo.com/Computers_and_Internet/Internet/
   World_Wide_Web/CGI_Common_Gateway_Interface/

Java
http://java.sun.com/
http://www.javaworld.com/javaworld/jw-06-1996/jw-06-vm.html

Java Applets
http://www.gamelan.com

Java Security
http://java.sun.com/sfaq/

JavaScript
http://www.netscape.com/comprod/products/navigator/
   version_3.0/building_blocks/jscript/index.html
http://home.netscape.com/eng/mozilla/3.0/handbook/
   javascript/index.html
http://www.freqgrafx.com/411/tutorial.html

JScript
http://www.microsoft.com/jscript/

Visual Basic Scripting Edition
http://www.microsoft.com/vbscript/

Keeping the
Site Fresh

Designing for Change

Contracting for Change

Imagine publishing in a medium where nothing is ever final, where mistakes can be fixed and new information can be published within minutes of hearing it, where ideas can be tested and discarded—or built upon—as soon as you test your audience's reaction to them, and to which readers can return time and time again and find new information at each visit. That's the world of the Web. For many designers, it's a world that takes a little getting used to, but understanding the fast pace of the Web is an important key to success in the medium.

On the Web, changing information, even after publication, is easily done. Unlike print, CD-ROM, video, or any other form of publishing, Web publications are never really "final." Making changes requires changing only one copy—the original on the server—and a simple change can be made, and be available to the reader, within moments.

Web publications continue to live and breathe after they're published. Changes aren't limited to refinements on the original content, though that's one benefit you'll quickly learn to appreciate (no more living with the embarrassing mistakes that can haunt you for years in print publications). You can post new features in response to reader requests, add new content as your company grows or launches new products, decorate your site for the holidays—even post content that changes minute by minute. Perhaps most importantly, though, Web publications, like magazines, need to constantly refresh their look and their content, both to stay up to date and to keep their readers interested and coming back for more.

The swift-moving pace of design technology is another strong impetus to completely revamp a Web site's design as often as every few months. In other media, the set of possible effects remains fairly constant, and technological advances mostly affect the ease with which those effects can be achieved. On the Web, new advances every few months completely change the way graphics, colors, sounds, and other media can be used, and Web sites that haven't changed in six months can look creaky and dated. There's every indication that the pace will accelerate rather than slow down over the next year or so. (In fact, our greatest quandary in planning this book has been the knowledge that our illustrations will seem dated by the time it hits the shelves.)

This capability for continuous change and refinement can't be overlooked when planning a Web site; it has repercussions for how you design your site, what features you include, and how you plan your contracts with clients or the scheduling and staffing requirements for in-house projects. In this final chapter, we'll go through some of the ways you can plan for and take advantage of this unique quality of the Web.

A "WHAT'S NEW" SECTION is a popular way to highlight new content on a site. At the Internet Underground Music Archive, a What's Brewin' button sends users to a list of upcoming events and new recordings.

BRANDEE AMBER SELCK
http://www.iuma.com/IUMA-2.0/brew/

I have this sign on my computer: "Process not product." When I first started working on the Web, I was so depressed. I was used to the print medium, where you would get to this moment of relief; you could open the final product and be done. Then I learned to change my attitude about the work.

SABINE MESSNER, HOTWIRED

LEADING WEB SITES change their look regularly to take advantage of what they've learned from reader responses and from their own hard-won experience, as well as new technology.

1996

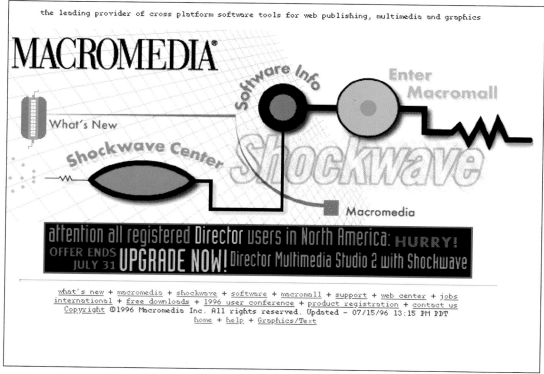

MACROMEDIA
http://www.macromedia.com/

1995

When you're developing the look of a magazine, it's a really big deal to change something about it. On the Web, it's not, and we can experiment. In fact, we should feel responsible to experiment and push the possibilities forward.

BARBARA KUHR, HOTWIRED

1996

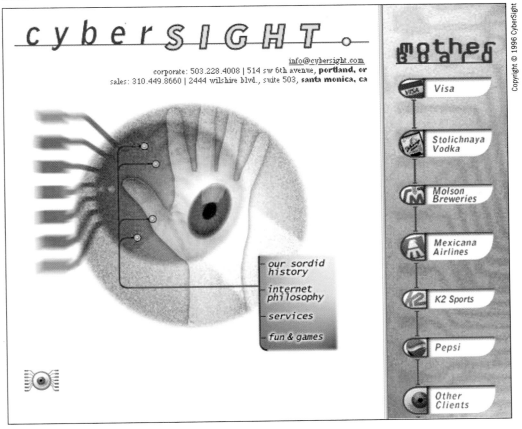

PETER BRAY/JOE WAKER
http://www.cybersight.com/

The idea is that you have to keep the information current, so you have repeated opportunities to redesign. Sometimes we say to our clients, "Here's what you can do now; here's something we may be able to do in the future."

JONATHAN NELSON, ORGANIC ONLINE

1995

1990 . . .

► NOV 1990
**World Wide Web
invented**

1993

► SPRING 1993
Mosaic
First graphical browser

1994

► FALL 1994
Netscape Navigator 1.0
JPEG support, simulta-
neous download of text
and images

1995

► SPRING 1995
Netscape Navigator 1.1
background colors, table
layouts, server push

► SUMMER 1995
**Microsoft Internet
Explorer 1.0**
font face and color

RealAudio
streaming audio

► WINTER 1995–1996
Netscape Navigator 2.0
Java, JavaScript, plug-ins,
frames, animated GIF

1996

► JAN 1996
Shockwave
Interactive multimedia
on Web pages

► SPRING 1996
VRML 2.0
Interactive 3-D

► SUMMER 1996
Liquid Reality/WebBurst
WYSIWYG Java animation tools

**Microsoft Internet
Explorer 3.0**
ActiveX controls, style sheets

► **Netscape Navigator 3.0**
Column layouts, streaming
QuickTime and VRML plug-ins

► FALL 1996
WebTV
Set-top boxes to receive Web
pages on TV

1997?

► **Frame-based layouts**
Layered page layouts created
via style sheets

► **Style sheet–based Web
layout applications**
Reliable, exact page layout
based on HTML style sheets,
created through WYSIWYG
applications

► **Adobe Vertigo**
Object-oriented animation and
graphics in Java

► **The Internet desktop**
Internet access built into desktop software

► **Cable modems**
High-bandwidth access from
the home

► **Interactive 3-D authoring**
WYSIWYG tools for interactive
VRML

► **Distributed applications**
Object-oriented programs for
interactive Web sites

NEW WEB DESIGN TECHNOLOGIES started
exploding after the invention of Mosaic, the first
graphical browser, in 1993. As the importance
of the Web as a publishing medium became
more apparent, software companies vied to
create tools. The pace of development was
explosive in 1996 and will continue to be so
for the foreseeable future. Keeping your Web
pages au courant requires constant study of
new technologies and rethinking your sites to
take advantage of them.

Designing for Change

Now that you know your site will be a living and breathing entity, your first task is making sure it has room to breathe. When we talked about structuring a site (→**53**), we discussed the need to plan for change by setting up departments that could house categories of content rather than a particular piece of information. Planning for change has other aspects as well. Careful up-front thinking about your site's directory structure and filenames will ensure that files will be easy to find and weed out at update time. Considering the maintenance effects of every decision will guard against implementing solutions—such as different versions of your page for each type of browser—that will be too costly or time-consuming to keep up over the long run. Technology can also help you automate the updating of your site. Java, ActiveX, and Unix file-management programs can be set up to swap out pages, or portions of pages, on regular schedules. Sites that offer product information or other data from company databases can take advantage of the database's features to churn out up-to-date HTML-formatted pages in various views.

In "Interactivity" we talked about ways to use HTML forms (→**150**) and the *mailto* feature (→**149**) to elicit feedback from readers. Wise designers take advantage of these features to create a partnership with readers in the ongoing development of the site. You

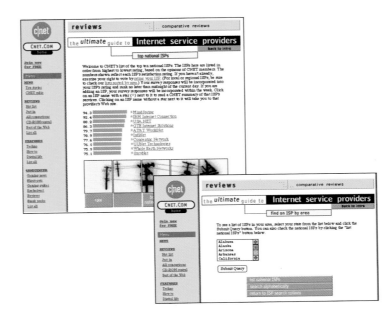

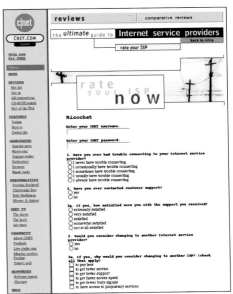

DATABASE-DRIVEN PAGES can be updated with each click of the visitor's mouse. CNET's comparative review of Internet Service Providers keeps a running tally of the top-rated ISPs in the country, based on users' own ratings (top). Readers can search the listings for the top-rated services in their own area (center) and add their own ratings to the database (right).

CNET
http://www.cnet.com/Content/ Reviews/Compare/ISP/

The bigger the site, the less often you need to change it. You could plot it on a matrix: the size of the Web site against the frequency of change. A site like Joe Boxer, a 400-page site, we change once every two months. The average user spends 9 to 15 minutes on the site, so it will take them awhile to work through everything that's up there.

STEFAN FIELDING-ISAACS, ART & SCIENCE

User FeedBack

This form allows you to send us your feedback about this server. All the items of this form are optionnal but we would appreciate any advice from you the users to improve this service.

☐☐General Information

Society: [   ]   Name: [   ]

Address:

```
┌──────────────────────────────┐⇧
│                              │
│                              │
│                              │⇩
└──────────────────────────────┘
◄ ▓                          ►
```

Tel: [   ]   Fax: [   ]

E-Mail: [   ]

Could you specify your opinion for the following items:

☐☐Service Information

Service usefulness:

○ Good ○ Medium ○ Bad ○ No Opinion

Easiness for access to information:

○ Good ○ Medium ○ Bad ○ No Opinion

Ease of use:

○ Good ○ Medium ○ Bad ○ No Opinion

☐☐Technology

Transfer Data Time:

○ Good ○ Medium ○ Bad ○ No Opinion

Usefulness of WWW facilities for this service:

○ Good ○ Medium ○ Bad ○ No Opinion

☐☐Overall Opinion

Could you indicate any other remarks you may have concerning this service:

```
┌──────────────────────────────┐⇧
│ |                            │
│                              │
│                              │
│                              │
│                              │⇩
└──────────────────────────────┘
◄ ▓                          ►
```

[Submit] [Reset]

ACRI
http://acri.cica.fr/CEO/cz_interests.html

Server Stats: Gathering Intelligence Behind the Scenes

Direct feedback from readers in the form of e-mail and HTML forms is just one way to find out what's working the way you want it to, and what isn't, on your site. You can also use software on the server to compile site-usage statistics that report what pages are visited most often and from what domains the visitors are arriving. Such statistics can provide valuable information about whether readers are using your site as you expected and whether the pages you want your readers to see are actually getting attention. It's a kind of information available from no other medium.

can use these methods to elicit feedback that will help you learn what works and what doesn't work on the site and to find out what readers want to see more of. It's become a common feature of many sites to have a *mailto* feedback link at the bottom of every page, encouraging readers to mail off their impressions as soon as they think of them. Using a form instead of *mailto* at the link allows publishers to pre-sort reader comments into categories, depending on the way the mail will be handled when it is received. Requests for new content can be sent to one mailbox, reports of broken links to another, for example. A series of questions can elicit the specific information the publisher is most interested in getting. If you have questions about your readers' preferences, put those into a feedback form. Visitors are usually happy to answer them, knowing that their answers will go toward creating a site that will more closely suit their needs.

The knowledge that change is inevitable and feedback will be swift also frees designers to take some chances they might not take in a less elastic medium. Trying a new layout, button design, department title, front page, or any novel approach has fewer risks on a Web site than in any other medium. If it doesn't work, your readers will let you know, and you can change it at great speed and comparatively little cost.

Contracting for Change

For freelance designers, the lack of an irrevocable end to their responsibilities—traditionally provided by the printing of the job—can lead to some confusing situations between the design shop and the client unless it is wisely prepared for. Above all, designers should make sure that the extent of their responsibilities is spelled out in the contract and understood by all parties. Knowing something about the evolutionary process of Web sites can help craft a contract that meets both the designer's and the client's needs.

The first order of business is to make sure both parties understand the need for **design specifications** and **design templates**, documents that are drawn up to explain and codify decisions made during the initial design process. Such specifications spell out things such as what font sizes, colors, and special fonts are used, and under what conditions. For a Web publication, these documents might also specfiy HTML coding styles (e.g., "all HTML tags typed in uppercase" or "all text paragraphs coded as <BLOCKQUOTE>"). Such documents will help the production department and any designers that do work on future editions of the site keep the look of the site consistent as it evolves. In the days when production departments and typesetters carried out a designer's plans, such written specifications were a common part of a designer's contract, but they are rarer now that

designers do their own production using desktop publishing. Creating a good set of specifications can take significant time and skill, in addition to the time and skill needed to create the design itself, and designers should make sure their contracts include sufficient payment for this extra step.

Designers should also be sure that their clients expect and have a plan for dealing with the inevitable design feedback that will occur once the site is on line. If the contract is not clear, clients may expect the designers to fix "mistakes" pointed out by visitors to the site. In some cases, that may be appropriate, of course, but in many others, the "mistake" may simply be one reader's opinion. A helpful way of dealing with the situation is to expect a certain number of requests for revisions and include a price for changes after publication in your bid.

New design work will also be required, of course, when new types of content are added to the site over time. Some sites will be taken over by in-house teams after the initial edition is complete, but some designers may want to be involved in the continued development of the sites they design. Having a hand in the evolution of your own design can be a great opportunity to learn about what works and doesn't work in Web design, as well as a way to make sure that work you're proud of doesn't deteriorate once it leaves your hands.

Of course, the constant change required of Web sites can create exciting opportunities as well as a few contractual pitfalls. No other medium gives designers a chance to experiment so freely with new approaches; collaborate so closely with their readers; know so surely, from instant feedback, what works and what doesn't in their designs; be so close to the forefront of the newest communication technology; and pioneer, so excitingly, new approaches to communicating in a brand new, interactive, animated medium.

Welcome to the World Wide Web.

design specifications
Documentation showing what design styles (typeface, size, indentation, and so forth) are to be used for each element of a publication.

design templates
Electronic documents that serve as starting points for new files. Templates include standard elements, styled according to the design specifications, that can be used or copied as a model for similar elements in the publication.

HTML
Reference

This quick reference to HTML lists the common tags you'll use to take advantage of the Web design features we've described in this book. Rather than providing a comprehensive guide to the language (as if that were possible, given its constant change), we focus here on the tags designers depend on most, in the versions most widely adopted. The tags are arranged in alphabetical order for quick access, and page references show where you can find more information about the tag or attribute in the book.

To use HTML wisely, you'll also need to know what kind of support each tag has in leading browsers (→**72**). The only way to really know whether a tag is supported in a particular browser is to test it with that software, but the Support column in this reference should help.

Many tag attributes are optional, but some attributes must be included whenever the tag is used. In this list, we've marked those with a bullet (•) preceding the attribute name.

While this table can help you quickly find the syntax for many useful tags, there are a few basic rules of HTML coding you'll need to bone up on before creating Web files. A list of online destinations at the end of this reference points out helpful resources.

START TAG	ATTRIBUTES	END TAG	EXPLANATION	SUPPORT	SEE PAGE
<A>		</A>	Creates a hyperlink	HTML 2.0	75–6
	• href="*URL*"		The file to be called by the hyperlink	HTML 2.0	75–6
	name=*name*		Names a section of an HTML document. That name can then be used in the *href=* attribute of another <A> tag.	HTML 2.0	
	target="*frame*" OR "_blank" OR "_parent" OR "_self" OR "_top"		Used with frames, names a frame or window in which the file should be displayed	EXT	96
<APPLET>		</APPLET>	Embeds a Java applet in the page	HTML 3.2	170
	align="left" OR "right" OR "top" OR "middle" OR "bottom"		The alignment of the applet's output in the window	HTML 3.2	
	alt="*text*"		Text that will be displayed if the applet doesn't load correctly	HTML 3.2	
	• code="*URL*"		The name of the Java applet	HTML 3.2	
	codebase="*URL*"		The directory the applet is stored in	HTML 3.2	
	• height=*n*, width=*n*		The height and width of the applet's output, in pixels	HTML 3.2	
	hspace=*n*, vspace=*n*		The horizontal and vertical space, in pixels, set between the applet and surrounding text	HTML 3.2	
	name="*name*"		A name by which other applets on the page can refer to this one	HTML 3.2	
<AREA>			Creates a hyperlink area within a client-side image map created with the <MAP> tag	HTML 3.2	110
	alt="*text*"		Text to be displayed in nongraphics browsers	HTML 3.2	
	• coords="*coord1, coord2, coord3 . . .*"		The coordinates of the area's boundaries. (Each shape has its own rules for specifying coordinates.)	HTML 3.2	
	href="*URL*"		The URL of the linked file	HTML 3.2	
	nohref		Defines the area as having no hyperlink	HTML 3.2	
	shape="rect" OR "circle" OR "poly"		The type of shape being defined	HTML 3.2	
	target="*frame*" OR "_blank" OR "_parent" OR "_self" OR "_top"		Used with frames, names a frame or window in which the linked file should be displayed	EXT	96
<B>		</B>	Marks text to be set in boldface type	HTML 2.0	85
<BASEFONT>			Names default font settings (used in the head of an HTML document)	EXT	
	color="#*RRGGBB*" OR "*name*"		A color for the text, using an RGB value expressed in hexadecimal or a color name	EXT	114
	face="*name*"		The name of a typeface	EXT	82

HTML 2.0
HTML 2.0, pretty much universally supported in graphical browsers

HTML 3.2
Part of HTML 3.2 specification, supported by major browsers or likely to be supported soon

EXT
An extension to HTML 2.0 supported by both Netscape and Microsoft, but not part of HTML 3.2

NSN
A Netscape extension that has not (so far) been supported by Microsoft

MSIE
A Microsoft extension that has not (so far) been supported by Netscape

START TAG	ATTRIBUTES	END TAG	EXPLANATION	SUPPORT	SEE PAGE
	size="*size*"		A type size, from 1 to 7; 3 is the default. The number can be an absolute number from 1 to 7 or relative size from –1 to +3.	NSN	
<BGSOUND>		</BGSOUND>	Plays a .wav (sound) file when the file is loaded	MSIE	146
	loop=*n* OR "infinite"		The number of times the sound clip will loop	MSIE	
	• src="*URL*"		The URL of the sound file	MSIE	
<BIG>		</BIG>	Marks text to be set in a large size	HTML 3.2	85
<BLOCKQUOTE>		</BLOCKQUOTE>	Marks text to be set as an indented quotation	HTML 2.0	84-7
<BODY>		</BODY>	Marks the text to be displayed in the browser window	HTML 2.0	69
	alink="*#RRGGBB*" OR "*name*"		A color for the active links (links being clicked on), using an RGB value expressed in hexadecimal or a color name	HTML 3.2	90, 113
	background="*URL*"		A graphics file to be used as the background	HTML 3.2	113
	bgcolor="*#RRGGBB*" OR "*name*"		A background color	HTML 3.2	113
	bgproperties="fixed"		Specifies that the background image should not scroll	MSIE	
	leftmargin=*n*		Sets a left margin, described as a number of pixels	MSIE	91
	link="*#RRGGBB*" OR "*name*"		A color for hyperlink anchors	HTML 3.2	90, 113
	text="*#RRGGBB*" OR "*name*"		A color for nonlinked text	HTML 3.2	90, 113
	topmargin=*n*		Sets a left margin, described as a number of pixels	MSIE	91
	vlink="*#RRGGBB*" OR "*name*"		A color for visited links	HTML 3.2	90, 113
** **			Creates a line break	HTML 2.0	
<CENTER>		</CENTER>	Marks elements that should be centered in the window	HTML 3.2	89-91
<CITE>		</CITE>	Marks text that should be set as a citation	HTML 2.0	85
<CODE>		</CODE>	Marks text that should be set as computer code	HTML 2.0	85
<DD>		</DD>	Marks text that should be set as a definition in a definition list (used with <DL> and <DT>)	HTML 2.0	84
<DFN>		</DFN>	Marks text that should be set as a definition	HTML 3.2	85
<DIR>		</DIR>	Creates a columnar list (up to 20 items)	HTML 2.0	84
<DIV>		</DIV>	Groups a set of elements, applying the attributes to all of them	HTML 3.2	
	align="left" OR "right" OR "center"		The alignment of the elements in the division		
<DL>		</DL>	Creates a definition list	HTML 2.0	84

START TAG	ATTRIBUTES	END TAG	EXPLANATION	SUPPORT	SEE PAGE
\<DT>		\</DT>	Marks text that should be set as a term in a definition list (used with \<DL> and \<DD>)	HTML 2.0	84
\<EM>		\</EM>	Marks text that should be emphasized	HTML 2.0	85
\<EMBED>		\</EMBED>	Embeds a plug-in or ActiveX control into the page	EXT	
	height=*n*, width=*n*		The height and width of the media, in pixels	EXT	
	name="*name*"		A name by which other objects can refer to this one	EXT	
	param="*value*"		Values to be passed to any parameters of the program	EXT	
	• src="*URL*"		The file to be displayed by the plug-in or ActiveX control	EXT	
\<FONT>		\</FONT>	Marks text to be set with special font attributes	HTML 3.2	82
	color="*#RRGGBB*" OR "*name*"		A color for the text, using an RGB value expressed in hexadecimal or a color name	HTML 3.2	89, 114
	face="*name*"		The name of a typeface	EXT	82
	size="*size*"		A type size, from 1 to 7; 3 is the default. The number can be an absolute number from 1 to 7 or relative size from –1 to +3.	HTML 3.2	89, 114
\<FORM>		\</FORM>	Surround all the tags that create a fill-in form	HTML 2.0	150–3
	• action="*URL*"		The script that should be run, and that the form data should be sent to, when the user clicks the Submit button	HTML 2.0	150
	method="get" OR "post"		Specifies a method for sending the data to the server	HTML 2.0	
\<FRAME>		\</FRAME>	Specifies the attributes of an individual frame within a frameset	EXT	96–9
	frameborder=1 OR 0 or "yes" OR "no"		Sets a border (*1* or *yes*) or omits a border (*0* or *no*) around a frame. (Microsoft's browser uses the numbers, Netscape's the words.)	EXT	97
	marginheight=*n*		The space between frames, in pixels	EXT	
	marginwidth=*n*		Creates a margin within the frame (specified in pixels)	EXT	
	name="*name*"		A target name for the frame (used by \<A>and \<AREA> tags to send linked files to that particular frame)	EXT	
	noresize		Prevents users from resizing the frame (by omitting the resize box)	EXT	
	scrolling= "yes" OR "no" OR "auto"		Includes or omits a scrollbar for the frame. By default (or using "auto"), a scroll bar appears if the frame's contents go beyond its borders.	EXT	
	src="*URL*"		The URL of the file to be placed in the frame	EXT	

HTML 2.0
HTML 2.0, pretty much universally supported in graphical browsers

HTML 3.2
Part of HTML 3.2 specification, supported by major browsers or likely to be supported soon

EXT
An extension to HTML 2.0 supported by both Netscape and Microsoft, but not part of HTML 3.2

NSN
A Netscape extension that has not (so far) been supported by Microsoft

MSIE
A Microsoft extension that has not (so far) been supported by Netscape

START TAG	ATTRIBUTES	END TAG	EXPLANATION	SUPPORT	SEE PAGE
<FRAMESET>		</FRAMESET>	Marks the tags that make up a set of frames	EXT	96-9
	cols="*col1, col2, col3,...*"		Sets up a frameset as a set of "columns." The set of columns is specifed by giving a width for each one. Widths can be specified in pixels, as a percentage of the window size, or as an asterisk (*), meaning that the column should take up the remaining space. If more than one column is specified withan asterisk, the space is divided evenly among them.	EXT	98
	rows="*row1, row2, row3,...*"		Sets up a frameset as a set of "rows." The set of rows is specifed by giving a height for each one. Heights can be specified in pixels, as a percentage of the window size, or as an asterisk (*), meaning that the row should take up the remaining space. If more than one row is specified with an asterisk, the space is divided evenly among them.	EXT	98
	frameborder=1 OR 0 OR "yes" OR "no"		Sets a border (*1* or *yes*) or omits a border (*0* or *no*) around a frameset. (Microsoft's browser uses the numbers, Netscape's the words.)	EXT	97
<H1>		</H1>	Marks text as a level-1 head (the largest head size)	HTML 2.0	84
<H2>		</H2>	Marks text as a level-2 head	HTML 2.0	84
<H3>		</H3>	Marks text as a level-3 head	HTML 2.0	84
<H4>		</H4>	Marks text as a level-4 head	HTML 2.0	84
<H5>		</H5>	Marks text as a level-5 head	HTML 2.0	84
<H6>		</H6>	Marks text as a level-6 head	HTML 2.0	84
<HEAD>		</HEAD>	Marks the tags in the HTML document's head	HTML 2.0	69
<HR>			Creates a horizontal rule	HTML 2.0	84
	align= "left" OR "right" OR "center"		The alignment of the rule in the window	HTML 3.2	
	color="*#RRGGBB*" OR "*color*"		A color for the rule, specified as RGB values (in hexadecimal) or as a color name	MSIE	
	noshade		Omits the default 3D shading for the rule	HTML 3.2	
	size=*n*		The length of the rule, in pixels	HTML 3.2	
	width=*n*		The width of the rule, in pixels	HTML 3.2	
<HTML>		</HTML>	Labels the document as an HTML document (introduces all other HTML tags)	HTML 2.0	69
<I>		</I>	Marks text to be set in italic	HTML 2.0	85

START TAG	ATTRIBUTES	END TAG	EXPLANATION	SUPPORT	SEE PAGE
\<IMG>		\</IMG>	Inserts an image file or video clip into the page	HTML 2.0	106
	align="top" OR "middle" OR "bottom" OR "left" OR "right" OR "center"		The alignment of the image or video clip relative to surrounding text	HTML 3.2	91
	alt="*text*"		Text that will display in text-only browsers or if the graphic or video clip doesn't load correctly	HTML 2.0	107
	border=*n*		The width of the border, specified in pixels (defaults to *border=1*; *border=0* omits the border)	HTML 3.2	
	controls		Used with *dynsrc=*, displays video controls	MSIE	
	dynsrc="*URL*"		Specifies an AVI file to be inserted	MSIE	142
	height=*n*, width=*n*		The height and width of the image or video clip, in pixels	HTML 3.2	119–20
	hspace=*n*, vspace=*n*		The horizontal and vertical space, in pixels, set between the image or video clip and surrounding text	HTML 3.2	91
	ismap		Specifies that the image is a server-side image map	HTML 2.0	110–1
	loop=*n* OR "infinite"		Used with *dynsrc=*, the number of times the video clip will loop	MSIE	
	• src="*URL*"		The URL of the image to be inserted	HTML 2.0	
	start="fileopen" OR "mouseover"		Used with *dynsrc=*, the event that starts the video clip running	MSIE	
	usemap="#*name*"		Names the map to be used for a client-side image map. The name is the one specified by the *name=* attribute of the \<MAP> tag.	HTML 3.2	110–1
\<INPUT>			Creates input controls within a form	HTML 2.0	150–3
	type="text" OR "button" OR "checkbox" OR "radio" OR "submit" OR "image" OR "reset" OR "hidden"		In an HTML form, the type of control to be created	HTML 2.0	152
	checked		For *type=checkbox* or *type=radio*, specifies that the box or button should be chosen as a default	HTML 2.0	
	maxlength="*length*"		For *type=text*, the maximum length of an entry, in characters	HTML 2.0	
	name="*name*"		A name for the control, used as a variable name when input is sent to a script for processing. (Used for all input types.) For *type=radio*, all the radio buttons in a group have the same name.	HTML 2.0	
	size="*size*"		For *type=text*, the length of the text box	HTML 2.0	
	src="*URL*"		For *type=image*, names an image to use as a Submit button	HTML 2.0	
	value="*name*"		For *type=checkbox*, a variable value to be sent when the box is checked. For *type=text*, the default entry in the text field. For *type=submit*, *type=reset*, or *type=button*, the text displayed on the button.	HTML 2.0	

HTML 2.0
HTML 2.0, pretty much universally supported in graphical browsers

HTML 3.2
Part of HTML 3.2 specification, supported by major browsers or likely to be supported soon

EXT
An extension to HTML 2.0 supported by both Netscape and Microsoft, but not part of HTML 3.2

NSN
A Netscape extension that has not (so far) been supported by Microsoft

MSIE
A Microsoft extension that has not (so far) been supported by Netscape

START TAG	ATTRIBUTES	END TAG	EXPLANATION	SUPPORT	SEE PAGE
<KBD>		</KBD>	Marks text to be set as keyboard input	HTML 2.0	85
<LI>		</LI>	Creates a new item in a list (<DIR>, <MENU>, <OL>, or <UL>)	HTML 2.0	84
	type="A" OR "a" OR "I" OR "i" OR "disc" OR "circle" OR "square"		Used with <OL> or <UL>, specifies a number or bullet style for the item. (See <OL> and <UL> for explanations of options.)	EXT	
	value=*n*		Used with <OL>, a number for that item	EXT	
<MAP>		</MAP>	Surrounds the map code for a client-side image map (referred to by the <IMG> tag's *usemap=* attribute)	HTML 3.2	110–1
	• name="*name*"		Provides a name for the map	HTML 3.2	110–1
<MARQUEE>		</MARQUEE>	Marks text that should scroll across the screen	MSIE	139
	align="top" OR "middle" OR "bottom"		Specifies an alignment of the marquee with the surrounding text	MSIE	
	behavior="scroll" OR "slide" OR "alternate"		Specifies a scrolling action: "scroll" (the default) scrolls from one side of the screen and off the other, "slide" scrolls just until it reaches the other side, and "alternate" scrolls back and forth across the window	MSIE	
	bgcolor="*#RRGGBB*" OR "*name*"		Names a color for the marquee's background, using an RGB value (expressed in hexadecimal) or a color name	MSIE	
	direction="left" OR "right"		The direction the marquee will scroll		
	height=*n* OR *n%*, weight=*n* OR *n%*		The height and width of the marquee, described in pixels or as a percentage of the screen height	MSIE	
	hspace=*n*, vspace=*n*		The horizontal and vertical space, in pixels, set between the marquee and surrounding text	MSIE	
	loop=*n* OR "*infinite*"		The number of times the marquee will loop	MSIE	
	scrollamount=*n*		The unit, in pixels, by which the marquee scrolls	MSIE	
	scrolldelay=*n*		The number of milliseconds between scrolls	MSIE	
<MENU>		</MENU>	Creates a menu list	HTML 2.0	84
<META>		</META>	Provides general information about an HTML document	HTML 2.0	136–7
	• content="*value*"		A value for use by the HTTP action specified with *http-equiv=*. For client pull, this is the number of seconds to wait before loading the next page.	EXT	
	http-equiv= "*http-action*"		The HTTP action that should be enacted. For client pull, use *http-equiv= "refresh"*.	EXT	
	url="*URL*"		Used with *http-equiv="refresh"*, the file that should be loaded next	EXT	

START TAG	ATTRIBUTES	END TAG	EXPLANATION	SUPPORT	SEE PAGE
<MULTICOL>		</MULTICOL>	Marks text that should be set in multiple columns	NSN	89–91
	• cols=*n*		The number of columns	NSN	
	gutter=*n*		The amount of space between columns, in pixels	NSN	
	width=*n*		The width of each column, in pixels	NSN	
<NOBR>			Joins elements that should not be separated by a line break	EXT	
<NOEMBED>		</NOEMBED>	Used with <EMBED>, marks elements that should be displayed in browsers that don't support plug-ins. (Browsers that support plug-ins ignore text marked by <NOEMBED>.)	EXT	
<NOFRAMES>		</NOFRAMES>	Used with the <FRAMES> tag, marks content that should be displayed in browsers that don't support frames. (The text is ignored by frames-capable browsers.)	EXT	
<NOSCRIPT>		</NOSCRIPT>	Used with the <SCRIPT> tag, marks material that should be displayed in browsers that don't support the scripting language. (This text is ignored by most script-capable browsers.)	EXT	
<OBJECT>		</OBJECT>	Inserts an object (e.g., an image, media file, or program)	EXT	106–7, 175
	align="left" OR "right" OR "center" OR "top" OR "middle" OR "bottom"		The alignment of the object in the window	EXT	
	border=*n*		The width of the border around the object, specified in pixels	EXT	
	classid="*class-identifier*"		A unique identifier for the plug-in or program. (The syntax depends on the type of object being inserted.)	EXT	
	codebase="*URL*"		The directory that holds the program	EXT	
	codetype="*MIME-type*"		The MIME type of the program	EXT	
	data="*URL*"		The URL for the object to be inserted into the page	EXT	
	height=*n* width=*n*		The height and width of the object, in pixels	EXT	
	hspace=*n*, vspace=*n*		The horizontal and vertical space, in pixels, set between the object and surrounding text	EXT	
	name="*name*"		A name by which other programs can refer to the object	EXT	
	shapes		Specifies that the object has shaped hyperlinks (as in an image map)	EXT	110–1
	standby="*text*"		Text that displays while the object is loading	EXT	
	type="*MIME-type*"		The object's MIME type. The browser uses this to determine whether it can display the object.	EXT	
	usemap="*name*"		Names the map to be used for a client-side image map	EXT	110–1

HTML 2.0
HTML 2.0, pretty much universally supported in graphical browsers

HTML 3.2
Part of HTML 3.2 specification, supported by major browsers or likely to be supported soon

EXT
An extension to HTML 2.0 supported by both Netscape and Microsoft, but not part of HTML 3.2

NSN
A Netscape extension that has not (so far) been supported by Microsoft

MSIE
A Microsoft extension that has not (so far) been supported by Netscape

START TAG	ATTRIBUTES	END TAG	EXPLANATION	SUPPORT	SEE PAGE
<OL>		</OL>	Creates an ordered (numbered) list	HTML 2.0	84
	type="A" OR "a" OR "I" OR "i"		Specifies alternate numbering styles: capital letters, lowercase letters, uppercase roman numerals, and lowercase roman numerals, respectively. (If no type is specified, the default Arabic numerals are used.)	HTML 3.2	
	start=n		Specifies a starting number	HTML 3.2	
<OPTION>			Used after the <SELECT> tag to create an option in a menu	HTML 2.0	153
	selected		Specifies that the option should be selected by default	HTML 2.0	
	value="text"		The value to be sent if the option is selected	HTML 2.0	
<P>			Inserts a paragraph break	HTML 2.0	84
	align="left" OR "right" OR "center"		The alignment of the paragraph in the window	HTML 3.2	
<PARAM>		</PARAM>	Used with the <OBJECT> or <APPLET> tags to pass parameter values to a program	HTML 3.2	
	• name="name"		Names the parameter the value should be assigned to	HTML 3.2	
	• value="value"		Provides a value for the parameter	HTML 3.2	
	valuetype="data" OR "ref" OR "object"		Describes how the value should be interpreted: as data (the default), as a URL (ref), or as the URL of an object in the same document (object)	HTML 3.2	
	type="MIME-type"		The MIME type of the data	HTML 3.2	
<PRE>		</PRE>	Marks text that should be laid out exactly as typed, including spaces and carriage returns	HTML 2.0	88
<S>		</S>	Marks text that should be set as strikeout (same as <STRIKE>)	HTML 2.0	85
<SAMP>		</SAMP>	Marks text that should be set as a sample	HTML 2.0	85
<SCRIPT>		</SCRIPT>	Marks a client-side script	HTML 3.2	16–7
	language="name"		Names the language the script is written in	HTML 3.2	
	src="URL"		Names an external script file	NSN	
<SELECT>			Creates a menu of choices, either a pull-down menu (the default) or a scrolling menu	HTML 2.0	153
	multiple		Allows multiple selections from a scrolling menu	HTML 2.0	
	• name="name"		Creates a name for the menu, used as a variable name when the input is sent to a script for processing	HTML 2.0	
	size="size"		Creates a scrolling menu of the depth specified	HTML 2.0	

START TAG	ATTRIBUTES	END TAG	EXPLANATION	SUPPORT	SEE PAGE
\<SMALL>		\</SMALL>	Marks text that should be set in a small size	HTML 3.2	85
\<SPACER>		\</SPACER>	Creates a blank space in the page layout	NSN	89
	align="left" OR "right"		For *type=block*, tells the browser to wrap the adjoining text left or right around the space	NSN	
	height=*n*, width=*n*		For *type=block*, the width and height of the empty space	NSN	
	size=*n*		For *type=horizontal* or *type=vertical,* the size of the empty space, in pixels	NSN	
	type="horizontal" OR "vertical" OR "block"		Tells the browser to create a space in the current line (horizontal), to create a vertical space above the next item (vertical), or to create a rectangular space (block)	NSN	
\<STRIKE>		\</STRIKE>	Marks text that should be set as strikeout (same as \<S>)	HTML 3.2	85
_{		\}	Marks text that should be set subscript	HTML 3.2	85
\<SUP>		\</SUB>	Marks text that should be set superscript	HTML 3.2	85
\<TABLE>		\</TABLE>	Marks the set of elements that make up a table	HTML 3.2	92–5
	align="left" OR "right" OR "center"		Specifies the table's alignment in the window	HTML 3.2	
	bgcolor="#*RRGGBB*" OR "*name*"		The color of the table's background, using the RGB values (expressed in hexadecimal) or a color name	EXT	
	border=*n*		A width for the row's border, in pixels. *border=0* means no border.	HTML 3.2	
	bordercolor="#*RRGGBB*" OR "*name*"		A color for the table's border	MSIE	
	cellpadding=*n*		The space between each cell's border and its contents, specified in pixels	HTML 3.2	
	cellspacing=*n*		The space between adjoining cells	HTML 3.2	
	cols=*n*		The number of columns in the table		
	width=*n* OR *n*%		The table's total width, specified in pixels or as a percentage of the window size	HTML 3.2	
\<TD>, \<TH>			Marks the data (\<TD>) or a heading (\<TH>) that goes in a table cell	HTML 3.2	92–5
	align="left" OR "right" OR "center"		Specifies the data's alignment in the cell	HTML 3.2	
	bgcolor="#*RRGGBB*" OR "*name*"		A color for the cell's background	EXT	
	bordercolor="#*RRGGBB*" OR "*name*"		A color for the cell's border	MSIE	
	colspan=*n*		The number of columns the cell spans	HTML 3.2	

HTML 2.0
HTML 2.0, pretty much universally supported in graphical browsers

HTML 3.2
Part of HTML 3.2 specification, supported by major browsers or likely to be supported soon

EXT
An extension to HTML 2.0 supported by both Netscape and Microsoft, but not part of HTML 3.2

NSN
A Netscape extension that has not (so far) been supported by Microsoft

MSIE
A Microsoft extension that has not (so far) been supported by Netscape

START TAG	ATTRIBUTES	END TAG	EXPLANATION	SUPPORT	SEE PAGE
	height=*n*		The height of the table cell, in pixels	HTML 3.2	
	nowrap		Disables line-wrapping in the cell	HTML 3.2	
	rowspan=*n*		The number of rows the cell spans	HTML 3.2	
	valign="top" OR "middle" OR "bottom" OR "baseline"		The vertical alignment of the cell's contents relative to its borders	HTML 3.2	
	width=*n*		The cell's width, specified in pixels or as a percentage of the table size	HTML 3.2	
\<TEXTAREA\>		\<TEXTAREA\>	Creates a multiline text field	HTML 2.0	153
	• cols=*n*, rows=*n*		The width (rows) and height (cols) of the text area, in characters	HTML 2.0	
	• name="*name*"		A name for the text area, used as a variable name when the input is sent to a script for processing	HTML 2.0	
\<TR\>		\</TR\>	Creates a new table row	HTML 3.2	153
	align="left" OR "right" OR "center"		The alignment of the contents of the row's cells	HTML 3.2	
	bgcolor="#*RRGGBB*" OR "*name*"		A color for the table row's background	EXT	
	bordercolor="#*RRGGBB*" OR "*name*"		A color for the row's border	MSIE	
	valign="top" OR "middle" OR "bottom" OR "baseline"		The vertical alignment of the row's contents relative to the cell's borders	HTML 3.2	
\<TT\>		\</TT\>	Marks text that should be set in teletype (monospaced) text	HTML 2.0	85
\<U\>		\</U\>	Marks text that should be set underlined	HTML 2.0	85
\<UL\>		\</UL\>	Creates an unordered (bulleted) list	HTML 2.0	84
	type="disc" OR "circle" OR "square"		A shape for the bullets	EXT	
\<VAR\>		\</VAR\>	Marks text that should be set as a variable	HTML 2.0	85

HTML 2.0
HTML 2.0, pretty much universally supported in graphical browsers

HTML 3.2
Part of HTML 3.2 specification, supported by major browsers or likely to be supported soon

EXT
An extension to HTML 2.0 supported by both Netscape and Microsoft, but not part of HTML 3.2

NSN
A Netscape extension that has not (so far) been supported by Microsoft

MSIE
A Microsoft extension that has not (so far) been supported by Netscape

Online: HTML Resources

For more information on how to work with HTML, turn to the Web itself. Here are some online resources that should help you create HTML that looks good and works well with a variety of web browsers.

Official HTML

The official documentation from the Internet Engineering Task Force's HTML Working Group.

HTML 2.0
http://www.w3.org/pub/WWW/MarkUp/html-spec/

HTML 3.2
http://www.w3.org/pub/WWW/MarkUp/Wilbur/

Current Tags

A number of online sources compile current HTML codes into handy lists you might find more useful than the official specifications. These also take into account tags that aren't official but are in wide use.

The Bare Bones Guide to HTML
http://werbach.com/barebones/barebone.html

HTML Elements List (Sandia National Labs)
http://www.sandia.gov/sci_compute/elements.html

HTML 3.2 Unofficial Reference
http://www.htmlhelp.com/reference/wilbur/

Microsoft Internet Explorer HTML Reference
http://www.microsoft.com/workshop/author/newhtml/
    default.htm

Netscape's Extensions to HTML
http://www.netscape.com/assist/net_sites/
    html_extensions.html
http://www.netscape.com/assist/net_sites/
    html_extensions_3.html

Tag Support by Leading Browsers
http://www.browserbydesign.com/resources/appa/apa1.htm

General Resources

Pointers to general information on HTML and Web authoring.

The Art of HTML
http://www.taoh.com/

HTML Obsession
http://www.cnmnet.com/~ksdurbin/index1/

WebMastery
http://union.ncsa.uiuc.edu/HyperNews/get/www/html/
    guides.html

Tutorials

How to compose HTML files: the basics.

A Beginner's Guide to HTML
http://www.ncsa.uiuc.edu/General/Internet/WWW/
    HTMLPrimer.html

Crash Course in HTML
http://www.nashville.net/~templedf/crash/CrashCourse.html

An Introduction to Frames
http://www.netscape.com/assist/net_sites/frames.html

Dos and Don'ts

Mistakes to avoid and good practices to follow in creating HTML files.

The HTML Bad Style Page
http://www.earth.com/bad-style/

Composing Good HTML
http://www.cs.cmu.edu/People/tilt/cgh/

Style Guide for Online Hypertext
http://www.w3.org/pub/WWW/Provider/Style/Overview.html

The Ten Commandments of HTML
http://www.visdesigns.com/design/commandments.html

Web Wonk
http://www.dsiegel.com/tips/

Newsgroups

An online forum for answers to your questions.

comp.infosystems
www.authoring.html

Glossary

A

ActiveX
Microsoft's technology, based on *OLE,* for allowing software components to interoperate.

ActiveX control
A program, based on *ActiveX* technology, that adds new features to an ActiveX-compatible program.

ActiveX document
A special type of *ActiveX control* that gives browsers and other programs that support *ActiveX* the ability to read a certain document format.

adaptive palette
A palette created by choosing the most-used colors in an image.

AIFF
Audio Interchange File Format, a cross-platform digital sound format.

animated GIF
A graphic file, in GIF89a format, that includes multiple layers that can be played in succession to create an animation. See also *GIF.*

anti-alias
To blur the edges of a graphic to reduce the stair-stepping pattern ("jaggies") that often appears on low-resolution output devices such as computer screens.

AppleScript
A scripting language developed by Apple to offer a standard method of automating Macintosh programs.

applet
A *Java* program designed to be distributed over the Net.

ASCII
Stands for American Standard Code for Information Interchange. ASCII files, sometimes called "pure text" files, can contain only information included in that code set, which consists of the 26 letters of the alphabet (both uppercase and lowercase), numbers from 0 to 9, and a few common symbols.

attribute
Values provided within an HTML tag to specify additional information about how the tagged element should be treated.

.au
A sound file format commonly used on Unix computers.

avatar
In graphics-based *chat systems,* a figure that represent a participant.

AVI
Audio-video interleave, the standard video format for Microsoft Windows.

B

bit depth
The number of bits used to record each pixel of information in an image file. Common formats are 8-bit (256 colors or shades of gray) and 24-bit (16.7 million colors). Also often used to refer to the number of bits per *sample* in a sound file.

bitmap
A graphics format that creates an image using an array of pixels of different colors or shades. See also *object-based graphics.*

bookmark
A record of a particular page's URL, stored with a user's browser Preferences, allowing the user to choose the page's name from a menu to return to the page.

branching diagram
In Web design, a diagram that shows what pages a Web site contains and how they are related to one another.

browser
Client software designed to communicate with Web servers and interpret the data received from them. Many different browsers are available, each with different features. Some common browsers include Netscape Navigator, Microsoft Internet Explorer, NCSA Mosaic, and lynx.

browser-safe palette
A palette of 216 colors (based on 6-bit color) used by most browser manufacturers to display color on 8-bit (256-color) systems. Mapping graphics to the browser-safe palette before posting them on a Web site avoids the danger that Web graphics will be subject to *dithering* on the viewer's system.

C

cache
An area of memory or disk reserved for holding data that is expected to be used again, making that data faster to retrieve the next time it's used.

cascading style sheets
A format for style sheets that can be attached to *HTML* documents, so called because style sheets defined in one way (e.g., with a <STYLE> tag) overrule those set in another (e.g., in the <BODY > tag), and style definitions can be inherited by sub-classes of a style. The first draft of the proposal is referred to as *CSS1*.

CGI
Common Gateway Interface, a set of rules by which *browsers* can request the services of programs stored on a *server* and the server can return files based on the program's results.

CGI script
A *script* or program saved on the server and available to Web clients via *CGI*.

chat system
A system, usually based on *IRC*, that allows Internet users to exchange messages with other visitors to a site in real time.

client
In a *client-server system* such as the Web, the user's computer.

client pull
A method of animation created when an HTML page automatically calls the next page to be down-loaded. Client pull is accomplished via an attribute to the <META> tag *(http-equiv=)* that simulates an *HTTP* call. See also *server push*.

client-server system
A networking system in which processes are split between *server* computers, which hold files for dis-tribution, and *client* computers, which can request files and other services from the servers.

client-side image map
An *image map* for which the map information and the map processing program resides on the client (user's) computer.

client-side processing
Running programs on an Internet *client*, rather than on a *server*.

client software
A term used to describe *browsers*, mail readers, and other software used on the *client* machine to read files obtained over a *client-server system* such as the Web.

code-signing
A method of ensuring the safety of downloadable programs, such as ActiveX controls, in which the pro-gram's creator "signs" the object, and client systems check for the signature before running it.

content negotiation
A method by which servers can check which client software is avail-able on the client machine and download a page appropriate to that software.

creative brief
A statement of the goals of a design process.

D

design specifications
Specifications describing how each element of a document is to be laid out.

design templates
Standard designs that can be reused for a set of similar pages.

dithering
A method of creating a color by com-bining two or more discrete colors.

domain name
A name by which an Internet *server* is known (e.g., "peachpit.com"). The first part of the domain name pro-vides a unique, plain-language iden-tifier for the Internet server. The second part (following the period) is usually a three-letter code signify-ing the type of site: e.g., *.com* for commercial, *.edu* for educational institution.

E

e-mail
A sytem for exchanging electronic messages over a network.

end tag
In HTML, the tag that marks the end of an element. The end tag is usu-ally the same as the start tag but preceded by a slash (/) character.

F

floating frames
Frames that are not part of a frame-set, but are defined individually.

frames
An *HTML* feature that lets designers split the browser window into sepa-rate units, each of which can hold a separate HTML file and can scroll and be updated separately from the rest of the window.

frameset
The set of frames that make up a page. A <FRAMESET> tag defines the number of rows and columns for the window.

Frontier
A scripting language developed by UserLand, used as an alternative to AppleScript to script actions in Macintosh programs.

FTP
File transer protocol, a method for sending files over the Internet.

G

GIF
Graphics Interchange Format, a compressed *bitmap* format created by CompuServe. The oldest version, called GIF87a or CompuServe GIF, has been superceded by a newer version, called GIF89a, which sup-ports *transparency* and animation. See also *animated GIF, JPEG*.

gopher
A protocol used to create hierarchi-cal menus, allowing users to move through information by moving through the directory structure until they find the information they need.

H

helper application
An application launched by a browser to display files it can't read itself. See also *plug-in, ActiveX control*.

hexadecimal
A numbering system using base-16 (rather than the base-10 of the decimal system). In hexadecimal, the numbers from 10 to 16 are indicated by the letters A–F. Hexa-decimal numbers are used to spec-ify RGB (red/green/blue) values in *HTML* tags such as <BGCOLOR>.

history list
A list of pages that the user has visited during an online session, usually listed in a browser menu so that the user can choose the page's name to return to it.

home page
Sometimes used as a generic name for a Web site, but now usually referring to the top page of a site structure, which provides access to all other pages on the site.

HTML
Hypertext Markup Language, a set of tags developed by the creators of the Web to mark the structural elements of text documents. A defin-ing feature of HTML is its inclusion of tags that create *hyperlinks* to other documents on the Internet. HTML is an application of *SGML*.

CSS1
The abbreviation used to refer to the first version of the *cascading style sheets* proposal.

HTML 2.0

The specification, finalized in September 1995 by the HTML working group of the *IETF*, that codifies the basic set of *HTML* tags.

HTML 3.2

A working draft, under development by the HTML working group of the *IETF*, that proposes an extended set of *HTML* tags.

HTML editors

Word processing programs designed to create *HTML* files.

HTML filters

Programs that translate an application's files into *HTML*-coded text files.

HTTP

Hypertext transfer protocol, the communications *protocol* on which the World Wide Web is based. HTTP sets rules for how information is passed between the server and the browser software.

hyperlink

In a *hypertext* document, such as a Web page, an electronic link that, when chosen, calls up a piece of linked information.

hypertext

An electronic Information structure through which the reader navigates via hyperlinks.

I

IETF

Internet Engineering Task Force, a consortium of industry and educational interests that oversees the development of standards for the Internet.

image map

A type of graphic in which different locations in the file (specified by pixel coordinates) are linked to particular destination *URLs*.

indexed color

Mapping an image's original colors to a new, reduced color palette.

information architect

For any publishing project, the person responsible for determining how information will be organized. In Web design, the information architect is usually responsible for deciding how the information will be arrayed on the pages of a Web site and how it will be accessed by the user.

inline graphic

A graphic loaded into a browser window as part of an *HTML* document.

interlacing

A feature of some graphics formats that allows the graphic to be *streamed* into a Web page in alternate rows and/or columns, allowing visitors to see a rough version of the image before it is completely downloaded.

Internet

A worldwide computer network that links thousands of smaller networks. Initially developed by the U.S. government to link its suppliers and the Pentagon, it is now used by millions of businesses and individuals.

Internet Relay Chat

An Internet protocol for exchanging text messages in real time among multiple simultaneous users. Abbreviated as *IRC*.

Internet Service Provider

A company that provides a connection to the Internet.

InterNIC

The service that registers *domain names* for Internet users.

IRC

See *Internet Relay Chat.*

ISP

See *Internet Service Provider.*

J

Java

A cross-platform programming language developed by Sun Microsystems. Because Java programs can run on any processor, it is a standard for programs, or *applets,* that are distributed over the Web.

JavaScript

A *scripting language,* developed by Netscape and Sun Microsystems, specialized for controlling Web *browser* processes.

Java Virtual Machine

A software layer that executes compiled *Java* code. The existence of the "virtual machine" is the key to Java's cross-platform capabilities.

JPEG

A compressed *bitmap* format, developed by (and named for) the Joint Photographic Experts Group of the International Standards Organization. JPEG is generally used for photographic images. An alternate version, called *progressive JPEG,* supports *interlacing.*

JScript

A JavaScript-compatible scripting language developed and supported by Microsoft.

L

Lingo

The scripting language used by Macromedia Director, a popular multimedia authoring package.

linked graphic

A graphic loaded into the *browser* window as the target of a *hyperlink.*

lossless compression

A graphics compression scheme, such as that used by GIF, that reduces file sizes without discarding any image information.

lossy compression

A graphics compression scheme, such as that used by *JPEG,* that reduces file sizes by discarding nonessential image information.

M

map file

For *server-side image maps,* a file (stored on the *server*) that holds the map information, linking specific regions of the image to specific target *URLs.*

MBONE

A virtual network, based on the IP Multicast protocol, that offers a method for broadcasting multimedia data over the *Internet*. MBONE and IP Multicast depend on "propagation servers," which retransmit a signal at strategic locations, so that a single transmission can be multiplied exponentially as it travels the network.

MIDI

Musical Instrument Digital Interface, a standard for recording and playing synthesized sounds on electronic instruments.

MIME

Multipurpose Internet Mail Extensions, a method of specifying the format of a file for Internet software such as mail readers and Web browsers. The software uses the MIME code to determine how to interpret the file.

monospaced

A term used to describe a typeface in which every character has the same width. Such typefaces are useful for setting tables, program documentation, or other texts in which vertical alignment is crucial.

MPEG
A compressed video format, created by and named for the Motion Picture Experts Group of the International Standards Organization.

navigation bar
On a Web page, a set of *hyperlinks*, usually in the form of icons or text links, that offers access to a standard set of pages—usually the top pages of the site's main sections.

newsgroup
An *Internet* service that allows users to post comments that can be read by any other visitor. The set of Internet newsgroups is sometimes referred to as "Usenet" for the network on which they reside.

object-based graphics
Graphics created as an assembly of shapes, or "objects." Object-based graphics are suitable only for illustrative (line-based) images. Sometimes referred to as *vector graphics*.

OLE
A technology developed by Microsoft to allow programs to share files and functions. The term originally stood for Object Linking and Embedding. OLE is the basis of Microsoft's *ActiveX* technology.

OpenType
A new font technology, developed by Microsoft and Adobe, that will combine the features of Type 1 and TrueType fonts, making the different font formats compatible across different systems and platforms.

page architecture
In Web design, a plan for the placement of information on a page.

PDF
Portable Document Format, an electronic document format, created by Adobe Systems and based on *PostScript,* used by Adobe Acrobat.

perl
A *scripting language* often used to create *CGI scripts.*

plug-in
A special kind of helper application that displays special formats inside the browser window.

PNG
A 24-bit, compressed graphics format, which can support multiple levels of *transparency* and two-dimensional *interlacing.*

PostScript
A page-description language developed by Adobe Systems, used widely by desktop publishing programs and output devices.

Progressive JPEG
A version of the *JPEG* graphics format that supports *interlacing.*

protocol
A set of rules for exchanging information between computers over a network or via a modem connection.

Q

QuickTime
A video and sound format created by Apple Computer and supported on the Macintosh and Windows platforms.

QuickTime Conferencing
A version of Apple's QuickTime software that supports duplex, real-time transmission.

QuickTime VR
A technology created by Apple Computer for creating and viewing 3-D scenes.

R

real-time motion
In digital animation or video, the effect of natural motion achieved by using a frame rate of 24–30 frames per second.

S

sample
In digital media, a digital recording of sound or visual data, taken and played back at high frequencies to create the illusion of natural sound or motion.

script
A simple program that lists a sequence of actions to be followed by the computer. See also *scripting language.*

scripting language
A programming language, such as *JavaScript* or *perl,* designed to control a particular environment or set of tools.

search engine
A program that searches through electronic information. Web search engines such as Lycos and Info-Seek search through indexes of the entire Internet in response to user queries. Search engines can also be set up to search the contents of individual sites.

server
In a *client-server system*, the computer that holds the data to be distributed.

server push
A method of animation created by the automatic downloading of pages from the server, activated by a *CGI script.* See also *client pull.*

server-side image map
An *image map* for which the *map file* and the map processing program reside on the *server,* and the coordinates of a user's click are sent to the server for processing.

SGML
Standard Generalized Markup Language, a language, widely used by government and educational institutions, used to mark the structural elements of text documents, so that the documents can be read and displayed appropriately by a variety of software. *HTML* is one application of SGML. SGML is codified by the International Standards Organization as ISO 8879.

Shockwave
Software created by Macromedia to allow files from its Director, Authorware, and FreeHand programs to be published on the Web. Shockwave includes a compression utility (called Afterburner) for each program, plus client software that can be used to view the "shocked" files.

staging server
A *server* that has the same directory structure as the server that will be used to publish Internet files, used to test pages online before they are made publicly available.

start tag
In HTML, the tag that marks the beginining of an element. Many tags also require *end tags* to mark the element's end.

storyboard
A document that shows the planned sequence of frames for a video or film project.

streaming
Describes technologies that feed media files to a player progressively, so that a file can begin playing as it is downloaded.

T

TCP/IP
Stands for Transmission Control Protocol/Internet Protocol, the communication *protocol* developed for use over the Internet and now supported by most computer systems.

technical specification
A document that describes the expected user experience and the way the site should respond to users' actions. A technical specification clarifies the expectations for programmed interaction on a site.

Telnet
A protocol that allows an Interent user to run programs stored on another Internet computer, or a program that uses the protocol.

tile
To arrange an object or graphic across an area by repeating it in contiguous, adjacent areas. On the Web, small background graphics are tiled to fill the browser window.

transparency
A feature of an image file in which certain colors can be made invisible against a background. *GIF* and *PNG* graphics support transparency.

U

URL
Universal Resource Locator, a standard method of naming files on the World Wide Web. Sometimes referred to as URI (Universal Resource Identifier) or URN (Universal Resource Name).

V

VAG
The Virtual Architecture Group, the group in the *IETF* responsible for creating standards for *VRML*.

variable
In programming, a placeholder for a value that can be reassigned based on user input or other changing conditions.

vector graphics
Another name for *object graphics*, reflecting the fact that the objects that make up the images are created from mathematical splines, or vectors, rather than described as individual pixels. EPS and FreeHand files are common vector graphics formats.

VBScript
See *Visual Basic Scripting Edition*.

videoconferencing
Systems in which video images of the participants are displayed on the other participants' screens. Conversations may be held via text or audio, depending on the system and the available bandwidth.

Visual Basic
A programming language developed by Microsoft especially for creating Windows programs.

Visual Basic Script
See *Visual Basic Scripting Edition*.

Visual Basic Scripting Edition
A *scripting language* based on Microsoft's Visual Basic programming language, specialized for controlling Web processes, *ActiveX controls,* and *Java* programs. Sometimes referred to as *Visual Basic Script* or *VBScript.*

VRML
Virtual Reality Modeling Language, a *scripting language* used to define 3-D shapes for use on the Web. VRML (often pronounced "ver'-mul") supports *hyperlinking* and programmed behaviors.

W

WAIS
Wide Area Information Service, a protocol used to build indexes of Internet pages, allowing quick searches for information.

.wav
The native sound format for Microsoft Windows.

webmaster
The person in charge of managing a Web site. The name is used for a variety of functions, including but not limited to the role of head editor, lead producer, or site engineer.

world
The word used for a *VRML 3-D* environment, to differentiate it from the "page" interface of 2-D formats.

World Wide Web
An *Internet* service, based on the *HTTP protocol,* that allows publishers to post data in richly formatted pages and allows users to navigate information on *servers* around the world through a system of *hyperlinks.*

X

XTension
A program that extends the capabilities of QuarkXPress, a popular page layout program.

Index

DARCY DINUCCI (darcy@tothepoint.com) has written about design and technology for over a decade, as an editor for *PC World, NeXTworld,* and *Publish* magazines, as a contributor to *MacWeek, Print,* and *U&lc,* and as editor of *The Little PC Book* and *The Macintosh Bible, 5th edition,* for Peachpit Press. In addition, she now runs To the Point Publishing, a publishing services company in San Francisco.

MARIA GIUDICE (maria@yodesign.com) and **LYNNE STILES** (lynne@yodesign.com) have been partners in YO, a San Francisco information design office, since 1991. YO's projects have included books for Addison-Wesley, HarperCollins, Peachpit Press, and projects for Apple Computer, *Publish* magazine, Gray Line Tours, and RIDES for Bay Area Commuters. YO designs and produces the Digital Color Prepress series of books for Agfa, and was profiled in *Information Architects* (Graphis Press, 1996.) YO's Web design work has included sites for Peachpit Press (http://www. peachpit.com/), Big Book (http://www.bigbook.com/) and Match.com (http://match.com/).